DATA MINING WITH
SAS ENTERPRISE MINER

THROUGH EXAMPLES

CÉSAR PÉREZ LÓPEZ

INTRODUCTION

This book presents the most common techniques used in data mining in a simple and easy to understand through one of the most common software solutions from among those existing in the market, in particular, SAS ENTERPRISE MINER. Pursued as initial aim clarifying the applications concerning methods traditionally rated as difficult or dull. It seeks to present applications in data mining without having to manage high mathematical developments or complicated theoretical algorithms, which is the most common reason for the difficulties in understanding and implementation of this matter.

Today data mining is used in different fields of science. Noteworthy applications in banking, and financial analysis of markets and trade, insurance and private health, in education, in industrial processes, in medicine, biology and bioengineering, telecommunications and in many other areas. Essentials to get started in data mining, regardless of the field in which it is applied, is the understanding of own concepts, task that does not require nor much less the domain of scientific apparatus involved in the matter. Later, when either necessary operative advanced, computer programs allow the results without having to decipher the mathematical development of the algorithms that are under the procedures.

This book describes the simplest possible data mining concepts, so that they are understandable by readers with different training. The chapters begin describing the techniques in affordable language and then presenting the way to treat them through practical applications. An important part of each chapter are case studies completely resolved, including the interpretation of the results, which is precisely the most important thing in any matter with which they work.

The book begins with an introduction to mining data and its phases. In successive chapters develop the initial phases (selection of information, data exploration, data cleansing, transformation of data, etc.).

Subsequently elaborates on specific data mining, both predictive and descriptive techniques.

Predictive techniques covers all models of regression, discriminant analysis, decision trees, neural networks and other techniques based on models.

The descriptive techniques vary dimension reduction techniques, techniques of classification and segmentation (clustering), and exploratory data analysis techniques.

INDEX

Chapter 1

DATA MINING. CONCEPTS, TECHNIQUES, AND SYSTEMS

1.1 APPROXIMATION THE CONCEPT OF DATA MINING

Data mining can be initially defined as a process of discovery of new and meaningful relationships, patterns, and trends to examine large amounts of data.

The availability of large volumes of information and the widespread use of computer tools has transformed data analysis orienting it towards certain specialized techniques included under the name of mining data or *Data Mining*.

Data mining techniques pursue the auto-discovery of the knowledge contained in the information stored so ordered in large databases. These techniques aim to discover patterns, profiles and trends through analysis of data using recognition technologies, patterns, neural networks, fuzzy logic, genetic algorithms and other advanced techniques of data analysis.

However, data mining is already a very evolved concept that needs to be conceptually approximate by stages. Initially the purpose of information systems was gathering information about a specific plot to aid in decision-making. With the computerization of organizations and the emergence of applications software operational on the information system, the main purpose of information systems is to give support to the basic processes of the Organization (sales, production, staff...). Once satisfied the need of having a computer support for the basic processes of the Organization (*management information systems*), organizations require new capabilities of the information systems (*information systems for decision-making*).

In this way have appeared different business tools for the taking of decisions (DSS or *Decision Support Systems*) that *coexist*: EIS, OLAP, queries and reports, and own data mining tools.

An EIS (*Executive Information System*) is an information system and a set of associated tools that provides management access to information of State and its management activities. Specializes in analyzing the daily status of the Organization (through key indicators) to quickly inform about updates to managers. The requested information tends to be, in large measure, numerical (weekly sales, stocks, part, etc.) and represented graphically in the style of spreadsheets.

OLAP (*On-line Analyitical Processing*) tools are more generic, work on an information system (or transactional data store) and allow to perform aggregations and combinations of data in ways far more complex and ambitious, with more strategic analysis goals. OLAP tools are based, generally, systems or multidimensional interfaces, presenting the information in a matrix manner. OLAP tools provide facilities to "manage" and "transform" data, produce other "data" (more added, combined) and are a great help to analyze data because they produce different views of the same.

The *reporting systems* or *Advanced queries* are usually based, relational or object-relational systems and the result is presented in tabular form. They are usually implemented in relational databases.

Data mining tools allow you to extract patterns, tendencies and regularities to describe and understand the data and to predict future behaviors. The data mining analyzes the data and the other tools listed above provide access to information to make the website more effective, i.e. are data mining support tools.

However the above mentioned tools often require the prior existence of a *warehouse of data (Data Warehouse)*. The data warehouse is the *central information system* throughout this process. A data warehouse is a collection of data domain-oriented, integrated, non-volatile and variant in time to assist in decision-making. A data warehouse is a set of historical, internal or external, and descriptive data of a context or study area, which are integrated and organized so that they allow to efficiently implement tools to summarize, describe, and analyze the data in order to help in the decision-making strategic.

Internal and external data sources are separated. Much of the data that are incorporated into a data store come from a transactional database that is the inner data source and whose information is the result of transactions arising from the daily activity, but there are also other external sources of information.

There is a specialized system for the loading and maintenance of a data warehouse, called *System ETL* (*Extraction, Transformation and Load*). This system is responsible for the reading of transactional data, the incorporation of external data, creation of keys, data integration, aggregation, cleaning and processing of data, creation and maintenance of metadata, load planning and maintenance, indexing, quality testing, etc.

However it must be clear that data warehouses are not essential to extracting knowledge from data. Data on a simple file of data mining can be done. But the advantages of organizing a data warehouse for data mining are well amortized medium and long term when we have large volumes of data, or these increase with time, or come from heterogeneous sources or are going to combine in ways not predefined and arbitrary.

1.2 THE PROCESS OF EXTRACTION OF KNOWLEDGE

But data mining is just one stage of the *process of extracting knowledge from data* (KDD). This process consists of several phases as the preparation of data (selection, cleaning, and transformation), his exploration and audit data mining itself such (development of models and data analysis), evaluation, dissemination and use of models (*output*). Also, the process of extraction of knowledge includes very different techniques (trees of decision, linear regression, artificial neural networks, Bayesian techniques, etc., support vector machines) of various fields (machine learning and artificial intelligence), statistics, databases, etc.) and it deals with a typology of problems (classification, categorization, estimate/regression, clustering, etc.).

KDD begins with the *collection and integration of information* from some initial data available (*data selection* phase). The early stages of the KDD determine that the successive stages are able to extract valid and useful knowledge from the original information. Generally, the information that you want to inquire about a certain domain of the organization is located in databases (*Database*) and other very different, both internal and external sources (in general information is ranked in data stores). Many of these sources are used for transactional work. The subsequent analysis will be much easier if the source is unified, accessible (internal) and disconnected from the transactional work. Apart from the Organization's internal information, data warehouses can collect external information such as demographics (census), yellow pages, psicografías (profiles by area), use of the Internet, information from other organizations and external databases purchased from other companies. The availability of large volumes of information at this stage leads to the need to use sampling techniques for the selection of data.

The next phase of the KDD integrates scanning, cleaning or screen of data (*Data Cleaning*) and the transformation of data. The greatest possible number of erroneous or inconsistent data (cleaning) and irrelevant (sieve) must be removed. Consultation tools are used in this phase (*Query tools*) and statistical tools (*Statistics tools*) almost exclusively. Exploratory analysis of data as histograms and diagrams of box, stem and leaves, which help detect abnormal or atypical data (*outliers*) are used in exploration. The presence of atypical data andmissing values(*missing*data) can lead us to use robust algorithms to atypical and missing data (e.g., decision trees), filter information, replace values through *imputation techniques* and to transform continuous data into discrete *Discretization techniques*. Among the advanced techniques of transformation we have reduction and increase of the dimension.

The next phase in the KDD is the own data mining which will take place from the development of predictive models and descriptive (*Model Development*) and through the analysis of data (*Data Analysis*). Once collected the data of interest, an Explorer can decide what kind of pattern you want to discover. The kind of knowledge that you want to remove will clearly mark the data mining technique to use.

To select and validate previous models is required a new phase consisting of the use of criteria of evaluation of hypotheses.The deployment of the model is sometimes trivial, but sometimes requires a process of implementation or interpretation. Statistical and visualization tools are additionally used in this phase (*Visualization tools*).

A later stage of the KDD is that relating to the dissemination and use of knowledge derived from data mining techniques on the corresponding models that usually lead to the generation of results (*Output Generation*). Model can have many users and need broadcast, be expressed in a comprehensible manner with which may require to be distributed in the organization. Visualization tools are used in this phase (*Visualization tools*), presentation (*Presentation tools*) and transformation of data (*Data transformation tools*).

Therefore, we observe in the KDD knowledge extraction process the following sequence of phases: selection $\rightarrow$ scan $\rightarrow$ cleaning $\rightarrow$ transformation $\rightarrow$ data mining $\rightarrow$ evaluation $\rightarrow$ broadcasting

In the *selection* phase are integrated data collected, determining the sources of information that can be useful and where to get them, are identified and selected the relevant variables in the data and apply the techniques of sampling suitable. All this is provided with a datastore with the information in a common format and without inconsistencies. Given that the data come from different sources, their *scanning* techniques of exploratory data analysis, looking for among other things, the distribution of the data, its symmetry and normality and correlations in the information is required. Then necessary *cleaning* of the data, since they may contain outliers, missing values and incorrect values. This phase analyzes the influence of atypical data, missing values are imputed and disposed of or correct the incorrect data. Then, if necessary, takes place the *transformation* of data, usually by means of techniques of reduction or increase in the size and scaling simple and multi-dimensional, among others. The first four stages are usually included under the name of *data preparation*. In the *data mining*phase, we decide what is the task to perform (sorting, grouping, etc.) and choose the descriptive or predictive technique that will be used. In the phase of *evaluation and interpretation* patterns evaluated was discussed by experts, and if necessary returns to the previous phases for a new iteration. Finally, in the phase of *dissemination* is made use of new knowledge and becomes part of it to all potential users.

However, the previous classification isn't the only one appearing in the literature on this subject. There are other interpretations of the concept of data mining, online consider phases of the process of extraction of knowledge previously expressed as data mining techniques. For example, SAS Institute defines the concept of *Data Mining* as the process of selecting (*Selecting*), explore (*Exploring*), modify (*Modifying*), modeling (*Modeling*) and rating (*Assessment*) large amounts of data with the aim of uncovering unknown patterns which can be used as a comparative advantage with respect to competitors. This process is summarized with the acronym SEMMA.

1.3 DATA MINING TECHNIQUES

The initial classification of data mining techniques to distinguish between predictive techniques, in which variables can be initially classified in dependent and independent (similar to the analysis of dependence or explanatory methods of multivariate analysis techniques), descriptive techniques, in which all the variables initially have the same status (similar to the analysis of interdependence or descriptive methods of multivariate analysis techniques) and auxiliary techniques.

Predictive techniques specify the model to the data based on theoretical knowledge. The model for data should contrast after the process of data mining before accepting it as valid. Formally, the application of all model exceed phases of *identification objective* (data apply rules that permit to identify the best possible model that fits the data), *estimate* (process of calculation of parameters of the model chosen for the data in the identification phase), *diagnosis* (contrast of the validity of the estimated model process) and *forecast* (process identified modelestimated and validated to predict future values of the dependent variables). In some cases, the model is obtained as a mixture of the knowledge obtained before and after the*Data Mining*and also must be tested before accepting it as valid. For example, the *neural networks* enable discover complex models and refine them as scan data progresses. Thanks to their learning abilities, they reveal complex relationships among variables without any external intervention. These techniques can include all types of regression, time series, analysis of variance and covariance, discriminant analysis, trees of decision, neural networks, genetic algorithms and Bayesian techniques. Both decision trees and neural network and discriminant analysis are *techniques of classification* that can extract behavior profiles or classes, being the objective to build a model that allows to classify any new information. Decision trees allow you to classify data into groups based on the values of the variables. Base mechanism is to choose an attribute such as root and develop the tree according to the most significant variables.

Descriptive techniques no default role is assigned to the variables. Not assume the existence of dependent and independent variables and also assumes the existence of a prior model for data. Models are created automatically on the basis of the recognition of patterns. *Clustering* and segmentation techniques are included in this group (who are also technical classification somewhat), the techniques of Association and dependence, exploratory data analysis techniques, and dimension reduction techniques (factorial, principal components, correspondences, etc.) and multidimensional scaling.

Both the descriptive techniques and predictive techniques are focused on the *discovery of knowledge* embedded in the data.

Auxiliary techniques are more superficial and limited support tools. It's new methods based on descriptive statistical techniques, queries, and reports, and generally focused on *verification*.

Classification techniques They can belong to the Group of predictive techniques (discriminant, decision trees and neural networks) and the descriptive (*clustering* and segmentation). Predictive classification techniques are often referred to as *ad hoc classification techniques* since they classified observations within previously defined groups or individuals. Descriptive classification techniques are referred to as *post-hoc classification techniques* because they perform classification without prior specification of groups.

1.4 SYSTEMS DATA MINING

Systems of data mining commonly used on the market along with techniques dealing with each of them, the platforms on which work and reading data interfaces are shown in Figure 1-5.

Product	Company	Techniques	Platform	Interface
Knowledge Seeker	Angoss	Decision trees	Win	ODBC
CART	Salford Systems	Decision trees	Win/UNIX	
Clementine	SPSS	Wide range	Win/UNIX	ODBC
Data Surveyor	Data Distilleries	Wide range	UNIX	ODBC
Gain Smarts	Urban Science	Graficos-ganancias	Win/UNIX	
Intelligent Miner	IBM	Wide range	UNIX (AIX)	IBM, DB2
Micostrategy	Micostrategy	Datawarehouse	Win	Oracle
PolyAnalyst	Megaputer	Symbolic	Win	Oracle, ODBC
Darwin	Oracle	Wide range	Win/UNIX	Oracle

Enterprise Miner	SAS Institute	Wide range	Win/UNIX/Mac	
SGI MineSet	Silicon Graphics	Association and classification	UNIX	Oracle, Sybase, Informix
Wizsoft/Wizwhy	Wizsoft			

Figure 1-5

The system of data mining we use throughout this book is *SPSS Clementine.*

SPSS Clementine provides different data sources (ASCII, Oracle, Informix, Sybase, Ingres, etc.), a simple visual interface and various tools for data mining (neural networks, trees decision, regression, time series, cluster, etc.). It works under the operating systems UNIX and Windows.

There are also market other usual tools. SAS implements data mining work by *SAS Enterprise Miner.*It is a complete tool that includes connection to databases (via ODBC and SAS datasets), sampling and inclusion of variables derived, partition of the evaluation of the model with respect to training, validation, and test sets, various tools for data mining (algorithms and types of trees of decision and *clustering*, neural networks, regression, etc.), comparison of models and models in SAS code conversion. It has a very simple graphical user interface and includes tools for process flow, trying the KDD as a process and process phases is they can repeat, modify and record.

There are also other systems that allow *Data Mining through data bases.* Specifically the database Oracle and SQL Server that have associated data mining systems.

Oracle has tools of "Business Intelligence" and "Data Mining" that have a more business-oriented and information systems. There are also tools for OLAP, Datawarehouse and advanced reports. It also has own data mining tools.

Microsoft SQL ServerAnalysis Services product that implements data mining features. It is based on the "OLE DB for Data Mining" and implements an extension of the SQL that works with DMM (*Data Mining Model*) that allows you to create the model, train it and make predictions. The SQL Server 2008 version, its module *Analysis Services* data mining algorithms has more advanced include that decision and regression trees, time series, clustering clusters, rules of Association, Naïve Bayes algorithm and text mining. It has a wizard and data mining designer that allows you to build sophisticated through an easy to use interface models. In addition, elevation charts and benefits, are provided so you can compare and contrast the quality of the models entities engage in the distribution.

PHASE OF SELECTION IN DATA MINING

2.1 SELECTION IN THE PROCESS OF EXTRACTION OF KNOWLEDGE

The extraction of knowledge (KDD) process begins with the *collection and integration of information* from some initial data available (*data selection*phase). The early stages of the KDD are very important because they determine that the successive stages are able to extract valid and useful knowledge from the original information. Generally, the information that you want to inquire about a certain domain of the organization is located in databases and other diverse sources, both internal and external. In general the information is ranked in data stores. The subsequent analysis will be much easier if the source is unified, accessible (internal) and disconnected from the transactional work. Apart from the Organization's internal information, data warehouses can collect external information such as demographics (census), yellow pages, psicografías (profiles by area), use of the Internet, information from other organizations and external databases purchased from other companies. The availability of large volumes of information at this stage leads to the need to use sampling techniques for the selection of data.

On the knowledge extraction process observe the following sequence: selection → scan → cleaning → transformation → data mining → assessment → broadcasting.

In the *selection* phase are integrated data collected, determining the sources of information that can be useful and where to get them, are identified and selected the relevant variables in the data and apply the techniques of sampling suitable. All this is provided with a warehouse of data (*Data Warehouse*) with information on common format and without inconsistencies.

2.2 COLLECTION AND DATA INTEGRATION: DATA WAREHOUSE

Generally, the information that you want to investigate is located in databases and other diverse sources, both internal and external. Many of these sources are used for the daily work (*operational or transactional databases*). On these same databases of work already can be extracted knowledge because they are used to maintain the transactional daily work of original information systems (known as OLTP, *On-line Transactional Processing*) and for analysis of the data in real time on the same database (known as *On-line Analytical Processing*, OLAP). But this analysis disturbs the daily of original information systems transactional work since this type of database is designed for transactional work, not for the data analysis, this last task that must be done at night or on weekends.

Stores data or *Data Warehouses* provide information systems support to decision-making (DSS or *Decision Support Systems*) and databases that allow to extract knowledge from historical information stored in the organization. Database designed with the aim of exploitation (analysis-oriented) is different from the from the databases of the operational systems (process-oriented). A data warehouse is a collection of data designed to support making decisions oriented towards the Organization's relevant information (is designed to efficiently find information relative to the basic activities of the Organization as sales, purchasing and production, and not to support the processes that are performed in it as order management, billing)(, etc.), integrated (integrated data from different operational systems of the organization or external sources), variable in time (data relate to a period of time and must be periodically increased) and non-volatile (the stored data are not updated, only increased).

Data warehouses are as clear for organizations advantages the profitability of investments for its creation, the increase of competitiveness in the market and increased productivity of the technicians of direction, being the main problems the underestimation of the effort required for your design and creation, the underestimation of the resources needed to capture, loading and storage of data, the continuous increase of the requirements of the users and the privacy of the data.

The typical components of a data warehouse is a*ETL system*(*Extraction, Transformation and Load*), a*Own data repository*with relevant information or metadata,*Interfaces and query management*that allow access to the data by connecting them more sophisticated tools (OLAP, EIS, mining of data) and*Systems integrity and security*in charge of maintenance global, backups, etc. The ETL system performs the functions of extraction of data sources (transactional or external), processing (cleaning, consolidation,...) and the load of the data warehouse.

The tools of exploitation of the data stores have adopted a *multidimensional data model*. They are typical *of OLAP tools*, which the user presented with a multidimensional view of data (multidimensional schema) for each activity that is the subject of analysis. User formulates query the OLAP tool by selecting attributes of this multidimensional schema without knowing the internal structure (physical schema) of the data store. The OLAP tool generates the corresponding query and sends it to the Manager of consultations of the system (e.g., using a SELECT statement). Thus favour the selection phase in the process of extraction of knowledge.

OLAP tools typically provide a multidimensional view of data (matrix), not to impose restrictions on the number of dimensions, offer symmetry for the dimensions, allow you to define flexible (without limitation) on dimensions: restrictions, aggregations and nests between them, offer intuitive manipulation operators and be transparent to the type of technology that supports the (ROLAP or MOLAP) data store. ROLAP systems are implemented on relational technology, but have some facilities to improve performance (indices of bitmap JOIN indexes *data partitioning*techniques, Query optimizers, extensions, SQL, etc.).

MOLAP systems have specific storage structures (*arrays*) and techniques of compaction of data that favor the performance of the store. MOLAP systems aim to physically store the data in multidimensional structures in such a way that the external representation and the internal representation match

Once a data warehouse designed and implemented using ROLAP or MOLAP technology, the *process of charging and maintenance* that store addresses. These tasks are addressed through an *ETL system* (*Extraction, Transformation and Load*).

If the operational data are maintained in a RDBMS (*Relational data Base System Manager*), extraction or selection of data it cannot be reduced to SQL queries or scheduled routines. If the operational data are in a proprietary system (data format not known) in external sources, text, hypertext or spreadsheets, extraction can be very difficult and may need to be made based on reports or dumps provided by the owners of data must be processed subsequently.

The transformation of the data extracted from the operational sources includes, among other things, cleaning, standardization, and calculation of derived data (integration).

Transport (loading) phase consists of moving data from the operational sources or intermediate storage to the data store and load the data into the corresponding data structures. The load can consume much time. In the initial load of the data warehouse move large volumes of data and in their periodic maintenance moving small volumes of data.

2.3 DATA WAREHOUSE Y DATA MINING

Once stored information in a *Data Warehouse* (data store), the techniques of *Data Mining* (data mining) apply on it optimally. Data warehouses are an ideal organization of information to apply the techniques of extraction of knowledge or data mining.

However, data warehouses are not essential to extracting knowledge from data. It is possible to mining data about a single data file. However, the benefits of building a data warehouse are written off easily, especially when we deal with large volumes of data, or when they come from heterogeneous sources and increase over time.

2.4 SELECTION SAMPLING DATA

Speaking of *sampling methods* , we refer to the set of statistical techniques that are studying the way to select a *shows as sufficiently representative* of a population whose information allows to infer the properties or characteristics of the population making a *measurable and undecideable error*. From the sample selected using a particular method of sampling, estimate population characteristics (media, total, ratio, etc.) with a measurable and controllable error. Estimates are made via mathematical functions of the sample called *estimators*, which become random variables by considering the variability of the samples. Errors are quantified using variances, standard deviations, or mean square errors of estimators, which measure the accuracy of these. The methodology that allows us to infer results, predictions and generalizations about the statistical population, based on the information contained in the previously chosen by formal sampling methods representative samples, is called *statistical inference*.

It is very important to note that to measure the degree of representativeness of the sample, it is necessary to use *probability sampling*. We will say that the sampling is probabilistic when the probability of obtaining each of the samples that can be selected, that is, where the selection of samples constitutes a random phenomenon probabilizable can be drawn. Such selection shall be verified in terms of gaming, being susceptible of measurement uncertainty for the same. This will allow to measure errors in the sampling process (through variance or other statistical measures).

There are several types of sampling, depending on which population statistics tica is finite or infinite, matter on which there is broad statistical literature, but we will consider only the *sampling in finite populations*. The initial finite population that you want to investigate is called *target population*, but target sampling of the entire population it is not always possible due to different problems that they do not allow to obtain information about some of its elements (inaccessibility of some of their elements, refusals to work, absences, etc.), with which the population which is really subject to study or *research population* does not match the target population.

On the other hand, to select the sample, we will need a list of so-called sampling *framework* that theoretically should match the target population units. A framework will be most appropriate how much better cover the population objective, i.e. the smaller the *error of coverage*. But frames the outdated, the omissions of some units, duplications of others and the presence of foreign units and other impurities requiring its purification (*purification of imperfect frames*) are inevitable. The target population by eliminating frame units erroneously included in it (strange units, mirrors, etc.) and adding the omissions could ideally be achieved.

Likewise, also would be a goal than to delete from the frame units for which no information can be (inaccessible, absent, not collaborating, etc.) will obtain the research population. The framework can be constituted by elementary units of sampling or compound units. A *elementary (or simple) unit* is the simplest possible sampling and a *unit composed (or primary)* consists of several basic units.

As in practice it is not easy to have frames of elementary units, tries to get frames of composite units which are more accessible. For example, to study a region inhabitants it is easier to have a list of homes that a list of individuals. You select a frame homes (composed of several individuals units) sample and then studied the properties of individuals with appropriate techniques.

2.5 SIMPLE RANDOM SAMPLING

It *without replacement simple random sampling* is a procedure of selection of samples with equal probabilities, which consists of obtaining the sample unit at random without replacement to the population of the previously selected units, bearing in mind that the order of the elements in the samples is not involved (i.e., that samples with the same elements in different order are considered equal). In this way, samples with repeating elements are impossible. The selection procedure is likely to equal, all samples are equiprobable, and also meets all the population units have the same probability of belonging to the sample $\pi_i = n/n$. Assumes that the size of the population is N and the sample size is n. As the sample is selected without replacement, the selection is made successive units for the sample with probability $1/(N-t)$ for values of $t= 0, 1,..., n$.

We could summarize the specifications of the sampling random simple without replacement or *unrestricted random sampling* as follows:

- It is a type of sampling of elementary units.

- It consists of obtaining the sample unit to randomly without replacement to the population of the previously selected units.

- The order of the elements in the samples is not involved; i.e., the samples with the same elements in different order are considered equal.

- Samples with repeating elements are impossible.

- It's a selection procedure with equal chances for all units of the population will have the same probability of belonging to the sample.

- All samples are equiprobable.

The *simple reset random sampling* is a selection procedure with equal probabilities which consists of obtaining the sample unit to randomly reset to the population of the previously selected units. Thus samples with repeating elements are possible, and any element of the population can be repeated in the sample 0, 1,..., n times. Suppose in all moment the size of the population is N and the sample size is n. As the sample is selected with replacement (previously selected units are reset to the population) and with equal probabilities, the successive selection of units for the sample with probability is $P_i = 1/N$ and all the samples are equiprobable, since:

$$P(u_1, u_2,..., u_n) = P(u_1)P(u_2) ... P(u_n) = (1/N)(1/N) ... (1/N) = 1/(N^n)$$

Happens that obtained the same unbiased estimators for the population parameters for the case of simple random sampling without replacement. Therefore, estimates of the mean and the population proportion are estimators by analogy (media and sample proportion), estimates of the total and the total of class population are the expansion through the population size of sample the mean and proportion.

The error of the estimates (variance) is always lower in the case of sampling without replacement, which tells us that *sampling without replacement is in general more accurate than sampling with replacement.*

In addition, *in the case of sampling without replacement less sample size is needed to make the same mistake as in the case of sampling with replacement*, so sampling without replacement is more efficient than sampling with replacement.

2.6 STRATIFIED SAMPLING

Suppose that the population under study, formed by N elementary units, is divided into L subpopulations or strata, which constitute a partition, i.e. do not overlap and the union of all of them is total.

Stratified sampling is a sampling type of elementary since sample stratified size units$n$is obtained by selecting$n_h$items ($h = 1, 2,..., L$) of each of the$L$strata that is subdivided the population independently. If the selection within each stratum is random simple and independently, the sampling is *called stratified random sampling*, but in general nothing prevents to use different types of selection within each stratum. If random sampling in each stratum is without replacement, stratified sampling is without replacement, and if random sampling in each stratum is reset, the stratified sampling is reset.

The main objective of the stratified sampling is to improve the accuracy of estimates by reducing the sampling errors. Try to minimize the variance of the estimators by strata creating more homogeneous possible between its elements (so that stratum estimates are accurate) and the more heterogeneous (to have the maximum of information). Other objectives of the stratified sampling are the following:

1. Provide separate estimates for each of the strata.
2. Make more rational use of the administrative organization.
3. Alleviate the framework defaults, isolating those defects in some strata.

It is very convenient to use stratified sampling when there is a precise variable for stratification whose values allow you to conveniently divide the population into homogeneous strata. The variables used for stratification should be correlated with the variables under investigation. For example, to carry out statistics on the income of the families in a city can Stratify according to the values of the variable professional qualification of the heads of its components (more qualifications normally have more revenue, so the layers will be homogeneous). If you want to study the turnover of establishments for sale to the public in a city, you can use your employees as a stratification variable, and classified (stratifying) settlements in hypermarkets, supermarkets, large stores, small shops and others, according to the number of employees; This is a division of settlements in homogeneous groups. If you want to study characteristics of hospitals can be variable stratification number of patients, to stratify them in large hospitals, clinics of middle and small clinics, resulting in groups of hospitals with similar problems. For statistics in the education sector the stratification variable level of education can be used, taking as strata levels of pre-school education, primary education, compulsory secondary education, high school and university education (each stratum has thus a very peculiar characteristics that make it homogeneous).

The estimate of the total population in random stratified sampling is the sum of the estimators of total in each stratum and elevation factors are N_h / n_h. The estimate of mean in stratified random sampling is the weighted average of the estimates of the average in eachstratum, being the weighting coefficients $W_h = N_h/N$ unitary sum, which, in turn, are the factors of lift. The estimator of random stratified sampling class total is the sum of the estimators of total class in each stratum. The estimate of the proportion in stratified random sampling is the weighted average of estimates of the proportion in each stratum, being Wweighting coefficients$_h$ $=N/n_h$unitary sum. The variances of the estimators and their mistakes are $(f_h = n_h / N_h)$.

In stratified sampling is called*affixation of the sample*to the distribution, allocation, award, secondment or distribution of the sample size$n$between different strata; that is, the determination of the values of$n_h$que verifiquen $n_1 + n_2$ + ... + n_L = n. They can set many afijaciones or ways to distribute the sample between the layers, but the most important are: uniform affixation, proportional affixation, affixation of minimum variance and optimal affixation.

Affixation uniform consists of assigning the same number of sample units to each stratum, which take all $n_h$equal to n, increasing or decreasing this size in a unit if n is a multiple of L, that is, $n_h = E(n) + 1$, where E denotes the entire part.

For this type of affixation, the variances of the estimators and their estimates are replacing General formulasf_h por k/N_h. This type of affixation gives equal importance to all levels, in terms of sample size, which will favour the smallest size strata and will hurt the large in relation to accuracy. It is only suitable in populations with layers of similar size.

Proportional affixation is to assign to each stratum a number of sample units in proportion to its size. The n the sample units are distributed proportionally to the sizes of the strata expressed in number of units.

In proportional affixation, we can ensure the following:

• Strata sampling fractions are equal and consistent with the overall fraction of sampling, its value being the constant of proportionality.

• Wweighting coefficients$_h$ are exclusively obtained from the sample, as they are only needed for its calculation sample values (n_h and n).

• The unbiased estimator for the population total can be expressed as the quotient of the total sample and the sampling fraction, or what is the same, as the product of the total sample by the inverse of the sampling fraction. Similar property is the unbiased estimator for the total of class (product of the total sample class by the inverse of the sampling fraction).

- The unbiased estimator for the population mean can be expressed as the ratio of the total sample and the sample size. Similar property is the unbiased estimator for the population proportion (ratio between the total number of sample class and the sample size).

- All units of the population have the same probability of inclusion in the sample of n units; in other words, we are autoponderadas specimens.

The **affixation of minimum variance or affixation of Neyman** consists of determining the values of n_n (number of units that are extracted from the stratum h- th sample) in such a way that for a sample size fixed n equals the variance of the estimators is minimal.

The usefulness of this affixation is greater if there are differences in the variability of the strata. In another case, greater simplicity and autoponderacion of proportional affixation make better employment of this.

Optimal affixation consists of determining values of n_h (number of units that are extracted from the stratum h- th sample) so that the variance of the estimators is minimum for a fixed cost C. The fixed cost C will be the sum of the costs of the selection of the sample units of strata; that is, if c_h is the cost per unit of sampling in the stratum h, the total cost of selection of the n_h sample units in the stratum will be $c_h n_h$. Adding costs $c_h n_h$ for the L strata we have the total cost of the stratified sample selection.

2.7 SYSTEMATIC RANDOM SAMPLING

We start from a population of size N, and grouped its elements in n areas (rows) of size k ($N = nk$). We could represent the population as follows:

$i \setminus j$	1	2	3	$\cdots$	j	$\cdots$	k
1	u_{11}	u_{12}	u_{13}	$\cdots$	u_{1j}	$\cdots$	u_{1k}
2	u_{21}	u_{22}	u_{23}	$\cdots$	u_{1j}	$\cdots$	u_{2k}
$\vdots$	$\vdots$	$\vdots$	$\vdots$		$\vdots$		$\vdots$
i	u_{i1}	u_{i2}	u_{i3}	$\cdots$	u_{1j}	$\cdots$	u_{ik}
$\vdots$	$\vdots$	$\vdots$	$\vdots$		$\vdots$		$\vdots$
n	u_{n1}	u_{n2}	u_{n3}	$\cdots$	u_{nj}	$\cdots$	u_{nk}

Below are numbered elements of the above table from left to right starting with the first unit of the first row and proceed to the first unit of the next row when any row is exhausted. We have the following structure:

$i \setminus j$	1	2	3	$\cdots$	j	$\cdots$	k
1	u_1	u_2	u_3	$\cdots$	u_j	$\cdots$	u_k
2	u_{k+1}	u_{k+2}	u_{k+3}	$\cdots$	u_{k+j}	$\cdots$	u_{k+k}
3	u_{2k+1}	u_{2k+2}	u_{2k+3}	$\cdots$	u_{2k+j}		u_{2k+k}
$\vdots$	$\vdots$	$\vdots$	$\vdots$		$\vdots$		$\vdots$
i	$u_{(i-1)k+1}$	$u_{(i-1)k+2}$	$u_{(i-1)k+3}$	$\cdots$	$u_{(i-1)k+j}$	$\cdots$	$u_{(i-1)k+k}$
$\vdots$	$\vdots$	$\vdots$	$\vdots$		$\vdots$		$\vdots$
n	$u_{(n-1)k+1}$	$u_{(n-1)k+2}$	$u_{(n-1)k+3}$	$\cdots$	$u_{(n-1)k+j}$	$\cdots$	$\underbrace{u_{(n-1)k+k}}_{u_N}$

To extract a sample of size n is chosen at random a unit in the first zone, and to select the $n-1$ remaining units to sample is taken in each area the unit that occupies the same place within its area which occupied the first unit selected within the first zone. For example, if the drive selected to sample at random in the first zone is the third, choose the $n-1$ remaining units for sample taking the third unit in each area. Systematic samples thus obtained (columns of the above table) are often referred to as *samples 1 in k*.

The probability of selecting any sample will be the probability to choose the unit that caused it in the first row by simple random sampling, i.e. 1 /k. Therefore, systematic sampling provides samples equiprobable. On the other hand, the probability that any unit of the population (of N units) belong to the sample (size k) is − k/n = k/nk = 1 /n; Therefore, systematic sampling is a type of sampling with equal probabilities. Samples from the sample space can be represented as follows:

$$\left(\widetilde{u}_1\right) = \left\{u_1, u_{1+k}, \cdots u_{1+(n-1)k}\right\}$$
$$\dots \dots \dots \dots \dots \dots \dots \dots \dots$$
$$\left(\widetilde{u}_j\right) = \left\{u_j, u_{j+k}, \cdots u_{j+(n-1)k}\right\}$$
$$\dots \dots \dots \dots \dots \dots \dots \dots \dots$$
$$\left(\widetilde{u}_k\right) = \left\{u_k, u_{k+k}, \cdots u_{k+(n-1)k}\right\}$$

Systematic sampling extends the sample to the entire population, collect the possible effect of stratification due to the order that contains the population units (each row can be considered a stratum), allows consideration of the population cluster (each column can be considered as a conglomerate), it is easy to apply and check, does not present problems of algebraic calculus and does not require distinction between replacement and not reset. In addition, if the arrangement of the elements in the population is random, systematic selection is equivalent to a simple random sampling. Finally, the sampling error tends to be lower than in simple random sampling or even that in stratified.

On the other hand, should bear in mind the possibility of increase of the variance if periodicity in the population and the theoretical problem that arises in the estimation of variances due to the fact that there is no independence in the selection of units in various areas, since the units extracted in each zone depend on the selected in the first zone. In general, there are only random selection for the first unit of the sample.

Shows that an unbiased linear estimator for the population mean is the average of the systematic sample obtained, for the population proportion is the proportion of the shows systematic, for the total population is N times the total systematic sample, and for the total of class is N times the total of class sample.

It is possible to *relate with sampling stratified systematic sampling* considering each zone k consecutive elements starting from the first as a stratum; i.e. can be divided the population into n strata constituted each of them by a table row (k units) of the picture that we have represented elements of the population numbered consecutively.

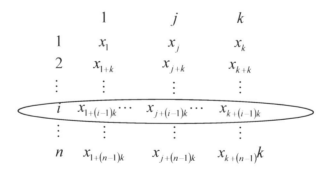

Obtain a systematic sample would then be equivalent to get a stratified sample with one unit per stratum. Please note, however, that in stratified random sampling is selected independently in each stratum, while in systematic sampling all selected items occupy the same place or order number within each area of k elements, with which there is no randomness in the selection. In addition, it would be desirable that the n systematic areas of k elements each (strata) are homogeneous within them and heterogeneous among them.

It is also possible to **relate the systematic sampling of conglomerates with sampling** whereas each column of n elements as a conglomerate; i.e. can be divided population into k clusters constituted each of them by a column in the table (n units). Obtain a systematic sample would then be equivalent to obtain a sample by conglomerates of size 1.

$$
\begin{array}{cccc}
 & 1 & j & k \\
1 & x_1 & x_j & x_k \\
2 & x_{1+k} & x_{j+k} & x_{k+k} \\
\vdots & \vdots & \vdots & \vdots \\
i & x_{1+(i-1)k} \cdots & x_{j+(i-1)k} \cdots & x_{k+(i-1)k} \\
\vdots & \vdots & \vdots & \vdots \\
n & x_{1+(n-1)k} & x_{j+(n-1)k} & x_{k+(n-1)}k
\end{array}
$$

Both in simple random sampling with replacement as without replacement, as well as stratified, systematic sampling and indirect methods of estimation, sampling units are the same as the object of study (simple or basic units) units, but in practice we find situations more general in which the sampling units comprise two or more units of study. In this case the sampling units are called primary or compound units.

2.8 CLUSTER SAMPLING

Cluster sampling is not needed a very specific framework such as simple random sampling in which it was necessary to have a list of units of the population, or as in stratified sampling, where it was necessary to have listings of units by stratum. Divides previously to sampling population in conglomerates or suitable areas, of which a certain number for sample is selected so it is only necessary to a framework of conglomerates that will be easier to get and cheaper. They can be used as frame territorial divisions established by administrative needs for which there is information. They can also be used as geographical areas whose characteristics are already very defined frame. It is clear that saving cost and time to pay visits to selected units. Moreover, the concentration of units decreases the need for travel.

On the other hand, in cluster sampling, we tend to have less precision in the estimates, since, although the ideal is that there is heterogeneity within, will always be a certain degree of homogeneity inevitable within conglomerates that will decrease the accuracy. This type of sampling efficiency decreases by increasing the size of the conglomerates, when in reality this type of sampling is more useful in the case of very large populations where large clusters can be built.

We consider a finite population with M elementary or latest units grouped in N larger units called clusters or primary units, in such a way that there are no overlaps between the conglomerates and containing these in any case to the population under study. We consider sampling the conglomerate unit, and extract a sample of n conglomerates from which we will estimate the population parameters of the population. The number of basic units of a conglomerate is called the cluster size. Conglomerates may be equal or different size, and should be as heterogeneous as possible within them and homogeneous among them, so that the ideal situation would be that a single conglomerate could faithfully represent the population (size one with minimum cost sample). Shown that the situation is now the complementary to the case of the strata studied previously.

Two of cluster sampling is a type of sampling in which a first stage is selected a sample of conglomerates of sizes $M_i$$i$ = 1, 2,n, n and in a second stage is selected, independently on each cluster of the first stage, a subsample of m_i elementary units between the Mi of the conglomerate. In both stages the selection can be with or without replacement, but in the second stage is often used sampling without replacement. In the second stage you can use any type of sampling of the already studied, but usually without replacement and equal chances.

In sampling two is not necessary to use all the elementary units of clusters selected in first stage. Neither is it necessary a complete framework of elementary units; just a more coarse framework for conglomerates, and within each conglomerate is enough with a submarco for the subsampling in second stage. In this way, as are considered stages of subsampling sub-frames more bastos, and therefore easier to obtain and manage, than complete frames of elementary units are used. When there is a certain degree of homogeneity within the cluster sample is absurd to select all its basic units for the sample. Just choose some of them causing the subsampling. In sampling two less resources are needed and the cost is less, since only visited some of the elementary units of clusters chosen in first stage for sample. However, in the two sampling precision is lower; the sub-frames within each cluster can cause complications to increase the number of stages of subsampling and are sources of variation that complicate the algebraic calculations (as many sources as stages have sampling). The first source is due to the selection of primary units and 2 source is due to the subsampling within each primary unit.

Two sampling is also called in two-stage sampling or sampling with subsampling (the subsampling is the second stage).

2.9 SAMPLING MULTISTAGE CLUSTER

In the multistage sampling consecutive submuestreos are made to a specified number of stages. For example, in sampling will select in a first stage a sample of primary units, in a second stage is subsampling in each of the first-stage sample units and in a third stage is subsampling in each of the second-stage sample units. Similarly it is generalizaría for a large number of stages, giving rise to the multistage sampling.

2.10 COMPLEX DESIGNS

In practice, it is usual to use polietapicos designs with different types of sampling at each stage. It is very common to use layering of primary units to select the primary units of the sample of first stage through stratified sampling. Then is the selection of the second stage within each unit of first stage units. For this type of sampling two stratification in first stage formulas of the estimators, variance and variance estimates are well known.

2.11 ANALYSIS OF CORRELATIONS

We already know that correlation analysis seeks to calculate the matrix of correlations between variables initial replacing those that are more related to each other by one of them. The *matrix of correlations*summarizes the correlations for all possible pairs of variables from n given $X_1, X_2..., X_n$. Is defined as:

$$R = \begin{pmatrix} r_{11} & r_{12} & r_{13} & \cdots & r_{1n} \\ r_{21} & r_{22} & r_{23} & \cdots & r_{2n} \\ . & . & . & \cdots & . \\ . & . & . & \cdots & . \\ r_{n1} & r_{n2} & r_{n3} & \cdots & r_{nn} \end{pmatrix}$$

where every r_{ij} is the correlation coefficient between X_i and X_j for all i, j.

If given a series of variables X_1, X_2,...,X_n, is studying the degree of simultaneous dependence among all of them, or between groups of them, the matrix of correlations can be used. If a function that explain a variable using all can be established on the basis of the intensity with which depend on others, which is are their influential causes, we are facing a problem of multiple regression, that will be studied later.

Using the multiple linear correlation coefficient is studied the degree of linear association between all the variables simultaneously, while that by means of correlation coefficients simple r_{ij} is measured the degree of association between variables X_i and X_j without taking into account other variables.

On the other hand, the *partial correlation matrix* summarizes the partial correlations for all possible pairs of variables between n given X_1, X_2,..., X_n. It is defined as:

$$P = \begin{pmatrix} r_{11} & r_{12} & r_{13} & \cdots & r_{1n} \\ r_{21} & r_{22} & r_{23} & \cdots & r_{2n} \\ . & . & . & \cdots & . \\ . & . & . & \cdots & . \\ r_{n1} & r_{n2} & r_{n3} & \cdots & r_{nn} \end{pmatrix}$$

where r_{ij} is the *coefficient of partial correlation* between X_i and X_j for all i, j.

While that by means of correlation coefficients simple r_{ij} is measured the degree of association between variables X_i and X_j without taking into account other variables, through coefficients of partial correlation measures the degree of association between X_i and X_j , bearing in mind the possible influence on these two variables from the rest of the variables.

When the variables are qualitative is very typical to consider the correlation coefficient between the ranks of the values of the variables. Refers to a value of a variable range place that occupies this value in the total set of values of the variable, so-called management of minor to major. *Are$_i$ and B$_i$ the different modalities of two qualitative variables X and Y*. Sean x_ie *and$_i$* ranges or order numbers that correspond to A_i and B_i, alleged ordered these modalities, the scale to be determined, with minor to major. It is defined *by ranges of Spearman correlation coefficient* for the qualitative variables *X* and *and* as the coefficient of linear correlation of variables whose values are x_i e *and$_i$*. This value is used to measure the degree of Association of qualitative variables *X* and *and*, based on the concordance or discordance of the classifications by ranges of its modalities.

The coefficient of correlation by ranges is also used for quantitative variables, with the clarification that the degree of Association retrieved is not the values of the variables, but the classifications by ranges of these values. The expression of this coefficient is given by:

$$\rho = 1 - \frac{6 \sum_i d_i^2}{N^3 - N}$$

siendo $d_i = x_i - y_i$. This coefficient is also called *ordinal correlation coefficient*, and for being a correlation coefficient varies between −1 and 1. When the concordance between the ranges is perfect then $d_i = x_i - and_i = 0$ and $\rho = 1$. When the disagreement is perfect $\rho = -1$. When there is no concordance or discordance $\rho = 0$.

WORKING ENVIRONMENT OF SAS ENTERPRISE MINER

3.1 INTRODUCTION SAS ENTERPRISE MINER

SAS Institute implements data mining in *Enterprise Miner*software, which will be used in this book, and other procedures and modules (STAT, STD,...) which will also be used throughout the text. SAS Institute defines the concept of *Data Mining* as the process of selecting (*Selecting*), explore (*Exploring*), modify (*Modifying*), modeling (*Modeling*) and rating (*Assessment*) large amounts of data with the aim of uncovering unknown patterns which can be used as a comparative advantage with respect to competitors. This process is summarized with the acronym SEMMA which are the initials of the 5 phases which comprise the process of *Data Mining* according to SAS Institute. Each of these stages has associated different nodes, as shown below:

- **Phase of selection (Selecting)**: carries associated data source (*Input Data Source*), sampling (*Sampling*), partition of data (*Data Partition*) and time Series (*Time series*) nodes. See Figure 3-1.

Figure 3-1

- **Phase of exploration (Explore)**: has been associated nodes distributions (*Distribution Explorer*) browser; Graphics (*Multiplot*); (*Insight*) multivariate analysis; Association (*Association*); Selection of Variables (*Variable Selection*), analysis of unions (*Link Analysis*). See Figure 3-2.

Figure 3-2

- **Phase of modification (MOD.)**: Definition of variables (*Data Set Attributes*); Transformation of Variables (*Variables Transform*); Treatment of outliers (*Filter Outliers*); Replacement of missing values (*Replacement*); Classification (*Clustering*); Self-organized neural networks (*SOM/Kohonen*), interactive grouping (*Interactive Grouping*) and time Series (*Time Series*). See Figure 3-3

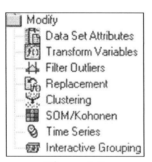

Figure 3-3

- **Modeling of phase (Model)**: regression (*regression*); Decision trees (*Tree*); Artificial neural networks (*Neural Network*); Neural networks and/or analysis of main components (*Princomp/Dmneural*); Model defined by the user (*User Defined Model*); Models Union (*Ensemble*); Memory-based reasoning (*Memory Based Reasoning*) and models in two stages (*Two Stage Model*). See Figure 3-4.

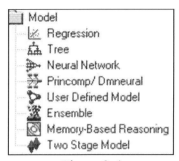

Figure 3-4

- ***Phase of assessment (Assess):*** Valuation (*Assessment*) and reports (*Reporter*). See Figure 3-5.

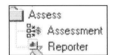

Figure 3-5

3.1.1 Starting with SAS Enterprise Miner

To access *Enterprise Miner* simply type ***miner*** in command of SAS Explorer (Figure 3-6) box.

Figure 3-6

You can also access *Enterprise Miner* from the SAS menu bar by selecting *Solutions → analysis → Enterprise Miner* (Figure 3-7).

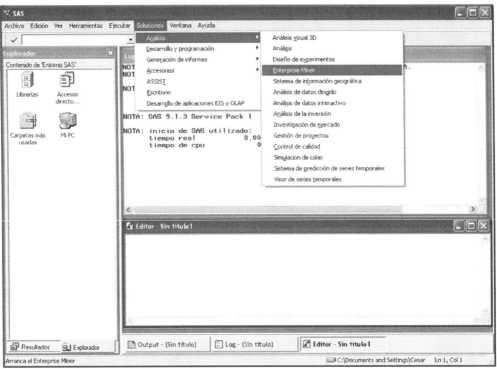

Figure 3-7

Both ways you reach the window of *Enterprise Miner*, in which stands out the work area, the toolbar and Navigator project with tabs for diagrams, tools and reports (Figure 3-8).

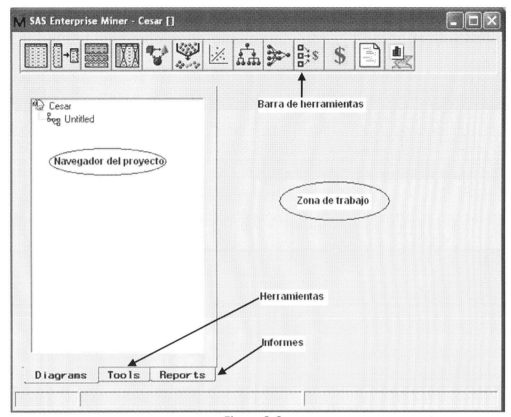

Figure 3-8

The diagrams (*Diagrams*) of the project Navigator tab allows you to select projects and open diagrams. The tab tools (*Tools*) displays the set of tasks that can be performed by *Enterprise Miner* (Figure 3-9). Reports (*Reports*) tab contains the generated reports that are to be created through the reports node (*Reporter node*) of *Enterprise Miner*.

Using the tab*Tools*we stand on the set of analysis tools for the*Data Mining.*Major entries in this menu (*Input Data Source, Sampling*, etc.) are nodes that contain different tools from*Data Mining*. The nodes are the basic elements that comprise all the analysis of *Enterprise Miner* as well as all the work comprising the cycle of *Data Mining*. All processes will therefore rotate around the use of them. Later we will describe the utilities of each of them.

Figure 3-9

In the working area of the figure 3-8 carry out all the tasks of the *Data Mining*process. It is here where the data are processed, models run and results are measured. This process is carried out by means of diagrams of flows. A flow diagram is nothing more than the orderly connection of all the nodes that make up a *Data Mining*problem.

The toolbar (Figure 3-10) contains the subset of tasks of *Enterprise Miner* which are frequently used by the user. The program allows you to add or delete the icons of the nodes of the toolbar according to your preferences.

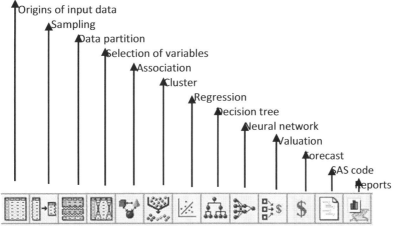

Figure 3-10

To add an item to the toolbar, select the icon in the area of the browser from the project and drag to the toolbar.

To delete an item which is not used, select the task with the right mouse button and choose *Remove from tool bar*.

The nodes that make up the toolbar can be added to the work area without the applications bar mainly in three ways:

- Click and drag the node to the work area from the toolbar.

- Click and drag the node to the work area from the toolset for analysis of SAS *Enterprise Miner*.

- Click with the right button on the working area and select *Add Node* from which a window is displayed to open the node.

Node can subsequently be opened by double clicking with the left button, well performing the selection with the mouse right button then press *Open*.

3.1.2 Home of a project new

SAS Enterprise Miner project is the document in which information, data, diagrams and a certain analysis results are saved. The projects are therefore associated with different *Data Mining* problems normally correspond to different databases. There is no restriction on the number of projects and *Enterprise Miner* allows up to 100,000 diagrams per project. Projects are saved with extension *.dmp* diagrams have extension *.dmd*.

To start a new project from the main menu select *File → New → Project* (Figure 3-11). This action opens the window *Create new project* (Figure 3-12). In this window it is necessary to specify the project name and the location of the same. Once made both options select *create*. The project is created with a diagram, that default will be called *untitled* until a new name is assigned to you when you save it (Figure 3-13). Once the project is created the next step is to perform an analysis following phases of *Data Mining*: selection, exploration, modification, modelling and evaluation of results.

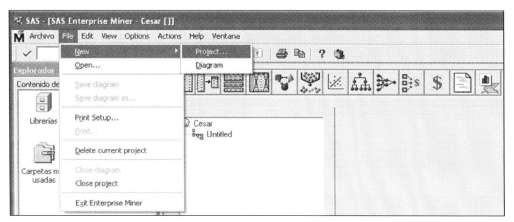

Figure 3-11

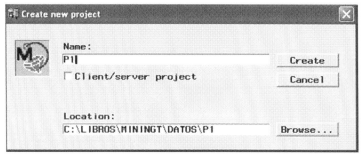

Figure 3-12

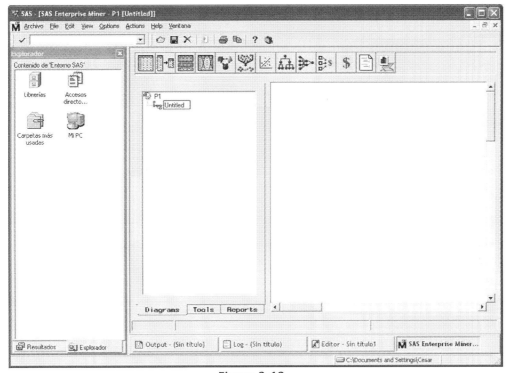

Figure 3-13

3.1.3 Main menu of Sas Enterrise Miner

*Enterprise Miner*contains a menu that lets you select and execute common tasks.This menu (top of Figure 3-13) presents the options *File, Edit, View, Options, Actions* and *Help* whose sub-items and purposes will be explored below.

The **File** option (Figure 3-11) presents the following sub-items:

New →Project: creates a new project that you can associate many diagrams.

New → Diagram: create a new diagram. To remove the lock of a diagram it is necessary to remove the file with extension *.*lck* associated diagram.

Open: open a new or existing diagram in the project in use. This task can also be performed with the icon ⌖ .

Save Diagram: saves the diagram that is being used within the project. This task can also be performed with the icon 💾 .

Save Diagram as: assigns a name and save the diagram used within the project.

Print Setup: specify the print options.

Print: prints the contents of *Enterprise Miner*. This task can also be performed with the icon 🖨 .

Delete current Project: removes the active project. This action is to also delete all the files that contain the project. This task can also be performed with the icon ✕ .

Close Diagram: saves and closes the selected diagram.

Close Project: closes the project currently in use.

Exit Enterprise Miner: ends the session with *Enterprise Miner* returning to the main setting of the SAS program.

The option **Edit** (Figure 3-14) presents the following sub-items:

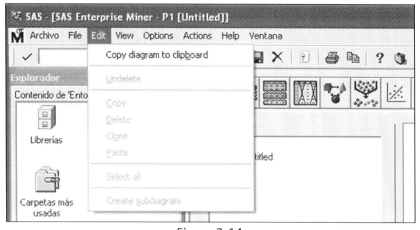

Figure 3-14

Copy Diagram to clipboard: allows you to copy the work area chart to then be stuck in a text document or to be presented in a report. This task can also be performed with the icon 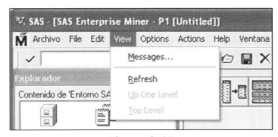 .

Undelete: retrieves the last deleted node.

Copy: copying a node, diagram or object of the work area.

Delete: deletes the node or the work area selected connection.

Clone: clones the selected node. Cloning involves copying the node and paste it in the folder *Custom* tools palette.

Paste: hits the node, object or diagram.

Select all: selects all the nodes in the work area.

Create subdiagram: creates a sub-diagram for grouping a set of nodes and connections selected within an icon node sub-diagram.

The option ***View*** (Figure 3-15) presents the following sub-items:

Figure 3-15

Messages: displays a window with messages for the active diagram.

Refresh: updated the project Navigator and diagrams of the work area.

Up One Level: shows the level immediately higher set of successive diagrams. If there is no subdiagrams considered diagram, we will only have a single diagram. If on the other hand there are subdiagrams diagram in use, then the subdiagrams may be displayed in your grouped shape (hiding its internal structure) or in its expanded form (showing its internal structure). The highest level shows the subdiagrams in grouped form.

Top Level: shows the diagram of process in its most grouped shape and therefore all the subdiagrams appear grouped.

The option **Options** (Figure 3-15) presents the following sub-items:

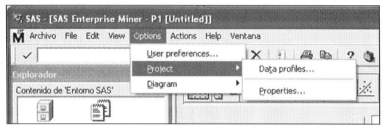

Figure 3-15

User preferences: opens the window of the user preferences (Figure 3-16) which allows you to specify various options at the start of *Enterprise Miner*. Also sets the directories that are used by default for new projects, sets the server for projects that need it and specifies the results HTML that you want to be displayed when using the results node (*Reporter node*). This task can also be performed with the icon    . After making the appropriate changes it is necessary to select *OK* to have this effect.

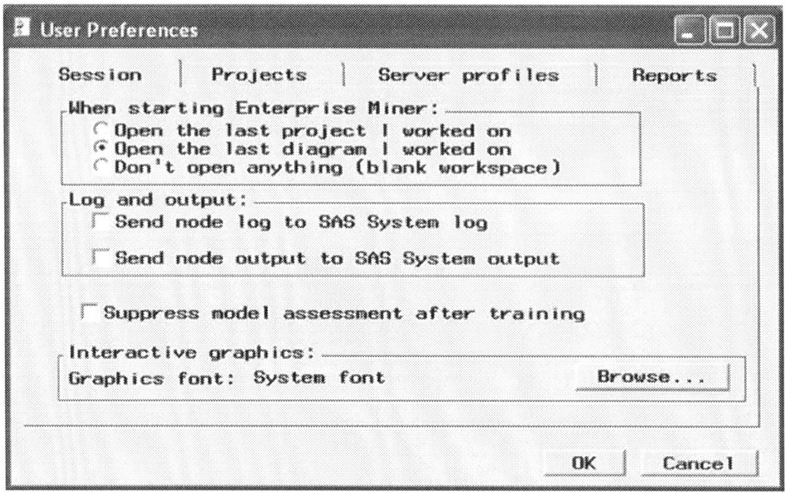

Figure 3-16

Project → Data Profiles: this option user-defined information about the objectives to achieve in the project.

Project → *Properties:* displays the project such as the name and type properties, if it is or not shared, its location (*General*tab) as well as the options of initialization (lapel *Initialization* of Figure 3-18), the *Data Warehouse* which feeds data (tab *Warehouse* of Figure 3-19) and the list of users who have open Project Server (*Server*tab), the route options (tab *Users* of Figure 3-20).

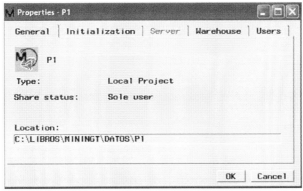

Figure 3-17

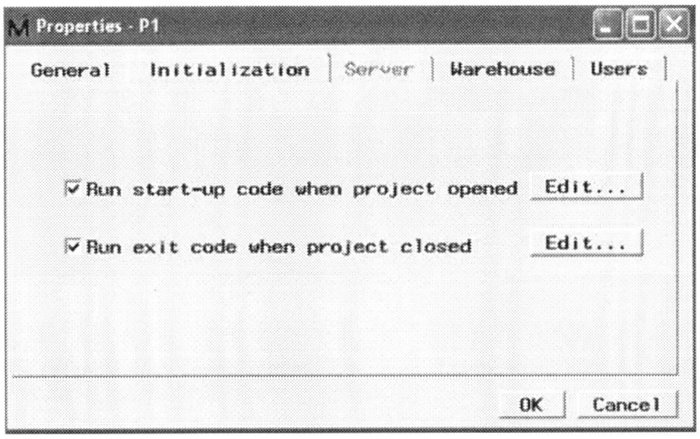

Figure 3-18

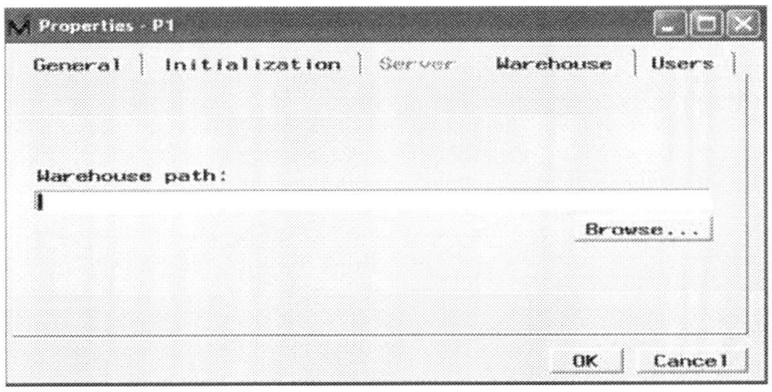

Figure 3-19

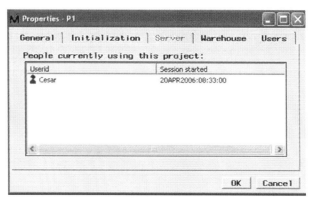

Figure 3-20

Diagram: presents several options work with diagrams (Figure 3-21).

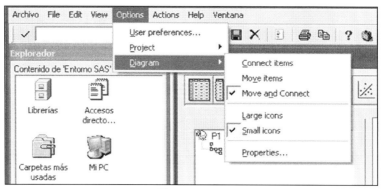

Figure 3-21

Diagram → *Connect items:* serves to establish connections between the icons of the nodes.

Diagram → *Move items:* serves to move the icons of the nodes within the work area.

Diagram → *Move and Connect:*(Default option): allows you to move and connect the icons of the nodes in the work area.

Diagram →*Large icons:* increases the size of the icons in the work area.

Diagram → *Small icons:* (default)*:* displays icons with a small size within the work area.

Diagram → *Properties:* opens the window of properties of the diagram (Figure 3-22). This option also allows protect diagram or create and store notes around it.

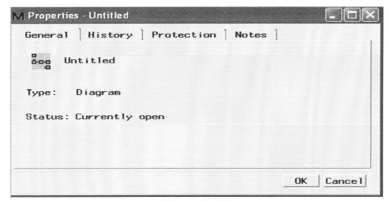

Figure 3-22

The choice of **Actions** (Figure 3-23) presents the following sub-items:

Figure 3-23

Open: opens the selected node.

Run: run the node selected as well as any previous connected node that has not been executed.

Results: open Manager results for those nodes that have generated results.

Add node: opens the window of *adding node* (Figure 3-24) that allows you to add a node within the work area.

Add endpoints: adds endpoints to the process flow.

Figure 3-24

The option **Help** (Figure 3-25) presents the following sub-items:

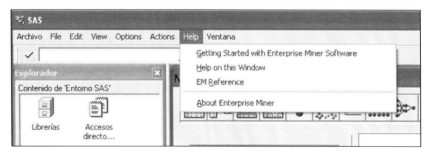

Figure 3-25

Getting Started withEnterprise MinerSoftware: opens a window with a tutorial for *Enterprise Miner* (Figure 3-26). This action can also be performed with the icon 🌑 .

Help on this Window: It opens a window with help on the selected topic (Figure 3-27). This task can also be performed with the icon ?.

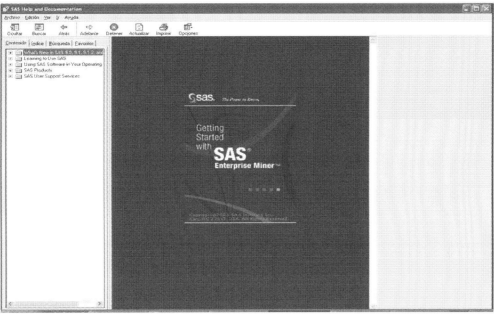

Figure 3-26

Figure 3-27

EM Reference Help: It provides specific help on each of the nodes of *Enterprise Miner* (Figure 3-28).

About Enterprise Miner: Information on the version of *Enterprise Miner* used (Figure 3-29).

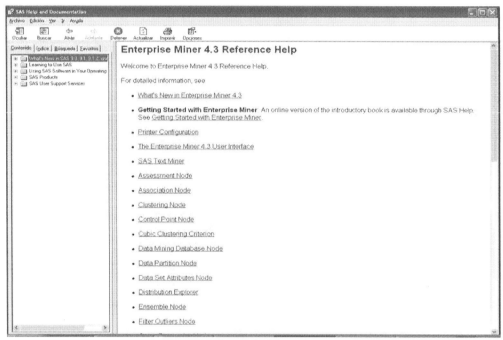

Figure 3-28

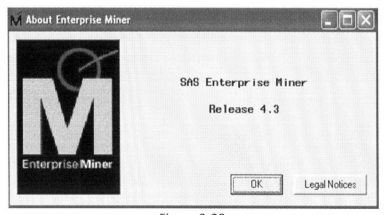

Figure 3-29

3.2 EXAMPLE WORKING WITH SAS ENTERPRISE MINER

With the data from the file in ASCII format of name *tenis.txt* located in *f:\libros\minigt\datos\tenis*, which contains information about the days that has been able to play tennis depending on meteorological aspects, is to build a model based on decision trees that allow pedecir if today it is possible to play tennis. The data shown in Figure 3-30.

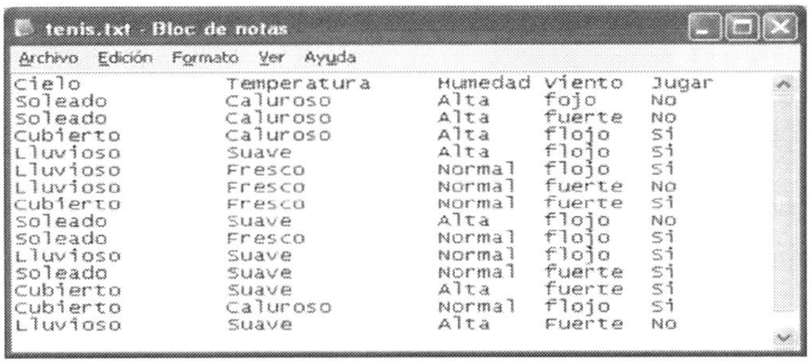

Cielo	Temperatura	Humedad	Viento	Jugar
Soleado	Caluroso	Alta	fojo	No
Soleado	Caluroso	Alta	fuerte	No
Cubierto	Caluroso	Alta	flojo	Si
Lluvioso	Suave	Alta	flojo	Si
Lluvioso	Fresco	Normal	flojo	Si
Lluvioso	Fresco	Normal	fuerte	No
Cubierto	Fresco	Normal	fuerte	Si
Soleado	Suave	Alta	flojo	No
Soleado	Fresco	Normal	flojo	Si
Lluvioso	Suave	Normal	flojo	Si
Soleado	Suave	Normal	fuerte	Si
Cubierto	Suave	Alta	fuerte	Si
Cubierto	Caluroso	Normal	flojo	Si
Lluvioso	Suave	Alta	Fuerte	No

Figure 3-30

3.2.1 Read data files and link them with Enterprise Miner through the node Input Data Source

The first task in the process of data mining is to read the set of baseline data. *SAS Enterprise Miner* performs this task through the *Input Data Source* (data node) node. The node's data is a fundamental, since it allows to read the analysis data and set its attributes. The node only reads the data in SAS format, so that if our data is in another format, in our case in ASCII delimited columns or tabs, we import it into any of the active libraries. If necessary, you create a new library.

To create a library press the icon 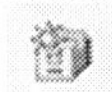 and in the fields of Figure 3-31 name the new library (*work*) and activate the picture *assigned to the home* so that it is available whenever we open SAS.

To import the ASCII file *tenis.txt* to SAS, SAS main menu select *file → import data* by choosing *file (.txt) Tab-delimited* according to of indicated in the figure 3-32. Press *Next* and choose the way in which the file is to be imported (Figure 3-33). Press *Next* again and will choose the library that will be staying the new imported SAS file and its name (Figure 3-34). Pressing *end* gets longer the imported file in SAS format *tenis.sas7bdat* which is hosted on the library *work* (*C:\libros\miningt\datos*).

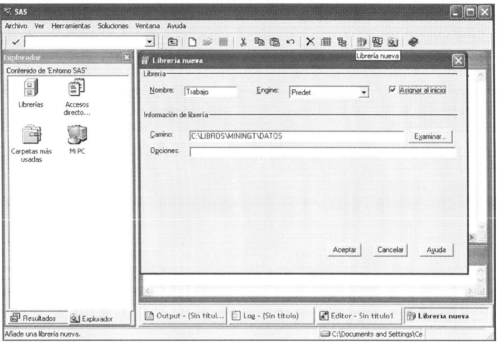

Figure 3-31

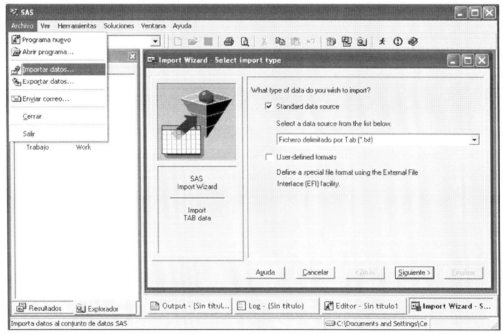

Figure 3-32

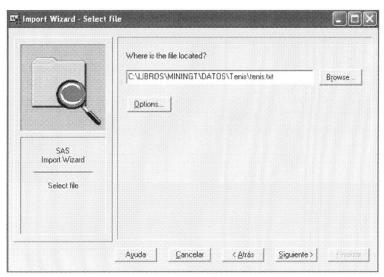

Figure 3-33

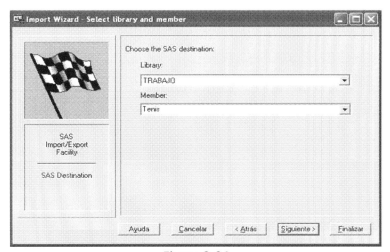

Figure 3-34

The SAS *log* Gets a message telling of the creation of the new file (Figure 3-35). If we want to see its contents simply click on the library *work* and double click on the file *tennis*. A window opens with the contents of the file SAS (Figure 3-36).

Similar data are imported from Excel, Access, dBase, Lotus, etc.

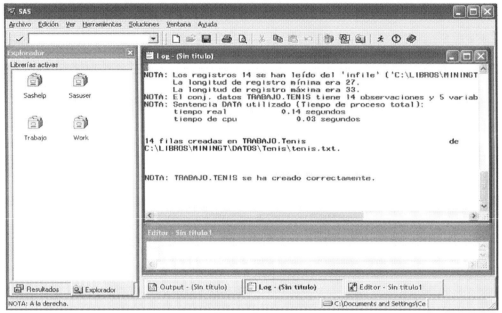

Figure 3-35

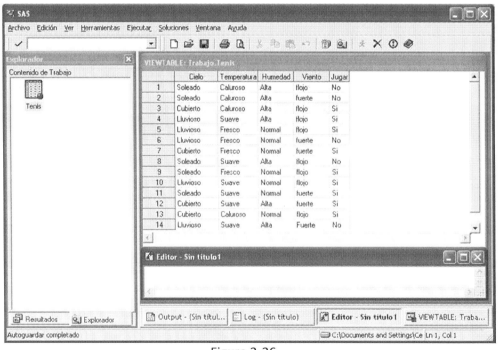

Figure 3-36

Once we already have our work data in SAS format in a particular library, run *SAS Enterprise Miner miner* in the SAS command box typing and pressing *Enter* or by *Solutions → analysis → Enterprise Miner*. When you click on the *Tools* of the project browser button gets the list of tools of *Enterprise Miner* , among which there is the node *Input Data Source* (Figure 3-37) as a sub-option of the *Sample*category. The node is inserted into the work area by dragging it up to it from the list of tools or the icon ▦ from the toolbar (Figure 3-38).

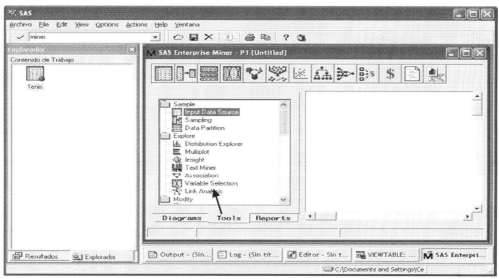

Figure 3-37

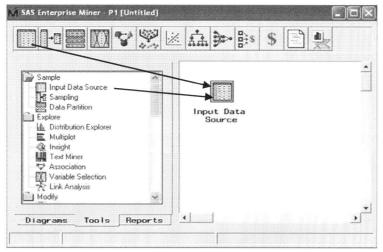

Figure 3-38

When you double click on the *Input Data Source* node in the area of work, gets the data entry screen. Click the *Data* tab and in the *Source Data* field we must indicate which library inside the data. Once these have been selected the node provides information about the number of rows and columns that contains the file (Figure 3-39). In addition, the node performs an assessment of the characteristics of the variables. If the sample is very large, and since the objective is only to define the type of variable, *Enterprise Miner* will take a sample which by default is set to 2000 data. If the database contains less than this amount then all data are selected. Data input with *SAS Enterprise Miner* file are already linked in this way.

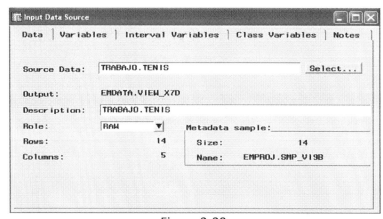

Figure 3-39

3.2.2 Define variables with the Input Data   Source node types

Tab *Variables* in the *Input Data Source* (Figure 3-40) screen allows you to assign types of variables following a series of patterns which can later be changed by the user. Our problem is to see if today we can play tennis. Addressing this problem have of defining the *sky, temperature, humidity* and *wind* as predictors or independent (input or *input*), while the *playing* field is the kind to predict (dependent variable), i.e. the result (of the destination or *target*). By default, *Enterprise Miner* set all variables as *input* and therefore the variable *target* or variable response are to be assigned by the user.To do this you click with the right button of the mouse over the variable change of type and you choose *Set Model role* in the resulting pop-up menu (Figure 3-41). To then choose the new type (*Target*) in the list of Figure 3-42. Figure 3-43 shows the variables with its final rate for this problem.

Therefore the aim of the *Input Data Source* node is both open data like defining the type of variable and its role in the analysis in a convenient way.

Input Data Source

| Data | Variables | Interval Variables | Class Variables | Notes |

Name	Model Role	Measurement	Type	Format	Informat	Variable Label
CIELO	input	nominal	char	$9.	$9.	
TEMPERATURA	input	nominal	char	$8.	$8.	
HUMEDAD	input	binary	char	$7.	$7.	
VIENTO	input	binary	char	$7.	$7.	
JUGAR	input	binary	char	$2.	$2.	

Figure 3-40

Input Data Source

| Data | Variables | Interval Variables | Class Variables | Notes |

Name	Model Role	Measurement	Type	Format	Informat	Variable Label
CIELO	input	nominal	char	$9.	$9.	
TEMPERATURA	input	nominal	char	$8.	$8.	
HUMEDAD	input	binary	char	$7.	$7.	
VIENTO	input	binary	char	$7.	$7.	
JUGAR	input	binary	char	$2.	$2.	

Set Model Role
Sort by Model Role
Subset by Model Role
Find Model Role
View Distribution of JUGAR

Figure 3-41

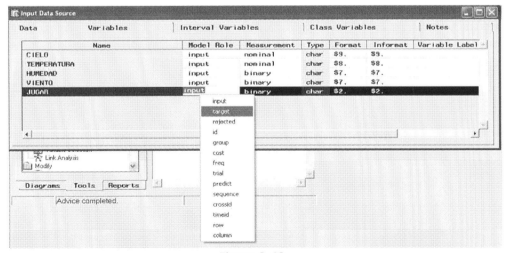

Figure 3-42

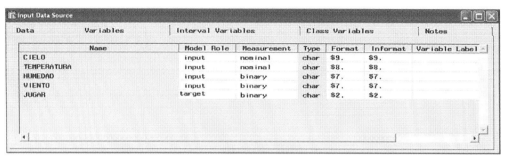

Figure 3-43

3.2.3 Link nodes in a diagram. The node Data Partition

Once the data node collects information of the problem it must be connected with other nodes to implement the process of *Data Mining*. The connection of different nodes will create a logical flow diagram (*process flow*) that will be completing the stages of sampling, descriptive statistics, coding, modeling and evaluation of results. The majority of the nodes can only be opened once they have been connected with data nodes.

In our case join the data (*Input Data Source*) node with the partition (*Data Partition*) in order to give training, 10% to validation and test 10% 80% data randomly. So drag the node *Data Partition* from the list of tools (*Tools*) or the icon to the area of work (Figure 3-44).

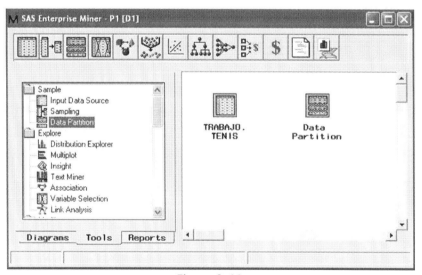

Figure 3-44

To connect two nodes just by clicking with the right button on the node that we want to connect and select *connect items* (Figure 3-45). Once you choose this option we will press on the source node and drag the arrow that originates to the node target (Figure 3-46).

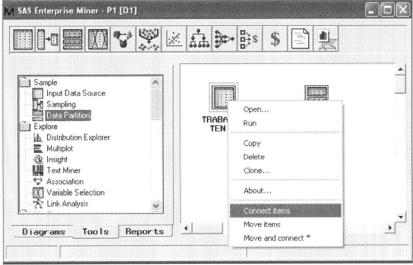

Figure 3-45

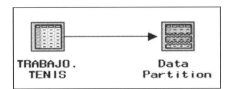

Figure 3-46

To delete a connection we click with the right button of the mouse on the arrow connecting the two nodes and select *Delete* (Figure 3-47).

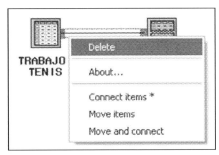

Figure 3-47

As the nodes to be created, it will be necessary to place them appropriately on the work area to achieve better organization and understanding of the flow chart. To move a node you click on the right button on the node that you want to move and select the *Move items* figure 3-45. Choose this option when we place the cursor over the node, we'll see how this takes the form of a hand. When this happens, we can take the node with the left button of the mouse and hold the node to move it to the new position. In general you would want to choose the option *Move and connect*. Thus, when the cursor is over the edge of the node, it will become a cross indicating that we can connect two nodes. Put the cursor over the center of the mouse you can move the selected node.

To assign randomly 80% data training, 10% to validation and test 10% we double click on the *Data Partition* node in the work area and fill the *Partition* tab as shown in Figure 3-48.

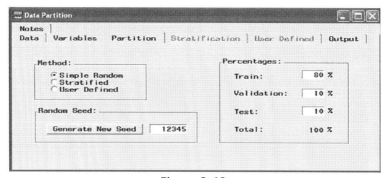

Figure 3-48

3.2.4 Use a node of modeling

Now we are in a situation of trying to use a model based on the data, in our case a decision tree. This will connect the node's data partition with a node of decision trees (*Tree*) that you drag to the work area from the list of tools or the icon ⚏ as shown in Figure 3-49.

Figure 3-49

Once you open the node *Tree* by double-clicking on it in the diagram, on the *Advanced* tab we specify as a measure for the estimation of the model the percentage of cases correctly classified. In addition we will define as enough observations to find a variable of division 14 (Figure 3-50).

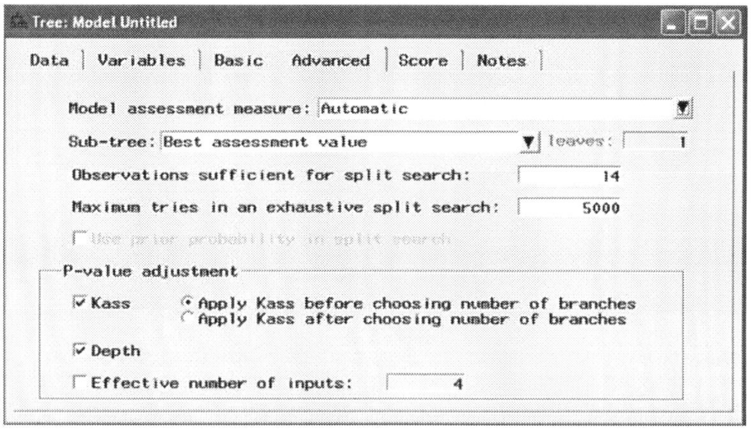

Figure 3-50

The *Score* tab we will indicate to save the response to training, validation, and test (Figure 3-51) data.

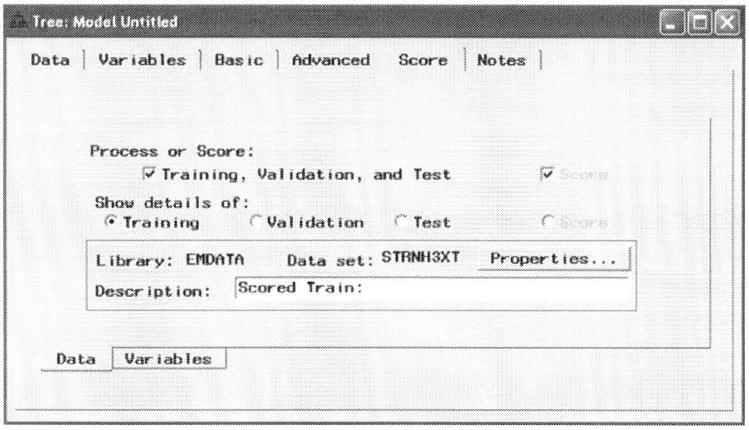

Figure 3-51

Once defined these options, and upon assignment of a name for the model (Figure 3-52), run through node *Actions* → *Run* (Figure 3-53) or by clicking with the right button of the mouse on the *Tree* node and choosing *Run* (Figure 3-54). After a vision of successfully (Figure 3-55) we can see the results of the adjustment (Figure 3-56) to be later interpreted.

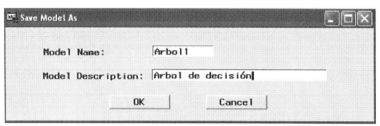

Figure 3-52

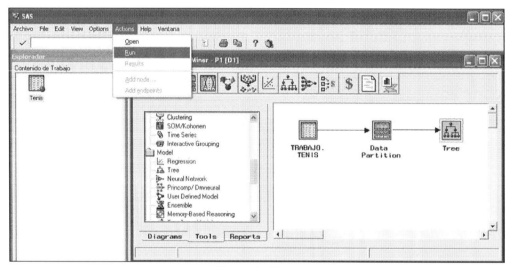

Figure 3-53

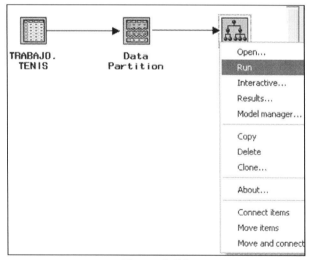

Figure 3-54

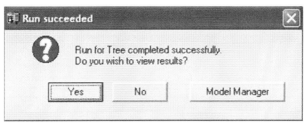

Figure 3-55

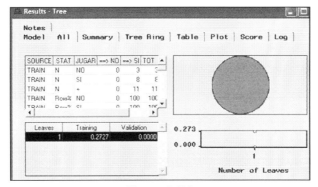

Figure 3-56

We can visualize the tree by selecting *View → Tree* (Figure 3-57). Given that the data set is very small, is a single branch (Figure 3-58).

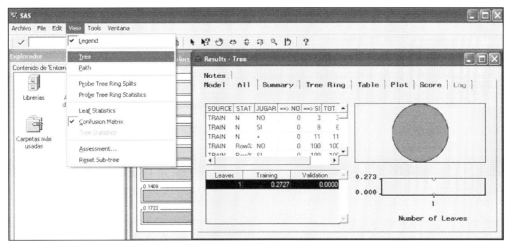

Figure 3-57

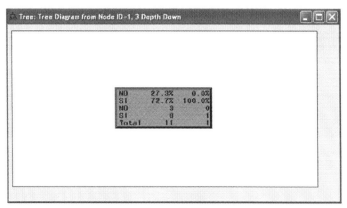

Figure 3-58

To solve the problem of a single branch, we eliminate the intermediate phase of partition of the data set and build the tree only with the *Input Data Source* and *Tree*nodes. To do so open a new diagram within our project using *File → New → Diagram* (Figure 3-59). Then insert the two nodes in the diagram and join them (Figure 3-60). When you now run the tree we get the results in Figure 3-61.

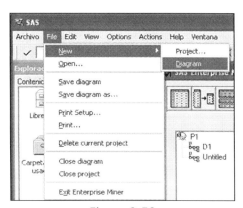

Figure 3-59

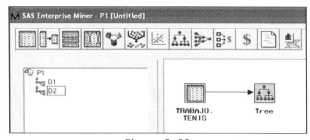

Figure 3-60

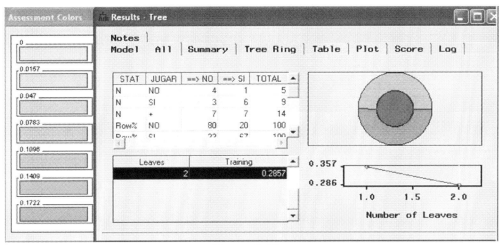

Figure 3-61

The *All* tab shows at the same time the following four tabs. Firstly it shows statistics of fit of the model (*Summary*tab). Secondly it shows the proportion of cases occurring in each of the nodes in each of levels or rings of the tree (*Ring*tab). Thirdly it shows the proportion of correctly classified cases, both training and validation, according to the number of leaves of each tree (*Table*tab). Finally is a graphical representation of the previous result (*plot*tab).

We can visualize the tree by selecting *View → Tree* (Figure 3-62).

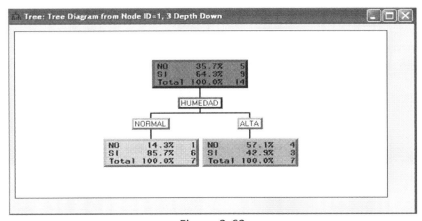

Figure 3-62

Chapter 4

PHASE OF SELECTION IN SAS ENTERPRISE MINER

4.1 LA PHASE OF SELECTION IN ENTERPRISE MINER

We remind that SAS Institute considers the process of *Data Mining* stages of selecting (*Selecting*), explore (*Exploring*), modify (*Modifying*), modeling (*Modeling*) and rating (*Assessment*) and that this process is summarized with SEMMA acronyms which are the initials of the 5 phases. Each of these phases is associated different nodes.

Initially the selection phase leads to partners nodes source of data (*Input Data Source*), sampling (*Sampling*) and partition of data (*Data Partition*) as shown in Figure 4-1, but are generally considered nodes selection of Variables (*Variable Selection*), appearing initially during the scan and time Series (*Time series*) that initially appears in the phase change also belonging to this phase.

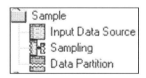

Figure 4-1

4.2 THE DATA SOURCE NODE

The data source node allows you to read the data for the analysis and define their attributes. The node only reads the data in SAS format, so that if our data is in another format, we will have to import it into any active libraries. If necessary, you create a new library. These tasks are explained in chapter three.

Once we already have our work in SAS (*creditos.sas7bdat*file) format data in a specific library (library *work* representing the subdirectory *c:\libros\miningt*), open the project P1 (*File → Open*) and using *File → New → Diagram* create diagram D3 (Figure 4-2). A_continuacion, the *Input Data Source* node is obtained by pressing the button *Tools* from the browser's project of Enterprise Miner as a sub-option of the *Sample* category Figure 4-1) or dragging the node itself about the area of work (Figure 4-3).

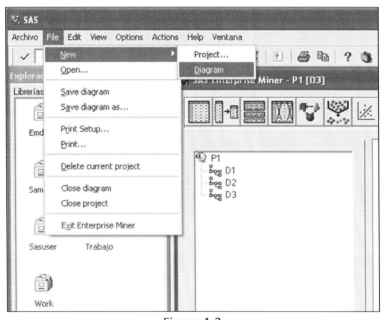

Figure 4-2

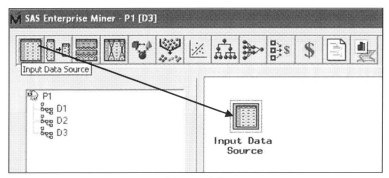

Figure 4-3

By double-clicking the *Data Source* node on the work area or by clicking with the right button of the mouse over the node and choosing *Open* from the resulting pop-up menu (Figure 4-4), the display of the node (Figure 4-5) opens.

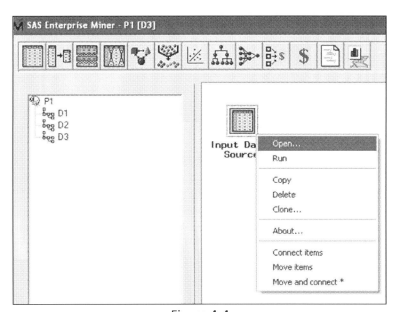

Figure 4-4

The *Input Data Source* node consists of tabs that are observed in Figure 4-5 and described below.

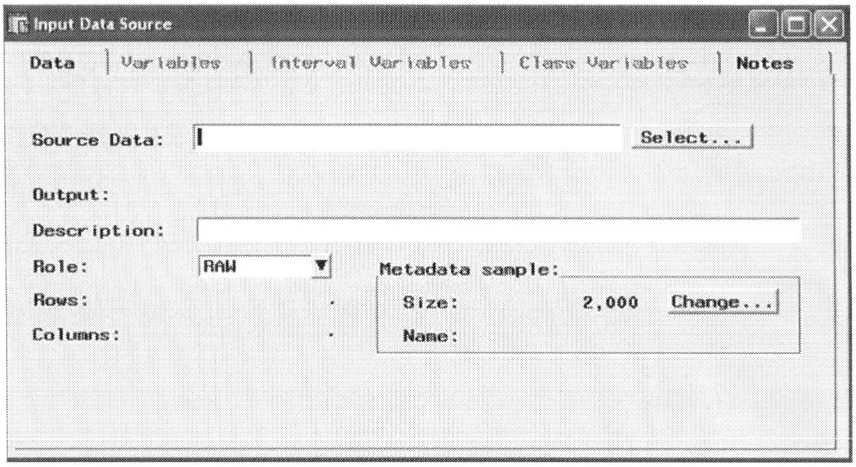

Figure 4-5

4.2.1 Tab Data

In the field *Source Data* we must indicate in what library data are. Once these have been selected the node provides information about the number of rows and columns that contains the file (Figure 4-6).

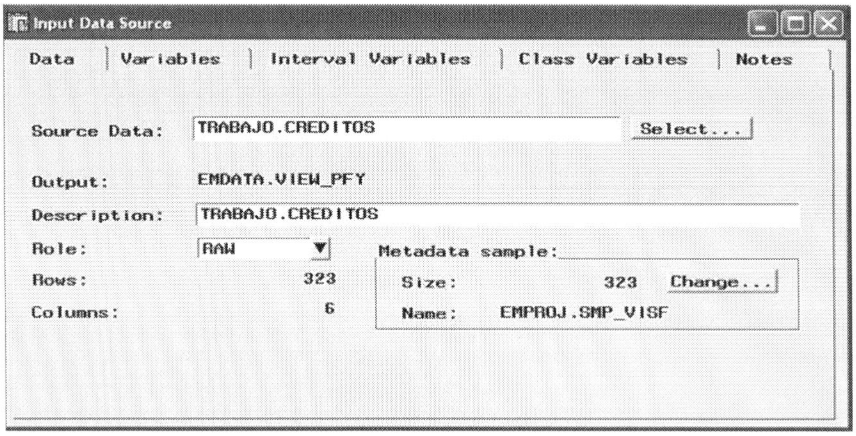

Figure 4-6

In addition, the node performs an assessment of the characteristics of the variables. If the sample is very large, and since the objective is only to define the type of variable, *Enterprise Miner* will take a sample which by default is set to 2000 data. If the database contains less than this amount then all data are selected.

4.2.2 Tab Variables

Used to establish the types of variables in the data file. The type of variable is assigned following a series of patterns which can later be changed by the user. By default, *Enterprise Miner* assigns the type of variable in the following way (Figure 4-7):

- Two values: binary
- Between three and 10 values: nominal
- More than 10 values: interval or continuous variable.
- The system defines all variables as *input* and therefore the variable *target* or variable response are to be assigned by the user.

Data	Variables		Interval Variables		Class Variables		Notes	
Name		Model Role	Measurement	Type	Format	Informat	Variable Label	
CLIENTE		input	interval	num	BEST12.	12.	CLIENTE	
CREDIT_V		input	binary	num	BEST12.	12.	CREDIT_V	
CAT_PROF		input	ordinal	num	BEST12.	12.	CAT_PROF	
PAGO_MES	Sort by Name	input	binary	num	BEST12.	12.	PAGO_MES	
EDAD	Find Name	input	ordinal	num	BEST12.	12.	EDAD	
AMEX	View Distribution of CAT_PROF	input	binary	num	BEST12.	12.	AMEX	

Figure 4-7

Therefore the aim of this node is both open data like defining the type of variable and its role in the analysis in a convenient way. In addition the node allows a quick scan of the variables. So you can click with the right button on the top of the variable (in our case CAT_PROF) and select option *View Distribution of* in Figure 4-7. Figure 4-8 is obtained.

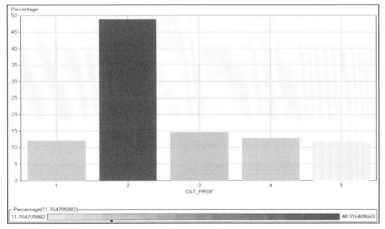

Figure 4-8

4.2.3 The profile of the target (Target profile)

By default, *Enterprise Miner* set all variables as *input* and therefore the variable *target* or variable response are to be assigned by the user.To do this you click with the right button of the mouse over the variable change of type (in our case CREDIT_V) and will choose *Set Model role* in the resulting pop-up menu (Figure 4-9). Then you choose the new type (*Target*) Figure 4-10 list. Figure 4-11 shows the variables with their definitive type in this case.

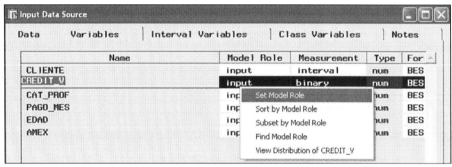

Figure 4-9

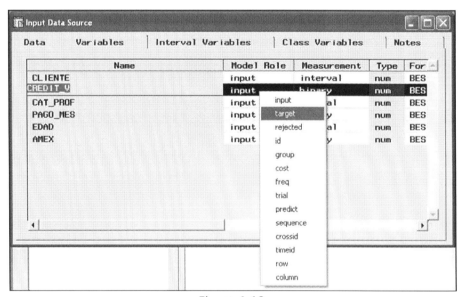

Figure 4-10

Data	Variables	Interval Variables			Class Variables		Notes
	Name	Model Role	Measurement	Type	Format	Informat	Variable Label
CLIENTE		input	interval	num	BEST12.	12.	CLIENTE
CREDIT_V		target	binary	num	BEST12.	12.	CREDIT_V
CAT_PROF		input	ordinal	num	BEST12.	12.	CAT_PROF
PAGO_MES		input	binary	num	BEST12.	12.	PAGO_MES
EDAD		input	ordinal	num	BEST12.	12.	EDAD
AMEX		input	binary	num	BEST12.	12.	AMEX

Figure 4-11

In *Data Mining* , most of the problems have a predictive goal. But what is meant by "best model" often depends on the aim pursued. For example, in the case of predicting a credit assessment, can think that it is also expensive to stop giving a credit to an individual who would pay him that grant credit to an individual who will not return. Depending on different circumstances, the cost of a wrong classification can be different. To vary this cost, it is necessary to define a cost-benefit matrix to select the best model according to this result. So, it is necessary to follow the following steps:

- With the arrow of the mouse on the name of the variable aim right button.

- Select the option *Edit Target Profile* (Figure 4-12).

- Select the *Assessment Information* tab to add cost-benefit matrix. To do this press the right button on the open area on the left and select *Add* to create a new array which we can rename after which press *Enter*.

- In the cells of the matrix we will define the values of costs and benefits of each of the possibilities that we can obtain in the confusion matrix.

- Click with the right button in the array defined in the area on the left and select *Set to use* (Figure 4-13).

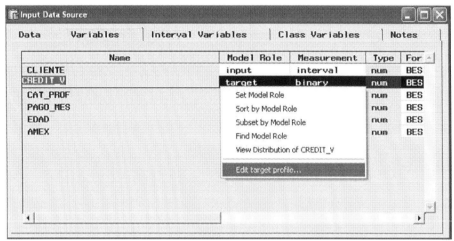

Figure 4-12

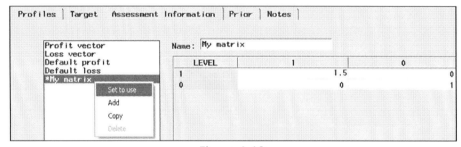

Figure 4-13

4.2.4 Specify to priori probabilities

It is advisable to have a sample of data with approximately the same number of cases in the response variable. However many times it happens that the odds in the sample does not correspond to probabilities *a priori* in the population. *Enterprise Miner* provides the possibility to modify these probabilities to reflect these differences between the sample and the population.

The main options are to assign likely equal or proportional to the sample size but we can also define them according to other criteria. So, it is necessary to carry out the following steps:

- Select *Prior* tab in Figure 4-13.

- Press the right button of the mouse in the area with the profiles of likely active and select *Add* to add a new vector of probabilities *a priori.*

- Define the new vector of probabilities corresponding to the population.

- Select the right button *Set to use* defined option is used (Figure 4-14).

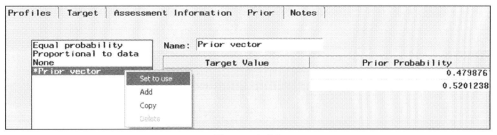

Figure 4-14

4.2.5 Tab Interval Variables

The *Interval Variables* tab presents descriptive statistics of continuous or interval (Figure 4-15).

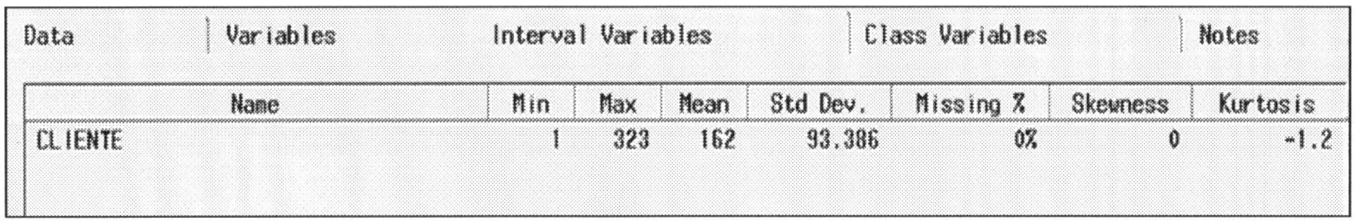

Data	Variables	Interval Variables			Class Variables			Notes
Name		Min	Max	Mean	Std Dev.	Missing %	Skewness	Kurtosis
CLIENTE		1	323	162	93.386	0%	0	-1.2

Figure 4-15

4.2.6 Tab Class Variables

The *Class Variables* tab shows statistics of the variables of the class (Figure 4-16).

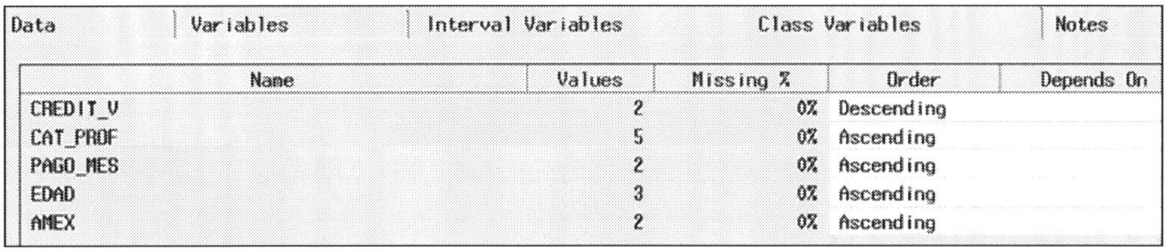

Data	Variables	Interval Variables	Class Variables		Notes
Name		Values	Missing %	Order	Depends On
CREDIT_V		2	0%	Descending	
CAT_PROF		5	0%	Ascending	
PAGO_MES		2	0%	Ascending	
EDAD		3	0%	Ascending	
AMEX		2	0%	Ascending	

Figure 4-16

4.2.7 Tab Notes

All nodes of *Enterprise Miner* have a tab called *Notes* in which we can gather different information about the used node. In the *Data Mining* process, it is important to point out the information and results that we go in order to optimize the time of analysis. In the case of using two equal nodes we can point at another node is different.

Finally, to exit the display of the *Input Data Source*node, the program allows to save or not changes made to variables (Figure 4-17).

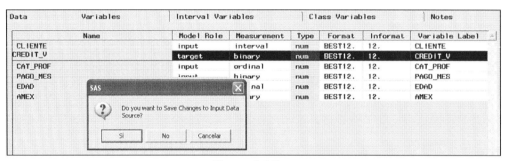

Figure 4-17

4.3 THE NODE SAMPLING

The node sampling (*Sampling*) to extract a sample of the data in cases where it is necessary. Its use is particularly indicated in very large databases in order to facilitate their treatment and decrease the analysis time.

After you open the project (P1) and work (D3) diagram, node *Sampling* is obtained by pressing the button *Tools* from the browser's project of Enterprise Miner as a sub-option of the *Sample* (Figure 4-1) category or by dragging the node itself on the work area (Figure 4-18).

It is then necessary to bind the *Input Data Source* node with the node *Sampling* to perform sampling on the data set. Pair this simply click with the right button on the *Input Data Source* node and choose *connect items* (Figure 4-19). Once you choose this option we will press on the source node and drag the arrow that originates to the node target (Figure 4-20).

By double-clicking the node *Sampling* on the work area or by clicking with the right button of the mouse over the node and choosing *Open* from the resulting pop-up menu, the display of the node opens. Your options can be implemented under the tab *General* (Figure 4-21).

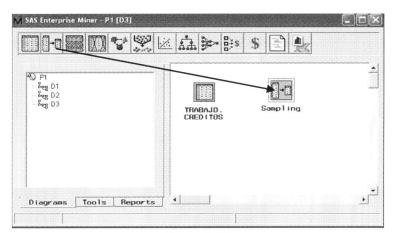

Figure 4-18

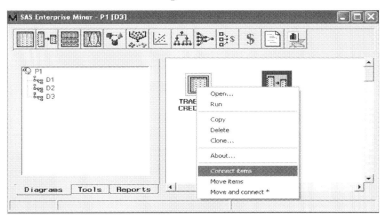

Figure 4-19

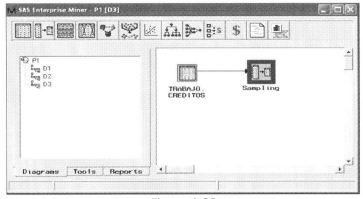

Figure 4-20

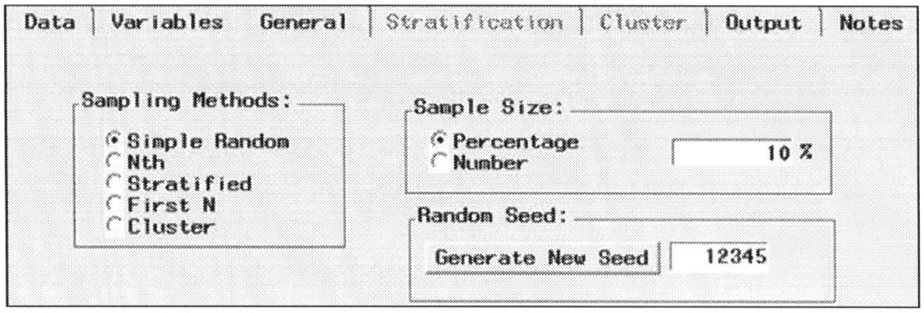

Figure 4-21

Sampling node allows the choice of different procedures for obtaining the sample through the *Sampling Methods* of Figure 4-21.

- **Simple Random (Simple random sampling):** each observation of the database has the same probability of being chosen and is therefore independent of other criteria. Along with the percentage of sampling data or absolute number to extract data (Figure 4-21) we should specify a number or random seed *Random Seed* to extract sample, which by default is 12345 and that must be greater than zero. The same random seed number ensures that we always draw the same sample. If the random seed is set to zero then whenever you launch the node we will obtain a different sample.

- **Each Nth notestions (systematic sampling):**once established the percentage of data to extract the system divides 100 between that percentage and then choose the data systematically. Suppose we want to select the 20% of the data, we divide 100/20 = 5. The system randomly chooses a fact in the top 5, let us suppose that selects the data 3, then to select successive cases will be data 8, 13, 18 and so on.

- **Stratified Sampling (sampling stratified):** this option must be selected on the tab *Stratification* a group of relevant variables for the stratified sampling. To choose these variables you click with the right button of the mouse over the *Status* of the variable, and select *Set Status* to later choose to *use* (Figure 4-22). In a sample stratified will keep the population proportion of values in the selected variables. The objective is to increase the capacity to adjust and generalization of the model or models that are subsequently built

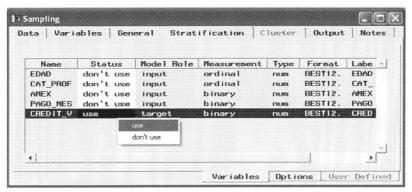

Figure 4-22

- **First N Observations**: the system simply selects the *N* first observations of the sample.

- **Cluster Sampling (Cluster sampling)**: based on a sample extracted using one of the simple methods are grouped cases in a certain number of *clusters*.

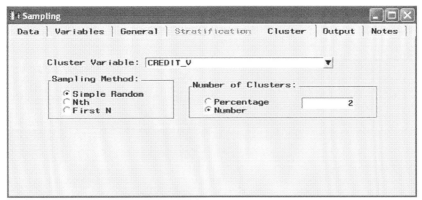

Figure 4-23

The *Output* (Figure 4-24) tab allows you to see the data set in which the sample will be saved (the EMDATA library file *SMP3WGM1*).

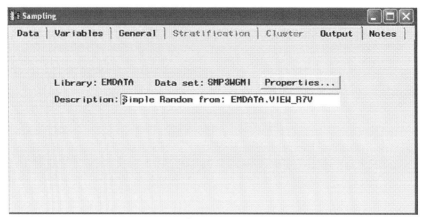

Figure 4-24

To run the selected sampling (in our case a simple random sample of 10%) the node *Sampling* with the right mouse button is clicked and you choose *Run* on the resulting pop-up menu (Figure 4-25). Figure 4-26 screen warns us that sampling has been done with success and offers the possibility to see the results (Figure 4-27).

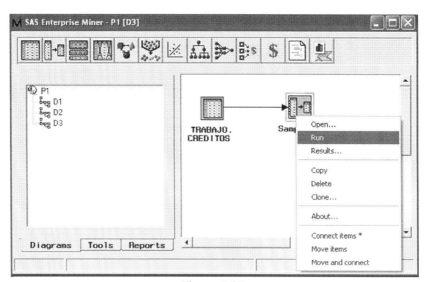

Figure 4-25

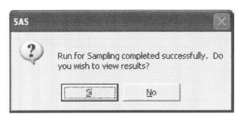

Figure 4-26

	CLIENTE	CREDIT_V	CAT_PROF	PAGO_MES	EDAD	AMEX
1	7	1	2	2	3	0
2	28	0	2	2	1	1
3	32	0	5	1	1	1
4	40	0	3	1	1	0
5	51	0	2	1	1	0
6	65	0	5	1	1	1
7	84	0	4	1	1	0
8	95	0	5	1	1	1
9	99	0	3	1	1	0

Results - Sampling
Notes
Table View: EMDATA.SMP3WGMI | Strata Information | Code | Log | Output

Figure 4-27

4.4 THE NODE OF DATA PARTITION

Data partition node (*Data Partition*) allows you to divide the data into subsets, suitable for analysis.A *data mining* process, it is often necessary to split the data for a correct generalization of the studied problem especially when the database is large enough. This method is especially needed in inductive powerful models such as decision trees or artificial neural networks whose algorithms can *learn by heart* the sample used to build the model but not be useful to predict or classify a different sample. While there are other methods to prevent the deterioration of the ability to generalize from a model, the data partition is the method most used in empirical practice. To carry out its implementation, the sample is divided into three subsamples that we will call:

- **Training** (*Training*): this sample is used to build various models varying the parameters of the same.

- **Validation** (*Validation*): this sample used to check the generalization of the model built. It is also used in various models, such as artificial neural networks, to control the learning process of the model.

- **Test** (*Test*): certain problems, once elected the final model that will process the *inputs*, this will be operating, and then is when the parameters or rules are fixed and ready for operation. It is at this time when the *test phase* where *a pattern of entries whose main characteristic is that it has never before been seen by model* is presented to model in order to obtain a prediction or unbiased data classification is made. He is evaluated as well, one time compared the real response and the estimated, the true accuracy of the model for the resolution of the problem.

Each of these three subsamples must include vectors of the entire distribution of the function that you want to close.

After opening the project (P1) and create a new diagram of work (D4), the node *Data Partition* is obtained through the button *Tools* from the browser's project of Enterprise Miner as a sub-option of the *Sample* (Figure 4-1) category or by dragging the node itself on the work area (Figure 4-28).

It is then necessary to bind the *Input Data Source* node with the node *Data Partition* for the partition of the data set. Pair this simply click with the right button on the *Input Data Source* node and choose *connect items*. Once you choose this option we will press on the source node and drag the arrow that originates to the node target (Figure 4-29).

By double-clicking the node *Data Partition* on the work area or by clicking with the right button of the mouse over the node and choosing *Open* from the resulting pop-up menu, the display of the node opens.

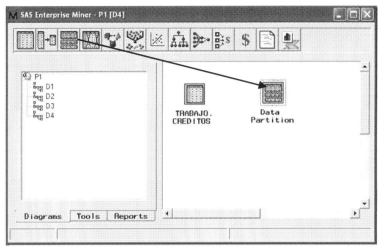

Figure 4-28

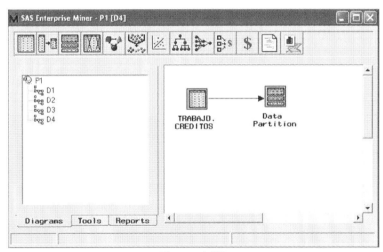

Figure 4-29

Once you open the node must select the tab *Variable Partition* where, together with the method of partition, we must specify the percentages of data that you want to dedicate to training, validation and test (Figure 4-30).

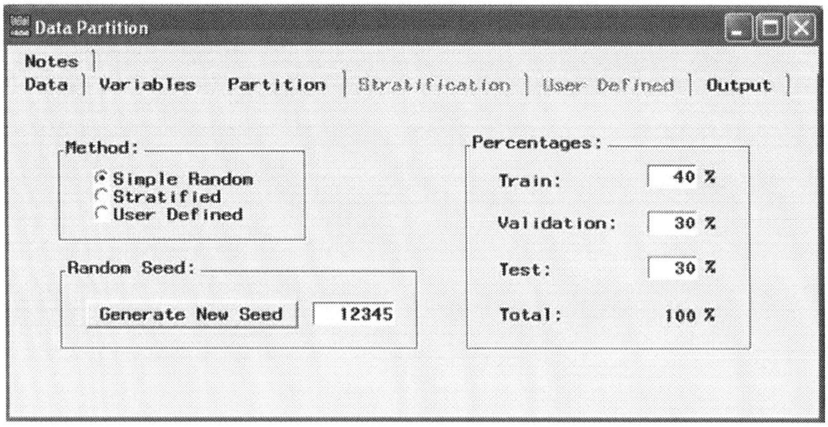

Figure 4-30

Although default *Enterprise Miner* allocates 40% of data training, 30% to validation and 30% to test, this rule is heuristic. A result is there clear statistical literature that says what is the best way of splitting a database. This result depends on the majority of the cases of the number of data, the noise that contain and its representativeness. In general the greater and more representative is the database, import less the percentage of the divisions. Finally it should be noted that the percentages to be specified should be integer values and that we can give the value zero if, for example, we consider that it is not necessary to take test data. In addition, the sum of the three specified percentages should be 100.

Unlike sampling node, this node presents the *User define* option. If we choose this option, the database must contain a variable that you specify for each data if it will be used to train, validate or prove the model (Figure 4-31).

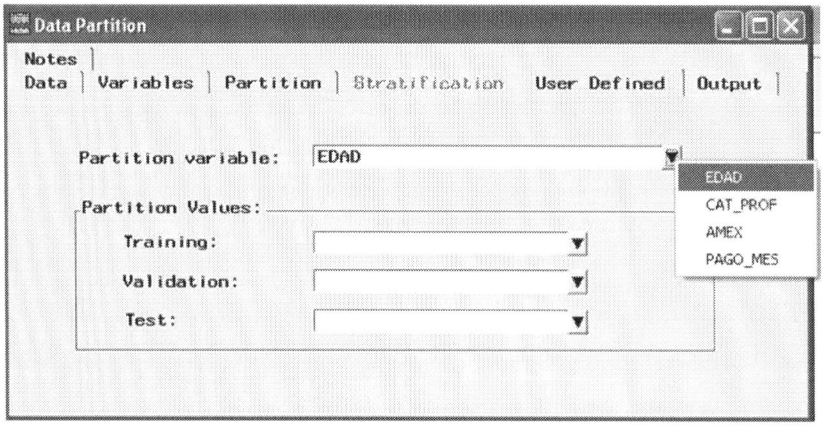

Figure 4-31

4.5 THE SELECTION OF VARIABLES NODE

Node selection of variables (*Variable Selection*) reduces the initial number of variables to one smaller number having the greatest possible relationship with the target variable of the analysis.Many problems of *Data Mining* have hundreds of potentially explanatory variables of the response or responses to evaluate. The selection of variables node is a useful tool to help reduce the number of *inputs* , eliminating those who have no relation with the variable aim of the problem. In principle this process could be done manually in the *Input Data Source* node by assigning the status *rejected* variables *input* that we don't want to consider. Through the Elimination of variables that do not contribute anything to the analysis we will remove redundant information and will increase the options for a more appropriate model. Therefore, that this node is often used in the flowchart from *Data Mining* problem before the model.

After opening the project (P1) and create a new diagram of work (D5), the node *Variable selection* is obtained through the button *Tools* from the browser's project of Enterprise Miner as a sub-option of the category *Explore* or dragging the node itself on the work area (Figure 4-32). It is then necessary to bind the *Input Data Source* node with the node *Variable Selection* to make your selection on the DataSet. Pair this simply click with the right button on the *Input Data Source* node and choose *connect items*. Once you choose this option we will press on the source node and drag the arrow that originates to the node target (Figure 4-33).

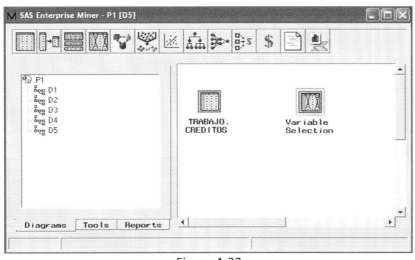

Figure 4-32

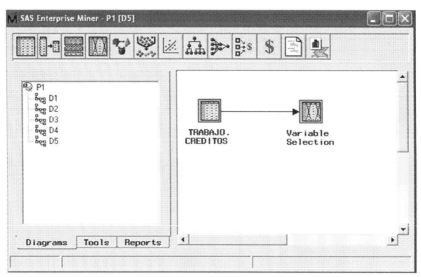

Figure 4-33

By double-clicking the node *Variable Selection* on the work area or by clicking with the right button of the mouse over the node and choosing *Open* from the resulting pop-up menu, the display of the node opens. Tab *Variables* (Figure 4-34) allows to observe what the variable target (has assigned *Target* as *Role Model*) that was defined as previously in the *Input Data Source* node.

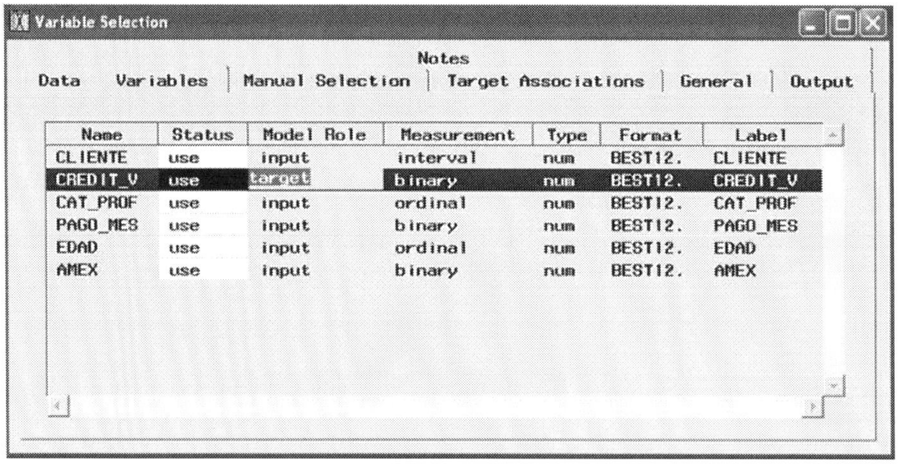

Figure 4-34

The *Target Associations* tab allows variables to be selected according to *criteria based on the R-cuadrado or Chi-square* (Figure 4-35) depending on the type of problem (continuous, binary or categorical variables).

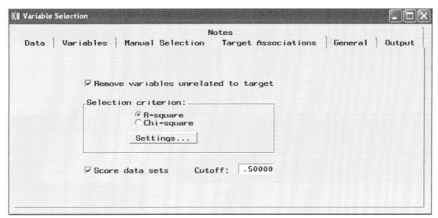

Figure 4-35

The criteria to reject or include a variable according to the R-cuadrado can be defined by clicking the button*Settings*(Figure 4-36).The *Squared Correlation* approach computes the correlation coefficient squared of each variable *input* response and rejects it if this value is less than the set as a cutoff. The remaining variables not removed after this first step are evaluated from a regression by successive steps with forward entry criteria. The variables that improve the coefficient of determination at one lower value than the cut-off point are also rejected.

In addition to the options listed above other criteria, can be set as include interactions of two variables, create interval variables for detecting nonlinear relationships or allow merging the categories of variables.

The Chi-square selection criterion is only available for target binary variables. The options for this criterion can be modified by pressing in *Settings* (Figure 4-37).The selection of variables is carried out to maximize the associations of a 2 x 2 contingency table. Each level of the ordinal or nominal variables is decomposed into binary variables. *Bins*, determines the number of categories in which a continuous variable is split. Default is set to 50 portions of the same size. The *Chi-square* option is the minimum value of the Chi-square statistical to decide whether the division is significant. This value marks as well the number of divisions to perform. *Passes* option specifies a maximum limit of assessments made by the system to determine the optimum number of categories. The default value is 6 but you can specify a number between 1 and 200. There is an *trade-off* in the choice since an increase in the number tends to improve the optimal partition if well at the expense of employing a longer analysis.

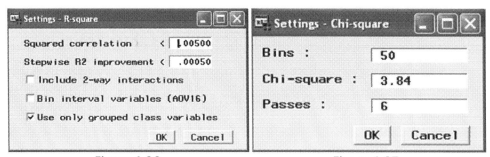

Figure 4-36   Figure 4-37

It is possible to *specify a breakpoint on variable binary target*. When the problem to be treated has a target variable binary, automatically is assigned a probability of belonging to class between 0 and 1. By default the value of cutting (*Cutoff*) is set to 0.5 (Figure 4-38) so that observations with one probability greater than 0.5 is classified as 1 while the sorting those below as 0. It is sometimes interesting to increase or decrease this value of cutting. To do this we vary the cell *Cutoff*.

Once all the options defined and executed the node (by clicking on it with the right mouse button and choosing Run from the resulting pop-up menu), the output window shows which variables are accepted as well as the reason for rejecting those variables that do not meet the conditions for entry defined (Figure 4-39).

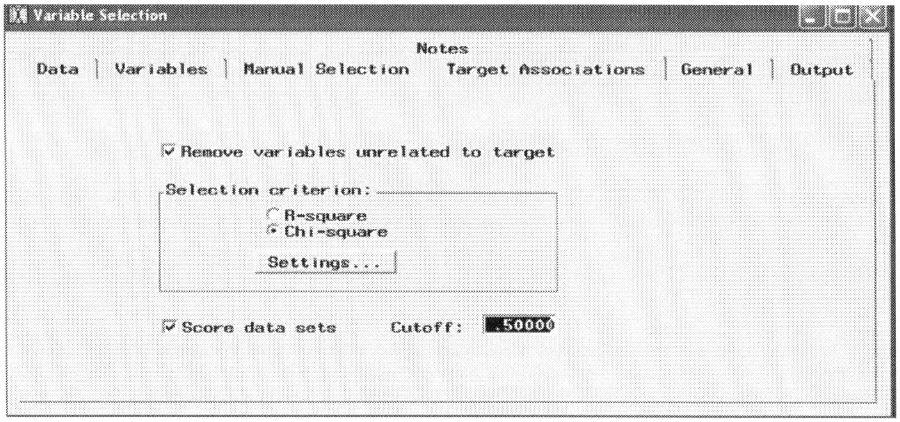

Figure 4-38

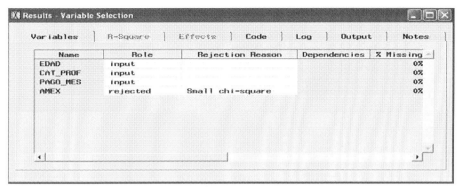

Figure 4-39

4.6 THE SERIES TEMPORARY NODE

Time series node (*Time Series*) allows you to select temporal characteristics for variables. This node can also inquire about the trends and cyclical or seasonal behaviour of certain variables. It is also useful to transform data with information from transactions at different moments of time in a time series with a certain frequency. Use the node requires a single variable objective, a temporary variable (*Timeid*). You can optionally specify a variable cross section (*Crossid*).

After opening the project (P1) and create a new diagram of work (D6), node *Time Series* is obtained through the button *Tools* from the browser's project of Enterprise Miner as a sub-option of the category *modify* dragging the node itself on the working area next to the node *Input Data Source* that this time will be assigned the AIR of the library data set work (Figure 4-40) by placing comma variable target (*Target*) *or* variable3 and the other variables with the characteristics seen in Figure 4-41.

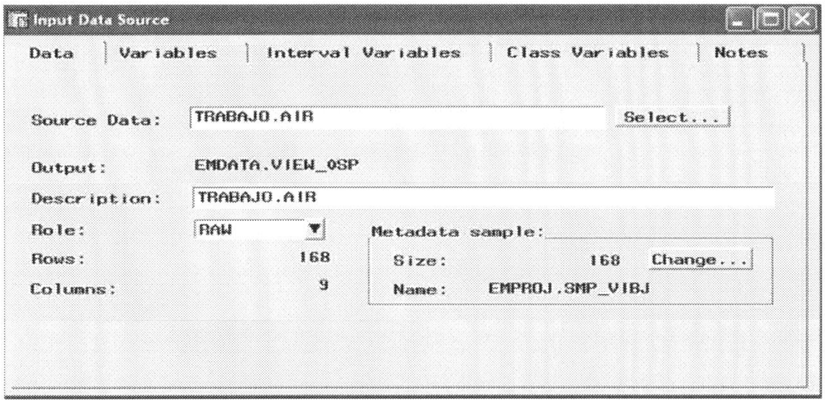

Figure 4-40

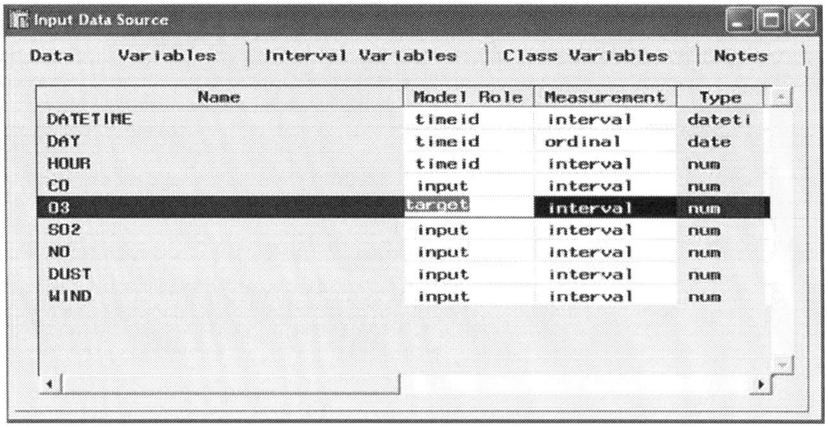

Figure 4-41

The database called AIR brings temporary information about the air quality measurements. The variables contained in this database are:

DATETIME: date and time of the measurement.

DAY: day of the week.

HOUR: time of day.

CO: carbon monoxide.

O3: ground-level ozone.

SO2: sulfur dioxide.

NO: nitric oxide.

DUST: dust in suspension.

WIND: wind speed.

It is then necessary to bind the *Input Data Source* node with the node *Time Series*. To do this simply click with the right button on the *Input Data Source* node and choose *connect items*. Once you choose this option we will press on the source node and drag the arrow that originates to the node target (Figure 4-42).

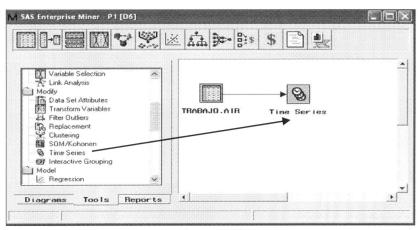

Figure 4-42

By double-clicking the node *Time Series* on the work area or by clicking with the right button of the mouse over the node and choosing *Open* from the resulting pop-up menu, the display of the node opens.

Once you open the node, it presents various options associated with different tabs of your screen (Figure 4-43) entry. These tabs are described below.

4.6.1 Data

The *Data* (Figure 4-43) tab allows you to place the set of data for analysis. By default this node only uses training (*Training*) data although other unused data are also passed to subsequent nodes.

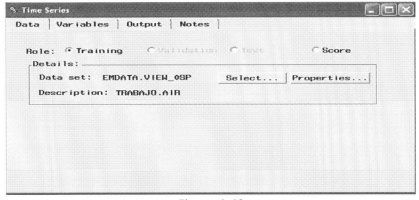

Figure 4-43

4.6.2 Variables

Variables (Figure 4-44) tab allows you to set the variables that will be used in the analysis.

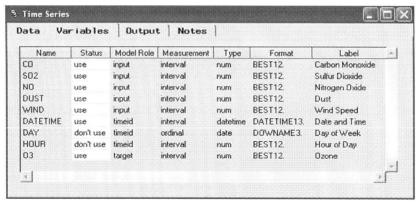

Figure 4-44

To access the scanning options have to press in the tool menu icon either in the main menu select *Tools → Settings...*

The Options window contains three tabs: *Time interval, Options* and *Output Data Set.*

4.6.3 Time Interval

In this window (Figure 4-45) must define which is the temporal range of the data.

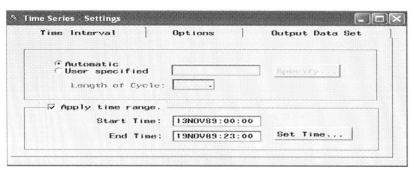

Figure 4-45

▪ **Automatic:** node looks for the variable *timeid* and tries to determine which is the range and relative cycle of the variable. If he could not define what the node will fail to be executed. If this occurs we will have to make the specification manually.

▪ **User Specified:** when you click the *Specify* button opens a window to specify temporary options. Before you ask a confirmation since the node must examine previously (Figure 4-46) data. The options in this window are described below.

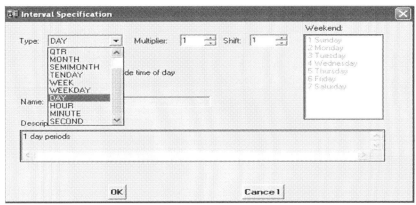

Figure 4-46

○ **Type:** displays a list of valid temporary options. The following table lists the length of these cycles.

Time interval	The cycle length
YEAR (YEAR)	1
SEMIYEAR (SEMESTER)	2
QTR (QUARTER)	4
MONTH (MONTH)	12
SEMIMONTH (FORTNIGHT)	24
TENDAY (TEN DAYS)	36
WEEK (WEEKS)	52
(WORKING) WEEKDAY	5
DAY (WEEK DAYS)	7
HOUR (HOURS)	24
MINUTE (MIN)	60
SECOND (SECONDS)	60

o **Multiplyer**: allows you to change the number of intervals that defines the type specified by default. For example to create intervals every two months, select MONTH and position the multiplier at 2. This will change the cycle to 6.

o **Shift**: if above instead of starting in the period January-February are to begin in July-August will select 4.

o **Weekend**: available only if we choose the WEEKDAY. Default on Saturday and Sunday are days of the week but you can choose different options by holding the CONTROL key while you select the days. This option is interesting, for example, a particular business rests on Monday whether measurements of an atmospheric phenomenon only occurs during certain days.

o **Gives you values include time of day:** includes the time of day data.

▪ **Length of cycle**: enter the desired duration of the cycle.

▪ **Apply Time Range**: select this option to specify a start and end in the analysis date. The node will only analyze dates contained in that period. The option *Set Time...* allows you to change this period graphically (Figure 4-47).

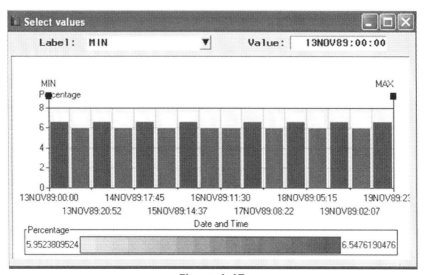

Figure 4-47

To do this select the square which lies under the MAX or MIN indicators and with the left button of the mouse pressed, move the square to the desired option.

4.6.4 Options

In the Options window, we will define the way in which data are accumulated, the method of imputation of missing data and statistics will print in the output of the results (Figure 4-48) Viewer window. The fields in this window are described below.

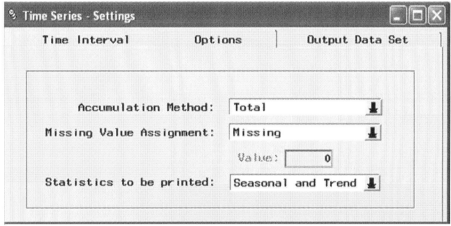

Figure 4-48

- **Accumulation Method:** this option is useful when the data are not spaced at defined intervals.

  o **Total:** observations are accumulated on the basis of the sum total of their values.

  o **Average:** observations are accumulated on the basis of the average of its values.

  o **Minimum:** observations are accumulated on the basis of the value is less than the total of their values.

  o **Median:** observations are accumulated based on the median of its values.

  o **Maximum:** observations are accumulated on the basis of the value greater than the total of their values.

o **First:** observations are accumulated on the basis of the first of its values.

o **Last:** observations are accumulated on the basis of the last of its values.

o **StdDev:** observations are accumulated on the basis of the standard deviations of their values.

o **N:** observations are accumulated on the basis of the number of non-missing data.

o **Nmiss:** observations are accumulated on the basis of the number of lost data.

o **Nobs:** observations are accumulated on the basis of the total number of data.

▪ **Missing Value Assignment**

o **Missing:** lost data are not imputed.

o **Average:** replaced by the media.

o **Minimum:** replaced the retail value.

o **Median:** replaced by the median.

o **Maximum:** replaced by the higher value.

o **First:** replaced by the first value.

o **Last:** replaced by the last value.

o **Previous:** replaced by the previous value.

o **Next:** replaced by the following value.

o **Constant:** replaced by a constant that we specify in the box *Value.*

▪ **Statistics to be printed:** Select if we want to print the results of Viewer node statistics of temporality (*Seasonal*), trend (*Trend*), or both.

4.6.5 Output Data Set

By selecting the square*Export transposed seasonal data set*(Figure 4-49) the node calculates the transposed matrix where the rows are transformed in columns in rows and columns.

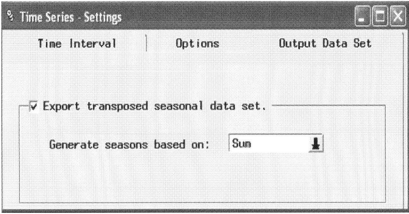

Figure 4-49

The variable used to generate temporary data can be changed by displaying the options in the box *Generate seasons based on*, which presents the following options.

- **Nobs:** the value of season is the total number of observations.

- **N:** the value of season is the total number of valid observations.

- **Nmiss:** the value of season is the total number of lost observations.

- **Min:** season is the minimum number.

- **Max:** season is the maximum number.

- **Range:** the value of the season is the range of values.

- **Sum:** the season is the sum of values.

- **Mean:** season is the average of the values.

- **StdDev:** season is the standard deviation of the values.

- **CSS:** season is the corrected sum of squares.

- **USS:** the season is the sum of squares not corrected.

- **Median:** the season is the median value.

If we intend to make predictions on the SAS Code node will need to disable the picture *Export transposed seasonal data set*

4.6.6 Output

In this window (Figure 4-50) we can examine the details of the output data.

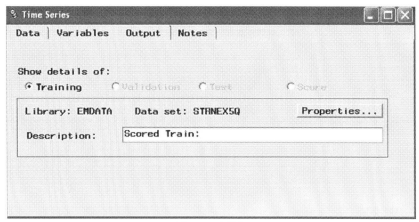

Figure 4-50

Chapter 5.

PHASE OF EXPLORATION IN DATA MINING

5.1 EXPLORATION IN THE PROCESS OF EXTRACTION OF KNOWLEDGE

After the selection phase, the process of extraction of knowledge includes the exploration phase. Given that the data come from different sources, his *exploration* using formal techniques of exploratory data analysis, looking for among other things, the distribution of the data, its symmetry and normality and correlations in the information is required.

Before applying any mining data or even multivariate analysis technique in general, is necessary to perform a preliminary analysis of the data available. It is necessary to examine the individual variables and the relationships between them, as well as evaluate and solve problems in research design and in data collection. The first task that is often addressed is *exploratory and graphic data analysis*. The majority of the statistical *software* has tools that provide graphic techniques prepared for the examination of the data that are enhanced with measures more detailed statistics for your description. These techniques allow the examination of the characteristics of the distribution of the variables involved in the analysis, bivariant (and multivariate) relations between them and the analysis of the differences between groups. It must be borne in mind that the graphic representations never replace the diagnostic measures formal statistical (contrasts of fit of the data to a distribution, contrasts of asymmetry, contrasts of randomness, etc.), but provide an alternative way to develop a perspective on the nature of the data and the interrelationships that exist, even if they are multivariate. Also is also task prior to the application of data mining techniques to the*checking of the underlying assumptions in the multivariate for the data mining methods*.

These assumptions depend on the particular technique that applies and often the contrast of *normalcy* of all and each one of the variables that are part of the study, the testing the *linearity* of the relationship between the variables involved in the study (the relationship between the possible dependent variable and independent variables which explain it must be a linear equation), checking the *homoscedasticity* of data consisting in seeing that the variation in the dependent variable that is attempts to explain through the independent variables are not concentrated in a small group of independent values (will be therefore see the equality of variances for data grouped according to similar values of the dependent variable) and the checking of the *multicollinearity* or existence of a relationship between the independent variables. It is sometimes necessary to check the absence of *waste or autocorrelation serial correlation*, which is to ensure that any errors of prediction is not correlated with the rest

5.2 EXPLORATORY ANALYSIS

Exploratory data analysis techniques allow to thoroughly analyze the information and detect possible anomalies presenting observations. J. W. Tuckey was one of the pioneers in the introduction of this type of analysis. Most commonly used descriptive statistics are the mean and the standard deviation. However, the automatic use of these indices is not very advisable. The mean and standard deviation are suitable indexes only when data distribution is approximately normal or, at least, symmetrical and unimodal. But the variables object of study not always meet these requirements. An in-depth review of the structure of the data is therefore necessary.

It is recommended to start an exploratory analysis of data with graphics that allow you to visualize the structure. We have the tools for *visual exploration*. However, for **formal exploration**, the use of *robust statistical* (or resistant) is strongly recommended if the data does not conform to a normal distribution. These statistics are those who are little affected by outliers. They tend to be based on the median and the quartiles and are easy calculation. Result of the exploratory analysis, is sometimes needed transformation of variables.

5.3 TOOLS VISUAL EXPLORATION

For quantitative data, it is advisable to start with stem and leaves or digital histogram graph. The next step is usually examine the possible presence of normality, symmetry and atypical values (outliers) in the data set. For this purpose they are used graphics box and moustache. However graphics box must always be accompanied by digital (or graphic) histograms of stem and leaves, since the former do not detect the presence of multimodal distributions. The scatter chart give us an idea of the relationship between variables and their adjustment.

5.4 HISTOGRAM OF FREQUENCIES

Anyway, it is always convenient to start the exploratory data analysis with the construction of the associated frequency histogram, for power so guess the probability distribution of the data, its normal, its symmetry and other interesting properties in the analysis of data.

As example we can consider the variable X defined as fuel consumption in litres to the 1000 kilometers of cars of a particular brand. The values for X are as follows:

43.1 36.1 32.8 39.4 36.1 19.9 19.4 20.2 19.2 20.5 20.2 25.1 20.5 19.4 20.6
20.8 18.6 18.1 19.2 17.7 18.1 17.5 30 27.5 27.2 30.9 21.1 23.2 23.8 23.9
20.3 17 21.6 16.2 31.5 29.5 21.5 19.8 22.3 20.2 20.6 17 17.6 16.5 18.2
16.9 15.5 19.2 18.5 31.9 34.1 35.7 27.4 25.4 23 27.2 23.9 34.2 34.5 31.8
37.3 28.4 28.8 26.8 33.5 41.5 38.1 32.1 37.2 28 26.4 24.3 19.1 34.3 29.8
31.3 37 32.2 46.6 27.9 40.8 44.3 43.4 36.4 30.4 44.6 40.9 33.8 29.8 32.7
23.7 35 23.6 32.4 27.2 26.6 25.8 23.5 30 39.1 39 35.1 32.3 37 37.7
34.1 34.7 34.4 29.9 33 34.5 33.7 32.4 32.9 31.6 28.1 30.7 25.4 24.2 22.4
26.6 20.2 17.6 28 27 34 31 29 27 24 23 36 37 31 38
36 36 36 34 38 32 38 25 38 26 22 32 36 27 27
44 32 28 31

To explore this information we prepare the table of frequencies associated with the data and study possible normality and symmetry of the distribution of the fuel consumption.

As it is a quantitative variable with 154 values ranging from 13 to 49, it will be necessary to group them into classes or intervals. For this purpose take 12 intervals of equal width (12 is an integer which approximates well the root cuatrada of N = 154). The width of the interval shall be (49 - 13) / 12 = 3. Gets the table of frequencies of the figure 5-1.

Interval	Limit lower	Limit top	Brand class	n_i	$f_i = n_i/N$	N_i	$F_i = n_i/N$
1	13.0	16.0	14.5	1	0,0065	1	0,0065
2	16.0	19.0	17.5	14	0,0909	15	0,0974
3	19.0	22.0	20.5	22	0,1429	37	0,2403
4	22.0	25.0	23.5	15	0,0974	52	0,3377
5	25.0	28.0	26.5	22	0,1429	74	0,4805
6	28.0	31.0	29.5	16	0,1039	90	0,5844
7	31.0	34.0	32.5	22	0,1429	112	0,7273
8	34.0	37.0	35.5	22	0,1429	53 °	0,8701
9	37.0	40.0	38.5	11	0,0714	145	0,9416
10	40.0	43.0	41.5	3	0,0195	148	0,9610
11	43.0	46,0	44.5	5	0,0325	153	0,9935
12	46,0	49.0	47.5	1	0,0065	55 °	1,0000

Figure 5-1

We have observed the 154 figures on consumption of automobiles which initially not provided much information. Obviously there is a variability in the use of automobiles; However, it is very difficult to detect what pattern is that variability to better determine the structure of the data. Therefore, first of all it has been suitable to perform a sort of the data according to its magnitude, i.e. a frequency table, should bring some light on the underlying distribution of frequencies.

The next task is the construction of the histogram of frequencies, graphic suitable for a quantitative variable with values grouped in intervals. Its representation is presented in Figure 5-2.

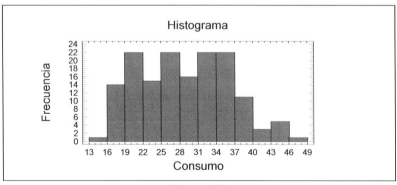

Figure 5-2

Shown that the underlying distribution modelling data on the variable consumption of automobiles is approximately symmetrical and bell-shaped, adjustable allowing you to believe in the existence of normality and symmetry on the distribution of X.

We see that the histogram gives a clear idea of the distribution of the variable, including a probabilistic for their modeling, in this case the normal distribution model. The simple examination of the data tabulated initially did not provide any information, however its graphics gives light to the process.

5.5 DIAGRAM OF STEM AND LEAVES

The stem and leaves is a semigrafico procedure to present information for quantitative variables, which is especially useful when the total number of data is small (less than 50). The principles for the realization of the diagram (due to Tukey) are as follows:

- Rounded data to two or three significant figures.

- Arrange them in two columns separated by a vertical line, so that data with two digits for the tens digit is found to the left of the vertical line (stem of the diagram), and right units (leaves or branches of the diagram). For example, 87 will write 8 7. For data with three-digit stem consists of the digits in the hundreds and tens, which will be written to the left of the vertical line, and the leaves will be formed by the digit of the units, which will be written to the right of the vertical line.

- Each stem defines a class, and it is written only once. Successive sheets corresponding to that stem will writing in order on your right. The number of sheets to each stem represents the frequency of each class.

The stem and leaves, also called *digital histogram*, is a combination between a bar histogram and a frequency table. To maintain the values of the variable, stem and leaf diagram is more informative than the classic bar histogram, preserving the original data, and at the same time, composed a profile that helps to study the shape and symmetry of the distribution. It is therefore a tool for exploratory analysis of data that shows the range of the data, where are most concentrated, its symmetry and the presence of atypical data. This procedure is not very advisable for large data sets.

Below is the diagram of stem and leaves (Figure 5-3) for the variable *X* defined on the variable consumption of cars in the previous section.

```
Diagrama de Tallo y Hojas para X: unidad = 1,0    1|2 representa 12,0

      23       1|56667777778888889999999
      51       2|0000000000011122233333333333444
    (31)       2|55555666667777777777788888899999
      72       3|000001111111122222222222233333444444444444
      34       3|5556666666667777778888889999
       9       4|00133444
       1       4|6
```

Figure 5-3

The range of *X* has been divided into 7 classes or intervals called *stems*, each of them represented by a row of the diagram. The first issue of each row (separated from others) presents the absolute frequency of the corresponding class. The second issue of each row presents the number of tens of each value of *X* in its corresponding class. The rest of the numbers in each row (called *leaves*) are the numbers of the units of all the elements of the class defined by the row. In this way, besides the distribution of elements in the form of horizontal histogram, in the diagram are the elements themselves. Leaves allow you to analyze the symmetry, normalcy and other features of the distribution in the same way that a histogram.

5.6 BOX AND WHISKERS CHART

Box and whiskers chart allows you to analyze and summarize a univariate data set given. This exploratory data analysis tool will allow to study the symmetry of the data, detect outliers and glimpses of a fit of the data to a given frequency distribution.

Box and whiskers chart divides data into four areas of equal frequency, a central box divided into two areas by a vertical line and two other areas represented by two horizontal segments (whiskers) that depart from the center of each vertical side of the box. The central box contains 50 percent of the data. The system draws the medium as a vertical line on the inside of the box. If this line is at the center of the box there is no asymmetry in the variable. The vertical sides of the box are located in the quartiles of the variable top and bottom. Starting from the center of each vertical side of the box are drawn two whiskers, one to the left and the other to the right. Moustache on the left has an end in the first quartile Q_1, and the other to the value given by the first quartile less 0.5 times the interquartile range, i.e., $Q_1-1.5 * (Q_3-Q_1)$.

Right mustache has one end in the third quartile Q_3 and the other at the value given by the third quartile more 1.5 times the interquartile range, i.e., Q_3+

1.5 * (Q_3-Q_1). The system is considered atypical values (*outliers*) that are to the left of the moustache left and to the right of the right mustache. System separates these data of the rest and represents them by means of points aligned with the horizontal centerline so they are easy to detect. Inside the central box represents the average with a plus sign.

Below is the graph of box and whiskers for the variable X relative to the variable consumption of automobiles (Figure 5-4).

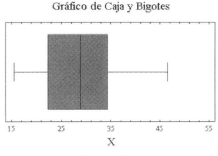

Gráfico de Caja y Bigotes

Figure 5-4

Graph allows you to assert that the variable X (consumption of automobiles per 1000 kilometers) varies between 15.5 and 46.6 and that 50% cars unit consumes between 22 (first quartile) and 34.5 (third quartile) litres to 1000 kilometres.

On the other hand, values of Xthereabnormally large*(outliers)* since in the figure do not appear points aligned with whiskers. The distribution is slightly asymmetric to the right, as right in the central area of the figure is larger than the left. The median corresponds approximately to the value X29.

Box and whiskers charts allow the option of representing *median notch*, which places two notches on the ends of the median.

The width of the notch represents a confidence interval about the median with a coefficient of 95% confidence (α= 0.05) which is determined by the expression $M\pm(1.25R1.35\sqrt{n})$ $(1 + 1 /\sqrt{2})Z_{\alpha 2}2$, where R is the variable interquartile range, M is the median and $Z_{\alpha 2}$ is the value of the normal distribution (0,1), which leaves to the right α 2 probability.

For our variable X, consumption of automobiles, have graphic box and whiskers with grooves in Figure 5-5.

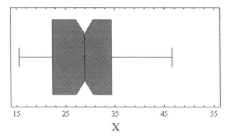

Figure 5-5

5.7 MULTIPLE BOX AND WHISKERS CHART

In statistics, it is typical to split the dataset of a variable in rational subgroups, which may for example be strata defined according to a particular variable of stratification. Multiple box and whiskers chart will allow to analyze, summarize and simultaneously compare multiple sets of univariate data given, corresponding to the different groups in which the values of a variable can be subdivided. This exploratory data analysis tool will allow to study the symmetry of the data, detect outliers and represent averages, medians, ranges and extreme values for all groups. Being simultaneous representation for all data sets, stockings, medium-sized, ranges, extreme values, Symmetries and outliers of all groups can compare. The graphic multiple horizontally represent a graph of box and whiskers for each group of values of the variable in study.

If classify the consumption of automobiles (variable X) according to its cubic capacity (variable and), we're doing subgroups with the values of X according to the stratification variable and. The possible values of and are 8, 6, 5, 4 and 3 cylinders. The values of X for each value of and are given below:

```
X    Y   X    Y   X    Y   X    Y   X    Y   X    Y   X    Y   X    Y   X    Y   X    Y
---------- --------- --------- --------- --------- --------- --------- --------- --------- ---------
43.1 4 36.1 4 32.8 4 39.4 4 36.1 4 19.9 8 19.4 8 20.2 8 19.2 6 20.5 6
20.2 6 25.1 4 20.5 6 19.4 6 20.6 6 20.8 6 18.6 6 18.1 6 19.2 8 17.7 6
18.1 8 17.5 8 30 4 27.5 4 27.2 4 30.9 4 21.1 4 23.2 4 23.8 4 23.9 4
20.3 5 17 6 21.6 4 16.2 6 31.5 4 29.5 4 21.5 6 19.8 6 22.3 4 20.2 6
20.6 6 17 8 17.6 8 16.5 8 18.2 8 16.9 8 15.5 8 19.2 8 18.5 8 31.9 4
34.1 4 35.7 4 27.4 4 25.4 5 23 8 27.2 4 23.9 8 34.2 4 34.5 4 31.8 4
37.3 4 28.4 4 28.8 6 26.8 6 33.5 4 41.5 4 38.1 4 32.1 4 37.2 4 28 4
26.4 4 24.3 4 19.1 6 34.3 4 29.8 4 31.3 4 37 4 32.2 4 46.6 4 27.9 4
40.8 4 44.3 4 43.4 4 36.4 5 30.4 4 44.6 4 40.9 4 33.8 4 29.8 4 32.7 6
```

23.7 3 35 4 23.6 4 32.4 4 27.2 4 26.6 4 25.8 4 23.5 6 30 4 39.1 4
39 4 35.1 4 32.3 4 37 4 37.7 4 34.1 4 34.7 4 34.4 4 29.9 4 33 4
34.5 4 33.7 4 32.4 4 32.9 4 31.6 4 28.1 4 30.7 6 25.4 6 24.2 6 22.4 6
26.6 8 20.2 6 17.6 6 28 4 27 4 34 4 31 4 29 4 27 4 24 4
23 4 36 4 37 4 31 4 38 4 36 4 36 4 36 4 34 4 38 4
32 4 38 4 25 6 38 6 26 4 22 6 32 4 36 4 27 4 27 4
44 4 32 4 28 4 31 4

The manifold box and whiskers d graphautomobile consumption (variable X) according to its cubic capacity (variable *and*), shown in Figure 5-6.

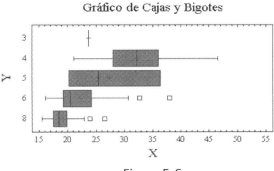

Figure 5-6

Graph allows you to assert that the variable X (liters consumed 1000 kilometers) *for 8 cylinder cars* varies between 15.5 and 23, and that 50% central these car consumes between 17.5 (first quartile) and 20 (third quartile) litres to the 1000 kilometers, there are 2 values of Xabnormally large*(outliers)* since in the figure are two points aligned with the right hand mustache. The distribution of X for 8 cylinder cars is slightly asymmetric to the right, as the area to the right in the central area of the figure is larger than the left, and the median corresponds approximately to the value X, being the average 19.5 approximately 18.5.

For 6-cylinder cars liters consumed per 1000 kilometers (variable X) vary between 16 and 31, focusing the central 50% of the values of X between 19 (first quartile) and 24 (third quartile), exist 2 abnormally large atypical X values *(outliers)* since in the figure are two points aligned with the right hand mustache. The distribution of X for 6-cylinder cars is asymmetric to the right, X median approaching 20.5 and the average at 22.5.

5-Cylinder cars the litres consumed per 1000 kilometers (variable X) vary between 20.2 and 36.5, concentrating 50% central values of X between the same values, there are no whiskers and *outliers*. The distribution of X for 5 cylinders cars is asymmetric to the right, X median 25.5 approaches and the average to 27.5.

For 4 cylinder cars liters consumed per 1000 kilometers (variable *X*) vary between 21 and 47, focusing the central 50% of the values of *X* between 28 (first quartile) and 36 (third quartile), there are no *outliers*. The distribution of *X* for 4 cylinder cars is almost symmetric with median values and average approximate to 32.

For 3-cylinder cars there is a single value of *X*, which does not build the box and whiskers chart.

If we compare different graphics, we see that the asymmetry of *X* is stronger for 5 and 6 cylinders cars, for the 8 is less and the 4 does not exist. Abnormally large *X* values appear only for 6 and 8 cylinder cars. Averages and medians vary enough for different groups of values of *X* certain values of *and*.

5.8 GRAPH OF SYMMETRY

The graph of symmetry is a tool that allows you to visually analyze the degree of symmetry of a variable. In the horizontal axis distances of the values of the variable are represented to the medium that they are below it, and on the y-axis represent the values of the variable distances median remaining above it. If the symmetry is perfect, the resulting set of points would be the main diagonal. While most approximates the graph to diagonal more symmetry exists in the distribution of the variable.

For the example of the variable *X*, variable defined by the number of litres consumed by cars every 1000 km that we have been considering during the whole chapter, have the graph of symmetry of Figure 5-7.

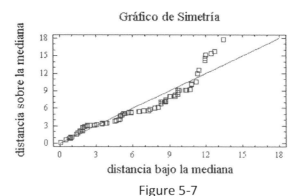

Figure 5-7

For the variable X, shown a degree of symmetry, since the points of the graph conform well to the diagonal.

Practical steps to prepare the chart of symmetry are the following:

1. It is estimated the median of the variable (in our case 28.9).

2. They are ordered values of the variable of greatest to lowest (descending order).

3. They are calculated the differences d_i between the ordered values of the variable and the median.

4. The positive values of d_i ordered from lowest are taken to larger and are called p_i. These values will be the *distances over the median*.

5. Negative values of d_i ordered minor are taken to larger and are called n_i. These values changed sign will be the *distances under the median*.

6. Are graphed points coordinates $(-n_i p_i)$.

In our example we started placing in a column values of X ordered from highest to lowest. Later formed a second column with the values $X-$ 28.9 resulting from subtracting X its median (28.9). Then we started this column in two different columns. In the first column, place negative values n_i of the column $X-$ 28.9 and change them sign, and in the second column put the positive values p_i of the column $X-$ 28.9. The next step is to sort both columns (the two already positive) of minor to major, resulting in values for the graph $(-n_i p_i)$ which is shown in Figure 5-8.

$-n_i$	p_i	$-n_i$	p_i	$-n_i$	p_i
0.1	0.1	4.6	3.8	8.7	7.2
0.5	0.6	4.7	3.9	8.7	7.5
0.8	0.9	4.9	4	9	8.1
0.9	0.9	5	4.1	9.1	8.1
0.9	1	5	4.6	9.5	8.1
0.9	1.1	5.1	4.8	9.5	8.3
1	1.1	5.2	4.9	9.7	8.4
1.4	1.5	5.3	5.1	9.7	8.8
1.5	1.8	5.4	5.1	9.7	9.1

1.7	2	5.7	5.2	9.8	9.1
1.7	2.1	5.9	5.2	10.3	9.1
1.7	2.1	5.9	5.3	10.4	9.1
1.9	2.1	6.5	5.4	10.7	9.2
1.9	2.4	6.6	5.5	10.8	10.1
1.9	2.6	6.9	5.6	10.8	10.2
1.9	2.7	7.3	5.6	11.2	10.5
2.1	2.9	7.4	5.8	11.3	11.9
2.3	3	7.8	6.1	11.3	12
2.3	3.1	8.1	6.2	11.4	12.6
2.5	3.1	8.3	6.8	11.9	14.2
2.9	3.1	8.3	7.1	11.9	14.5
3.1	3.2	8.4	7.1	12	15.1
3.5	3.3	8.4	7.1	12.4	15.4
3.5	3.4	8.6	7.1	12.7	15.7
3.8	3.5	8.7	7.1	13.4	17.7
3.9	3.5	8.7	7.2		

Figure 5-8

5.9 SCATTER CHART

It's a graphic that shows the relationship between two or more variables. It consists of points whose Cartesian coordinates are the pairs of values of two variables whose ratio you want to study represented on the vertical axis and horizontal axis. The positioning of the scatter chart points defines the relationship between the variables. If they are around a straight line, there is a linear correlation between the variables. If the points follow a non-linear pattern, the relationship between variables cannot be defined as linear. If the cloud of points is random and scattered, there was no any relationship between the variables. A graph of dispersion for an analysis of several variables which offers lots of information is that represents a matrix structure in the scatter chart of all pairs of variables (lower triangular matrix area), its histogram of frequencies (diagonal of the matrix) and correlation coefficients of all pairs of variables in study (upper triangular matrix area).

Figure 5-9 shows the matrix chart for variables, *consumption*, *power* and *price* of automobiles.

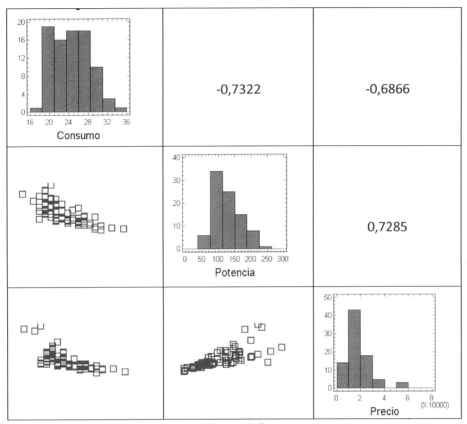

Figure 5-9

The graph of dispersion of the consumption power located in the element (2.1) of the matrix is easily adjustable to a line of negative slope, which indicates a strong negative relationship between both variables. Corroborates this information the coefficient of correlation between consumption and power (−0,7322) located in the (1,2) element of the array. The graph of dispersion of consumption with the price set in the element (3,1) of matrix is easily adjustable to a line of negative slope, which indicates a strong negative relationship between both variables. Corroborates this information the coefficient of correlation between consumption and price (−0,6866) located in the matrix element (1,3). The graph of dispersion of the power price in the array element (3,2) is easily adjustable to a straight line of positive slope, which indicates a strong, positive relationship between both variables. Corroborates this information the correlation coefficient between power and price (0,7285) located in the element (2,3) of the matrix. Histograms of the main diagonal of the matrix indicate normality and symmetry for consumption and the power, and some asymmetry for the price.

5.10 GRAPHICS FOR QUALITATIVE VARIABLES

Visual exploration of qualitative variables is usually carried out using rectangles diagrams, diagrams of sectors and pictograms.

Diagrams of rectangles They are constructed by assigning to each mode of the qualitative variable a rectangle with equal (or proportional) height to its absolute frequency n_i and with constant base.

As an example, Figure 5-10 presents a diagram of rectangles representing the assets according to the different categories of the variable branch of activity. On each rectangle is the absolute frequency n_i in thousands of assets of the relevant branch of activity. Own branches of activity are presented on the horizontal axis and on the y-axis different values of absolute frequencies by intervals that are used are presented as a reference to locate the height of each rectangle.

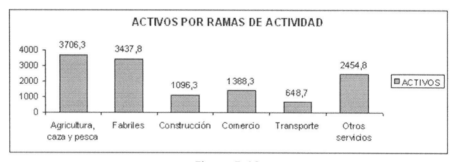

Figure 5-10

Diagrams of sectors (or cake) constitute the chart type used to represent frequency distributions of qualitative variables. The variable is represented in a circle whose portions (circular sectors) have a proportional area at the absolute frequencies of the variable modalities. To make the pie chart enough to assign to each form of the variable a sector circular whose central angle is proportional to the absolute frequency of the mode. Mathematically, the central angle mode α_i-th whose absolute frequency is n_i can be expressed as follows:

$$\alpha_i = kn_i \Rightarrow \frac{\alpha_i}{n_i} = k = \frac{\sum \alpha_i}{\sum n_i} = \frac{360}{N} \Rightarrow \alpha_i = \frac{360}{N} n_i = 360 \frac{n_i}{N} = 360 f_i$$

The calculations for our example are presented in the table of Figure 5-11.

BRANCH	ASSETS (n_i)	$f_i = n_i/N$	$\alpha_i = 360 f_i$
Agriculture, hunting and fishing	3706,3	0.29	104,79
Manufacturing	3437,8	0.27	97,20
Construction	1096,3	0.09	31,00
Trade	1388,3	0.11	39,25
Transport	648,7	0.05	18.34
Other services	2454,8	0.19	69,41
$N=$	12732,2		

Figure 5-11

Figure 5-12 shows the pie chart.

Figure 5-12

Another common way to construct pie charts consists of assigning to the pie relative to the mode i- th a percentage equal to percent that represents its absolute frequency n_i on the total frequency $N = \sum n_i$. Mathematically, the expression of the percentage p_i relative to the mode i- th is expressed as follows:

$$p_i = 100 \frac{n_i}{N} = 100 f_i$$

Figure 5-13 shows the above pie chart with percentages.

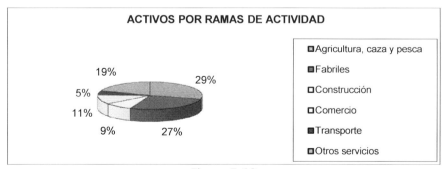

Figure 5-13

The *glyphs* are built of pictorial way representing each modality of the qualitative variable indicating the meaning of each character by a suggestive silhouette. For example, in Figure 5-14 a cylinder whose height is proportional to the number of facilities with hazardous waste in 1997 is represented on every State of the United States map.

Figure 5-14

In the glyphs you can use any silhouette to represent the frequency of each mode of the qualitative variable. The previous glyph with a cone on each State whose height indicates the frequency of hazardous waste facilities are shown in Figure 5-15.

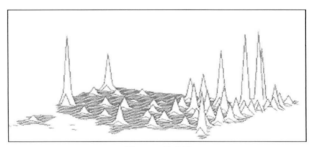

Figure 5-15

5.11 TOOLS FORMAL EXPLORATION

It is necessary to bear in mind that graphic representations, although they provide an alternative way to develop a perspective on the nature of the data and the interrelationships that exist between them even if they are multivariate, never replace the measures of statistical formal diagnosis as the contrasts of setting data to a distribution, the contrasts of asymmetry, the contrasts of randomness, the use of robust statistics, etc. The graphical exploration of data must always be accompanied by contrasts of formal exploration.

5.12 GOODNESS OF FIT TEST TO A DISTRIBUTION: TEST OF THE CHI -SQUARE

This kind of tests is comparing the data obtained in a sample we can deduce or which do not come from a population with a particular distribution (for example, of the normal distribution). These include contrast Chi-square goodness of fit which is described below.

Is a simple random sample of size N from a certain variable. The contrast of the Chi-square goodness of fit is carried out for sa ber if there are sufficient reasons to accept that this variable has a given probability distribution. Therefore, the null hypothesis H_{or} will refer that sampling observations constitute a set of N values from a random variable with a probability given by $P(S)$ distribution, and the alternative that this not happens. Let us study this contrast distinguishing two cases:

(a) the known population parameters

Probability $P(S)$ is fully specified, so that their expression does not display unknown parameters. If $H_{is\ certain}$, the distribution of the sample, which is the discrete uniform distribution obtained by assigning a probability $P_i = 1/N$ at each of the N values observed, can be considered a statistical picture of the fore population distri- $P(S)$.

However, due to random fluctuations in the treo mues, reason will be that the population and sampling distributions do not coincide, but for large samples can be expected that the distribution of the show cons tituya one approach to population distribution. In this sense, it seems natural to introduce some measure of deviation between both distributions and base our contrast on the properties of the dis contribution in the sampling of this measure.

Suppose that the random variable space is divided into r intervals $S_1, S_2,..., S_r$ disjoint, and is the probability that a value belongs to the interval i- th $p_i = P(S_i)$, where such intervals can be the r groups or classes in which have been arranged the sample values for purposes of tabulation. Sean $n_1, n_2..., n_r$ the corresponding absolute frequencies in the r groups sample, in such a way that n_i sample values belong to the class S_i, being $\sum n_i = N$ with $i =1,..., r$. Now made a measure of the deviation between the distribution of the sample and the distribution supposed to the population under the null hypothesis, whose expression is:

$$\chi^2 = \sum \frac{(n_i - Np_i)^2}{Np_i}$$

where n_i are the observed frequencies in the sample, and Np_i the estimation of frequencies expected pobla international distribution if that indicates H_0. The statistical χ^2 has, in the limit ($N \rightarrow \infty$), a Chi-square distribution with $r - 1$ degrees of freedom.

Determined the distribution of sampling for measurement of deviation χ^2, will build the contrast to H_0 in the following way: set the level of significance ▢, look in the tables of the Chi-square value C such that $P(\chi^2_{(r-1, ▢)} > C) = ▢▢$ and if the value of the statistical χ^2 is greater that C, then reject the hypothesis H_0 to the sample comes from the indicated population. If the value of the statistical χ^2 is less than C, then we accept H_0 and assure that the sample comes from the indicated population.

b) unknown population parameters

Suppose that according to the null hypothesis H_0 sample comes from a population where there are than previously estimated a series of k be unknown parameters. Fisher showed that if previously estimated the k parameters using the sample information, limit χ^2 statistical distribution is a Chi-square with $r - k - 1$ degrees of freedom, and the contrast is as in the previous case. The only difference are the degrees of freedom of the statistical χ^2.

Once exposed contrast χ^2 of goodness of fit, both for the case in which are not estimated parameters as for when is it does, we must point out that, for that there are no disturbances, Sintervals$_i$ should be such that the values of $P(S_i)$, for all i, they were about equal. In addition, when the number of intervals in which divides the space of the random variable is 2 test χ^2 should not be used if there is any expected rate of less than 5.

If the number of intervals is greater that 2 nor should be used the test χ^2 if more than 20% of the expected frequencies are less than 5 or any it is less than 1. However, sometimes expected frequencies can increase making joints of adjacent intervals, unions which, of course, make sense in reality.

5.13 LILLIEFORS KOLMOGOROV-SMIRNOV GOODNESS OF FIT TEST

The contrast of Kolmogorov-Smirnov test is a test for goodness of fit alternative to the of the Chi-square. Similar to the contrast of the Chi-square goodness of fit, we consider that the total mass of discrete probability is evenly distributed between the *N* values the sample so, ordered the sample values of less than wholesale, sample empirical distribution function $Fis_n(x) = N_i/N$.

The contrast of Kolmogorov-Smirnov applies only to continuous variables and tries to measure the fit between the empirical distribution of a sample function and the theoretical distribution function. It is therefore a contrast adjustment of the distribution of a sample to a given continuous distribution.

Function of empirical distribution of a sample $x_1, x_2,...x_n$, It is defined as:

$$F_n(x) = \frac{\text{number of values in the set } \{x_1, x_2,..., x_n\} \text{ which are } \leq x}{n}$$

To contrast the hypotheses that sample fits a distribution theoretical $F(x)$, the statistic is calculated:

$$D_n = Máx \, |F_n(x) - F(x)|$$

whose distribution is known and is tabulated. If the calculated distance D_n is greater to that found in tables, to a level of ▢, reject the distribution F (x) for the sample.

For given *n* and ▢ , find $D(▢,n)$ such that P $(D_n > D(▢,n)) = ▢$. The critical region of the test will be $D_n > D(▢,n)$.

This contrast has the advantage that it does not require grouping data and the drawback that if we calculate $F(x)$ estimating parameters of the population through the sample, the distribution of D_n is only approximate.

Typically used the statistical ▢nD_n instead of D_n, allowing us to compare tables for very large sample sizes.

We will take into account the following considerations:

- The Kolmogorov-Smirnov test is easier to apply than the χ^2.

- The Kolmogorov-Smirnov test is unaffected by regroupings of observations, while in the test of χ^2, by decreasing the groups, lost infor information, as well as degrees of freedom.

- The Kolmogorov-Smirnov test is applicable to small samples, while the χ^2 test is designed for large samples.

- The power of the Kolmogorov-Smirnov test is greater than the of the of the χ^2, although they tend to equalize when the sample size grows.

- The test of the χ^2 can easily be modified when there are parameters desco nocidos while the Kolmogorov-Smirnov test does not have such flexibility.

- The χ^2 test is applicable when the population is discrete or continuous and the Kolmogorov-Smirnov test requires continuity of $F\ (x)$.

It can be used for these contrasts (for all) the criterion of the p- value, rejecting the null hypothesis at the level ⍰ when the p- value is less than ⍰, and accepting it otherwise. When the distribution to adjust is a normal, the Kolmogorov-Smirnov statistic was studied and corrected by Lilliefors.

Chapter 6

PHASE OF EXPLORATION WITH SAS ENTERPRISE MINER

6.1 LA PHASE OF EXPLORATION ON ENTERPRISE MINER

We remind that SAS Institute considers explore phase within the process of *Data Mining* (*Exploring*), which takes place after the phase of selection (*Selecting*). Initially the exploration phase leads to partners the nodes shown in Figure 6-1, but are generally considered typically belonging to this phase distributions (*Distribution Explorer*) browser nodes, graphics (*Multiplot*) and multivariate analysis (*Insight*).

Figure 6-1

6.2 THE NODE EXPLORER DISTRIBUTIONS

It is a tool that allows you to examine distributions of variables and statistics of the data set in Studio. It is used to visualize and explore graphically large volumes of data. Its fundamental objective is to discover patterns, extreme values, or the limited influence of some variables. It also allows to create multidimensional histograms for discrete or continuous variables.

Once we already have our work in SAS (*creditos.sas7bdat*file) format data in a specific library (library *work* representing the subdirectory *c:\libros\miningt*), open the project P1 (*File → Open*) and using *File → New → Diagram* create diagram D7 (Figure 6-2). Then the node *Distribution Explorer* is obtained through the button *Tools* from the browser's project of Enterprise Miner as a sub-option of the category *scan* (Figure 6-1) or by dragging the node itself on the work area beside the *Input Data Source* node that is assigned the data set *creditos.sas7bdat* of the library work joining both (Figure 6-3).

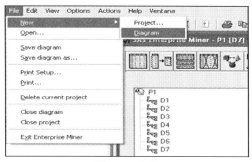

Figure 6-2

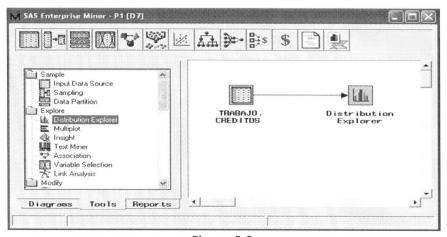

Figure 6-3

The next task is to double-click on the node *Distribution Explorer* to obtain your input screen. Once you open the node, select the *Variables* tab and in the column *Axis* set the axes on which we are going to represent each variable (Figure 6-4). Then run the node *Distribution Explorer* by clicking on it with the right mouse button and choosing *Run*. Can thus create histograms multidimiensionales to analyze relationships between data (Figure 6-5). On the tabs of each one of the axes will be able analyze Histograms correspond to the variables associated with the same (8-6 figures to 8-8).

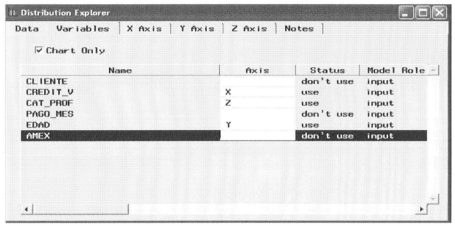

Figure 6-4

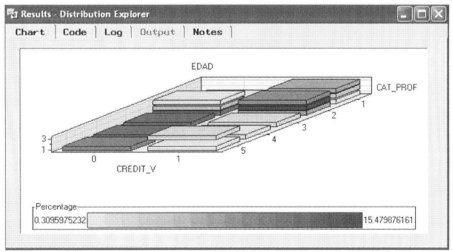

Figure 6-5

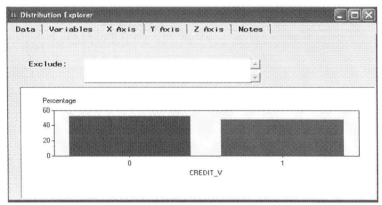

Figure 6-6

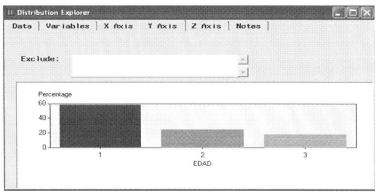

Figure 6-7

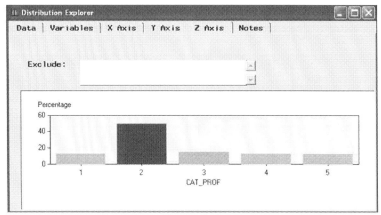

Figure 6-8

6.3 THE NODE MULTIGRAFICOS

The node Multigraficos (*Multiplot*) allows you to explore graphically large volumes of data. This node automatically creates bar graphs, histograms and scatter charts. With the multigraficos node data can be viewed from different perspectives to explore the existence or not of relationships between different variables. This node is useful also for detecting outliers in the data. In addition to its simplicity, it has an additional advantage over other similar *Insight*or *Distribution Explorer* nodes, and is that the node is able to generate the code necessary to create graphics in the SAS command environment.

Once we already have our work in SAS (*creditos.sas7bdat*file) format data in a specific library (library *work* representing the subdirectory *c:\libros\miningt*), open the project P1 (*File → Open*) and using *File → New → Diagram* diagram D8 created. Then the *Multiplot* node is obtained through the button *Tools* from the browser's project of Enterprise Miner as a sub-option of the category *Explore* (Figure 6-1), or by dragging the node itself on the area next to the *Input Data Source* node is assigned to which the data set *mundo.sas7bdat* of the library work. Then will be the union of the two (Figure 6-9).

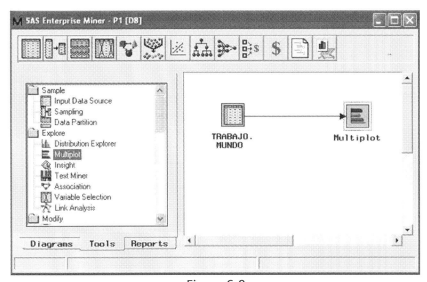

Figure 6-9

Below is double-clicked on the *Input Data Source* node to define those variables that you want to cross with each other (in our case the variable *GDP-CAP*) from the tab *Variables* (Figure 6-10) as a *Target* .

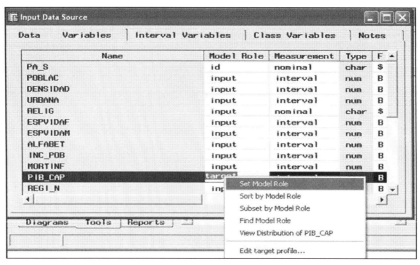

Figure 6-10

Then double click on the node *Multiplot*, is made we choose the *Variables* tab and select the variables that we are going to analyze (Figure 6-11). Then run the *Multiplot* node by clicking the *Run*icon✺. This produces the histogram of the first selected variable (Figure 6-12). By clicking with the right button of the mouse on any area of the graph and choosing *Graphs* → *Select* (Figure 6-13) Gets the *Selection* (Figure 6-14) screen in which you can choose the variables or pairs of variables to plot. If we choose *ALFABET* and *PIB_CAP* dispersion graph Figure 6-15 that includes the regression line is obtained. In this way we can analyze the relationships between the variables. If we choose your chart of averages (Figure 6-16) figure you get 6-17.

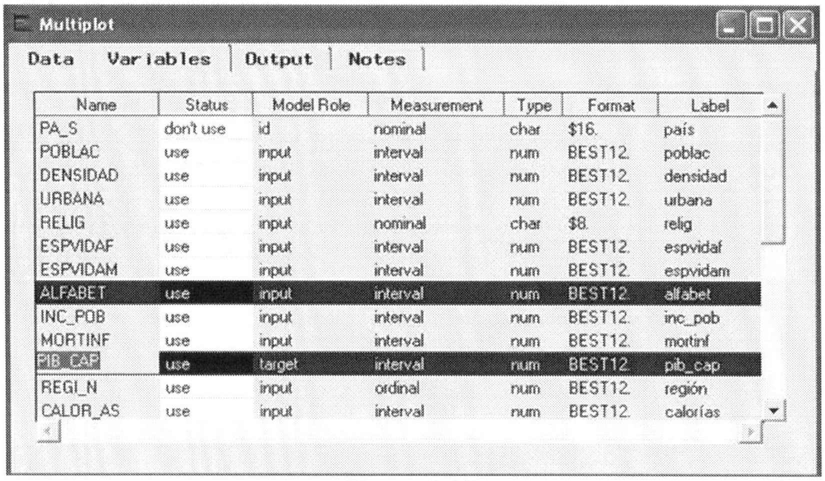

Figure 6-11

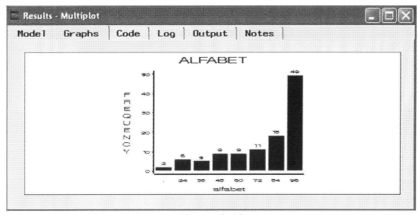

Figure 6-12

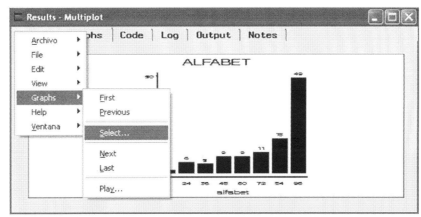

Figure 6-13

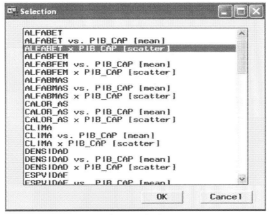

Figure 6-14

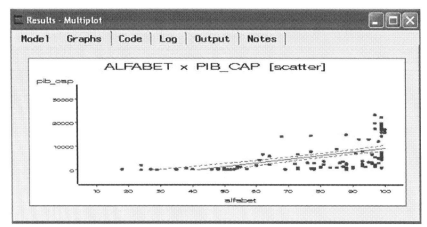

Figure 6-15

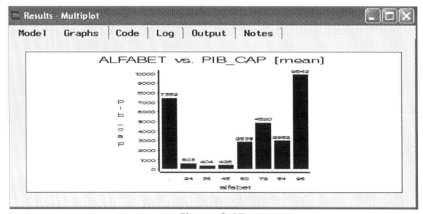

Figure 6-16

Figure 6-17

It is also possible to choose options for graphics and regression lines. To enable these options, however it is necessary to do it by default in the tools palette. So, it is necessary to push the right button in the *Multiplot* of palette Tools node and select *Properties* (Figure 6-18). Figure 6-19 properties of the graph whose tab Gets *Edit Defaults...* leads us to display options for graphics (Figure 6-18). On the tab *Bar Charts* are chosen for bars (Figure 6-20) graphics and options in the tab *Scatter plots* you choose the options for scatter charts and regression (Figure 6-21) lines including the type of regression, confidence intervals for the results and the possibility to show or not the equation of adjustment.

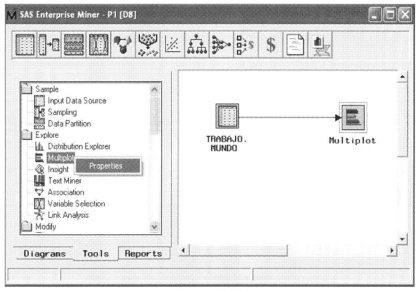

Figure 6-18

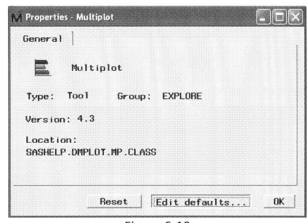

Figure 6-19

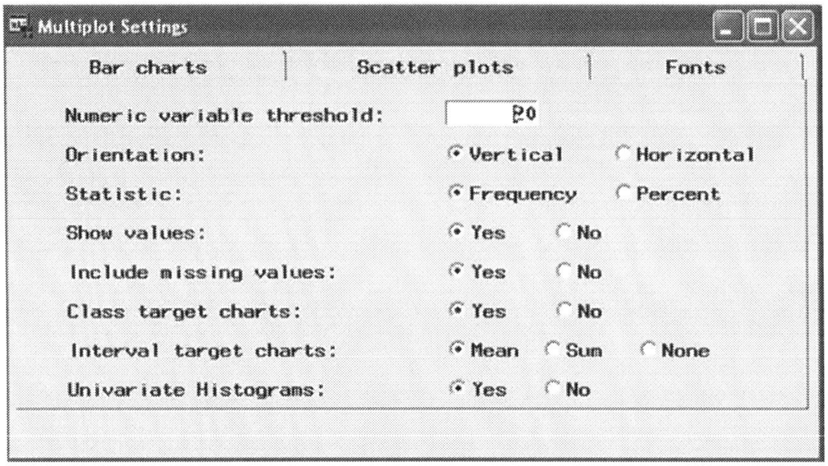

Figure 6-20

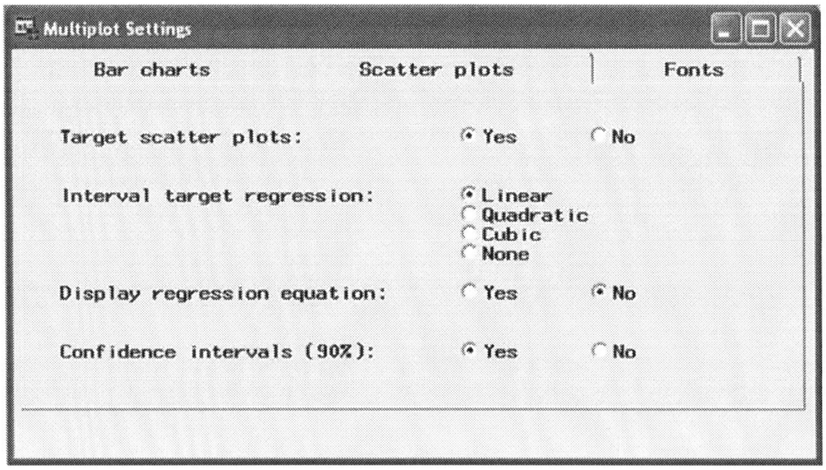

Figure 6-21

Choose one work data set variable in the variables tab of the *Multiplot* node and click on it with the right button of the mouse we can see its frequency distribution by choosing the option from the resulting pop-up menu (Figure 6-22) *View Distribution* . If we choose the variable *MORTINF* you get the histogram of Figure 6-23.

If on this histogram click with the secondary mouse button and choose *View → Frequency Table* (Figure 6-24) Gets the frequency table of the distribution of the variable *MORTINF* (Figure 6-25)

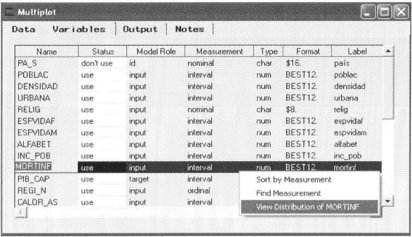

Figure 6-22

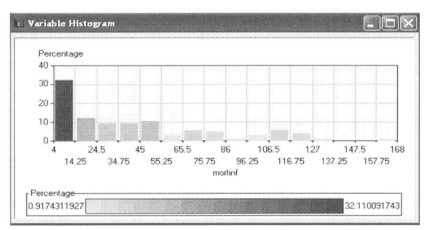

Figure 6-23

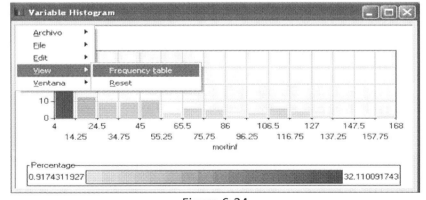

Figure 6-24

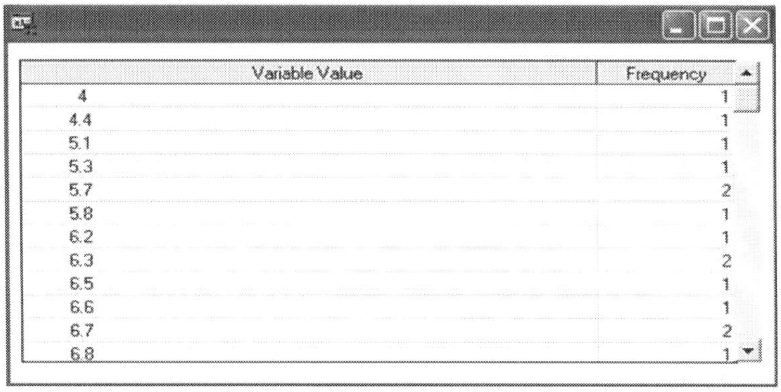

Variable Value	Frequency
4	1
4.4	1
5.1	1
5.3	1
5.7	2
5.8	1
6.2	1
6.3	2
6.5	1
6.6	1
6.7	2
6.8	1

Figure 6-25

6.4 THE NODE'S EXPLORATION OF PATTERNS

The exploration of patterns (*Insight*) node allows you to explore and analyze data interactively. It's a node that is in itself a tool for data analysis. It can carry out various functions of descriptive analysis and explore Univariate and multivariate distributions, create barcodes and 2D and 3D scatter charts and calculate correlations. It also allows to adjust explanatory models and perform multiple regression, analysis of variance, logistic regression, principal components analysis and canonical correlation analysis.

Once we already have our work in SAS (*educa.sas7bdat*file) format data in a specific library (library *work* representing the subdirectory *c:\libros\miningt*), open the project P1 (*File → Open*) and using *File → New → Diagram* create diagram D9. Then the node *Insight* is obtained through the button *Tools* from the browser's project of Enterprise Miner as a sub-option of the category *Explore* (Figure 6-1) or by dragging the node itself on the area next to the *Input Data Source* node is assigned to which the data set *educa.sas7bdat* of the library *work*. Then will be the union of the two (Figure 6-26).

Then double clicks on the node *Insight*, we chose the *Data* tab and choose between using a sample of the data set or all data (Figure 6-27). On the *Variables* tab can you click with the right button of the mouse on any of them and choose the option *View distribution* in the resulting pop-up menu (Figure 6-28) to obtain the corresponding frequency histogram (Figure 6-29). By double clicking on the *Input Data Source* node you can place one or more of the variables such as *Target* where a later analysis requires it to perform.

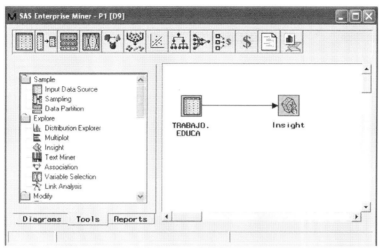

Figure 6-26

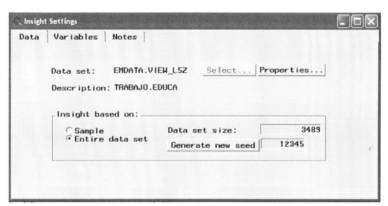

Figure 6-27

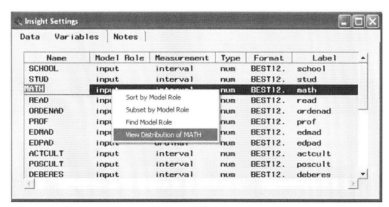

Figure 6-28

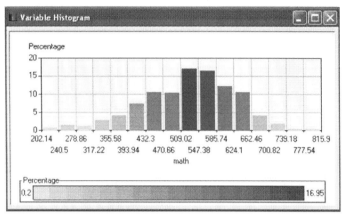

Figure 6-29

Then run the *Insight* node by clicking the *Run* icon ⚡ to obtain the general framework of *Insight* (Figure 6-30).

The **Edit** of the *Insight* menu bar option allows you to govern the editing options (Windows Presentation and management variables, observations and formats, etc.).

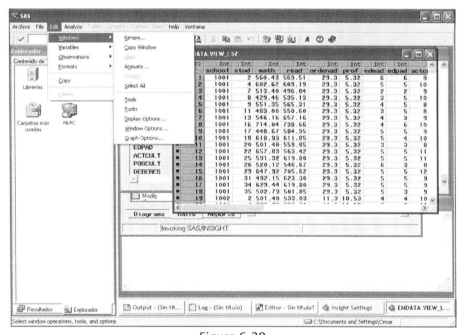

Figure 6-30

*Edit*options are seen in Figure 6-30. *Windows* option allows to modify the presentation of the Windows. The option *variable* allows a large number of transformations in the variables (Figure 6-31).The option*Observations* allows you to perform different actions to find and select data (Figure 6-32) how to find the data (or data) that coincides with assigned criteria, examine in detail the data of a selected case, labeling the variables that meet a desired characteristics, deselect the data that meet a given criteria, show or hide within a chart data that meet a chosen standardSelect or exclude the cases that will be included in the analysis according to a given criterion, etc. *Formats* (Figure 6-33) option allows you to change the width of columns and the number of decimal places of the data table. *Copy* and *Delete* options allow you to copy the image of the active window and delete the analysis or selected table.

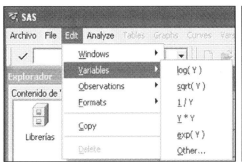

Figure 6-31

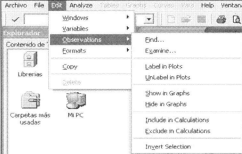

Figure 6-32

Figure 6-33

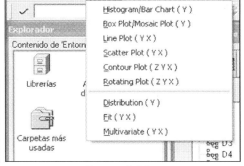

Figure 6-34

The option*Analyze* menu bar of *Insight* displays the analysis that can be carried out (Figure 6-34).The first group of options of *Analyze* are used for univariate and multivariate data analysis. The following options are used for the analysis of the distribution of variables, the adjustment of models and multivariate data analysis. These options are described below:

Histogram/Bar Chart (and): allows a histogram (Figure 6-36) for the variable that is selected in the screen of choice (Figure 6-35).

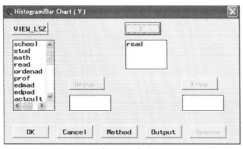

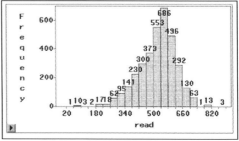

| Figure 6-35 | Figure 6-36 |

Box Plot / Mosaic Plot (and): allows a Diagram box and whiskers (Figure 6-38) of the variable selected in the screen (Figure 6-37).

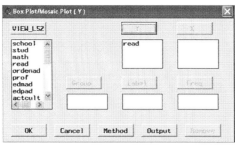

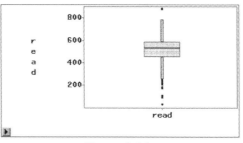

| Figure 6-37 | Figure 6-38 |

Also allows to superimpose several diagrams, box and whiskers (Figure 6-40) in accordance with the distribution of a second variable in a single graph (*X*) introduced on the screen (Figure 6-39).

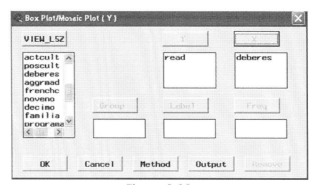

Figure 6-39

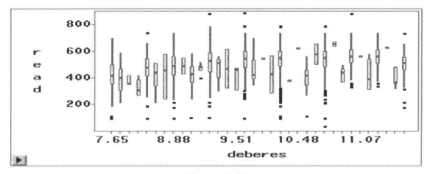

Figure 6-40

Line Plot (& X): allows the chart of lines joining the points situated in a plane defined by the coordinates of the two variables (Figure 6-41).

Scatter Plot (Y X): carries out the diagram of dispersion relative to the two variables (Figure 6-42).

Contour Plot (Z & X): performs a graphic of contour where an explained variable *Z* depends on two explanatory (*X* e) *and* (Figure 6-43).

Rotating Plot (Z and X): through this option can represent a dispersion diagram in three dimensions (Figure 6-44). The graph gives the option of rotating shafts to view in detail the relationships between the data.

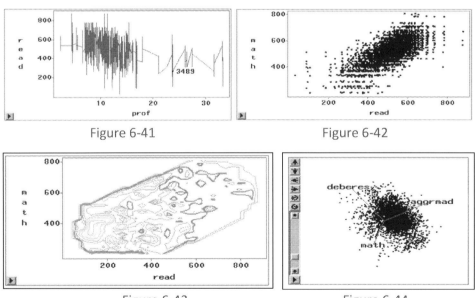

Figure 6-41   Figure 6-42

Figure 6-43   Figure 6-44

Distribution (and): allows to analyze the distribution of a variable and calculate different indicators and graphs of the same. In the *Distribution* (Figure 6-45) entry window we enter in the box *and* the variable or variables whose distribution you want to analyze. If it is a group formed by several variables we will introduce it in the *Group*window. We will introduce the variable *Label* if it is a string variable. We will use *Freq* when the variable represent frequencies. Finally we will use *Weight* if there is a variable that weigh the variable object of analysis to elevate the results to the population.

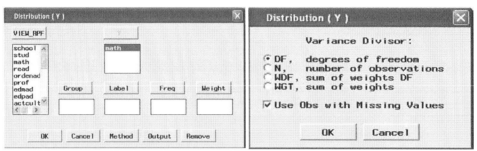

Figure 6-45   Figure 6-46

Then select the method of calculation of the distribution. For this we will make click in the option *Method*. This option allows you to choose four dividers to calculate the variance (Figure 6-46), the coefficient of asymmetry (*Skewness*) and kurtosis (*Kurtosis*). *DF* calculates the degrees of freedom that is uses *N*- 1 as the denominator to calculate the variance *N* uses the number of observations. Similarly to the case of weighted distributions can choose between *WDF* where to calculate the variance used as denominator the sum of weights less 1 or *WGT* where we use only the amount of pesos. By default the system choose *DF* , which is the first of the options. When we are looking at several variables and some of them have missing values, the option *Use Obs with Missing Values* introduces all the observations that have not lost to the variable *and* analyzed values in the analysis. If we eliminate this option, the values lost in any variable *and* will not be used for the analysis of any of the variables.

Once the method has been chosen, press *OK* and on the option *Output* of Figure 6-45 select the results that we want the system to calculate about Figure 6-47. In the option *Parameters* specify a value for α that represents the level of trust. The parameter μ_0 is only used in the calculation of adjusted averages (*Trimmed / Winsorized Means*) while the parameter θ is used in the estimation of the density (*Density Estimation*option) function and the cumulative distribution of the distributions of lognormal, exponential and Weibull (*Cumulative Distribution*option). In the *Descriptive Statistics*option, can calculate the moments, quantiles, confidence intervals, statistical t Student, the sign and the range of signs (*Tests for Location*). When you click *OK*, the results can be seen in Figure 6-48.

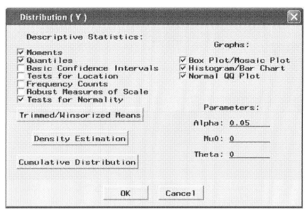

Figure 6-47

```
▶|                    Moments
N              3489.0000   Sum Wgts    3489.0000
Mean            528.0570   Sum       1842390.86
Std Dev          98.5763   Variance     9717.2913
Skewness         -0.5192   Kurtosis        0.3923
USS           1.007E+09    CSS        33893912.2
CV               18.6677   Std Mean        1.6689

▶|                   Quantiles
100% Max         815.9000         99.0%     721.0300
 75% Q3          602.2600         97.5%     686.8100
 50% Med         533.9800         95.0%     675.9500
 25% Q1          468.6200         90.0%     647.9200
  0% Min         202.1400         10.0%     398.9000
     Range       613.7600          5.0%     344.3000
     Q3-Q1       133.6400          2.5%     289.6900
     Mode        581.1500          1.0%     256.6000
```

▶	95% Confidence Intervals		
Parameter	Estimate	LCL	UCL
Mean	528.0570	524.7849	531.3291
Std Dev	98.5763	96.3166	100.9454
Variance	9717.2913	9276.8866	10189.9757

```
▶|    Tests for Location: Mu0=0
        Num Obs != Mu0:3489
        Num Obs > Mu0:3489
```

Test	Statistic	p-value
Student's t	316.42	<.0001
Sign	1744.50	<.0001
Signed Rank	3044152.50	<.0001

Figure 6-48

In the *Descriptive Statistics* option can also be calculated frequency tables, robust measures of scale as the mean difference of Gini, the interquartile range or the absolute deviation from the median (*Robust Measures of Scale*). Finally the option *Tests for Normality* calculates the statistics to compare normality of Shapiro-Wilk test, Kolmogorov-Smirnov, Cramér-von Mises and Anderson-Darling (Figure 6-49). In addition to the above options, with the options of *Graphs*, we can calculate graphic box and whiskers and mosaic, histograms and bar diagrams, already seen before, as well as graphic QQ to contrast normal (Figure 6-50).

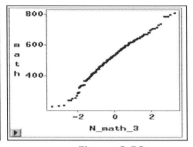

Robust Measures of Scale		
Measure	Value	Estimate of Sigma
Interquartile Range	133.6400	99.0674
Gini's Mean Difference	109.8968	97.3935
MAD	66.3500	98.3705
Sn	93.9292	93.9534
Qn	95.3639	95.3257

Tests for Normality		
Test Statistic	Value	p-value
Shapiro-Wilk	.	.
Kolmogorov-Smirnov	0.053074	<.0100
Cramer-von Mises	2.014930	<.0050
Anderson-Darling	14.05048	<.0050

Figure 6-49   Figure 6-50

Density Estimation option allows to calculate the function of density according to a series of parametric options: normal, lognormal, exponential, Weibull and non parametric (*Kernel Estimation*): normal, triangular, and quadratic (Figure 6-51). The results obtained allow interactively vary the parameter estimates (Figure 6-52)

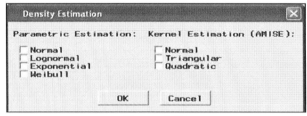

Figure 6-51

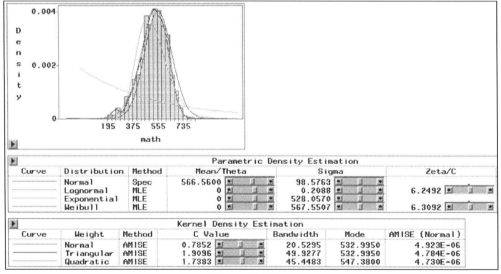

Parametric Density Estimation					
Curve	Distribution	Method	Mean/Theta	Sigma	Zeta/C
	Normal	Spec	566.5600	98.5763	
	Lognormal	MLE	0	0.2088	6.2492
	Exponential	MLE	0	528.0570	
	Weibull	MLE	0	567.5507	6.3092

Kernel Density Estimation					
Curve	Weight	Method	C Value	Bandwidth	Mode	AMISE (Normal)
	Normal	AMISE	0.7852	20.5295	532.9950	4.923E-06
	Triangular	AMISE	1.9096	49.9277	532.9950	4.784E-06
	Quadratic	AMISE	1.7383	45.4483	547.3800	4.730E-06

Figure 6-52

Finally, using the *Cumulative Distribution*option, we can calculate the distribution built from the various available options (Figure 6-53). When you click *OK*, the results in Figure 6-54 are obtained.

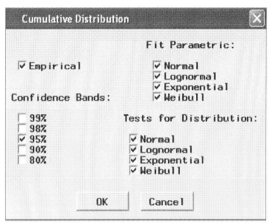

Figure 6-53

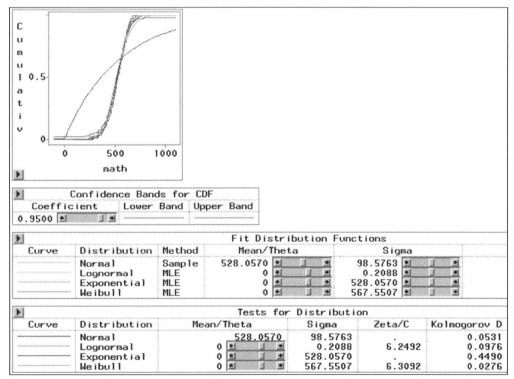

Figure 6-54

*Fit (Y, X):*allows to work with predictive and causal models. In the entry window of *Fit(Y,X)* Figure 6-55 must fill in the box *and* the variable or variables dependent or in box *X* the independent or explanatory variables in the model to adjust.Introducing the explanatory variables used*X* to introduce the variable as it is specified, used *Cross* to calculate the cross product of two or more variables and used *Nest* to create nested effects. In a nested effect a variable or cross effect is nested within the effects of one or more nominal variables. To use this function must select a variable or effect crossed with one or more nominal variables and press the *Nest*. Used *Expand* to create all the expanded effects of a variable with the specified degree of expansion (default is 2). For example, two nominal variables in an expansion of degree two generates three effects or variables *A, B* and *AB*. If the variables are continuous expansion of degree two generates five effects$X1,X2,X1 *X1,X1 *X2X2 *X2$. Option *Intercept* is used to include a constant in the model.   The *Apply* button displays the window results but without closing the Options window. In this way facilitates the modification of the model by adding or deleting interactively variables from analysis to the time we observe the consequences of these actions on Windows than for each analysis you go opening. The *OK* option calculates analysis but close the Options window. We can vary the analysis method by clicking on the button *Method* from Figure 6-55 for Figure 6-56.

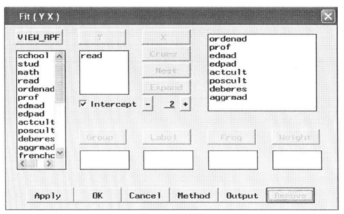

Figure 6-55

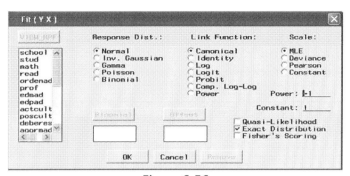

Figure 6-56

In the field *Response Dist.* Figure 6-56 will choose the distribution of the dependent variable. If the distribution is binomial we specify *and* with values 1 or 0 indicating success or failure, or a variable *and* that represents the number of successes in a number of attempts with a nominal variable that specifies the number of attempts. In the field *Link Function* you can choose a specific adjustment function (function link). The *Scale* field allows you to choose the parameter scaling of the distribution of the response variable. If we choose a scaling constant (*Constant*) is required to specify the value of the constant in the *Constant*box. If the model shows a huge spread, you can specify the *Quasi-Likelihood* option to adjust the generalized linear model using a quasi-likelihood function. If we choose a response with normal distribution and a canonical link function can also specify the *Exact Distribution* option to adjust the linear model using the exact distribution to calculate the statistics. *Fisher completo Scoring* option allows you to use the method of Fisher in the maximum likelihood estimates to estimate the parameters of the regression. Finally the option *Output* of Figure 6-55 displays 6-57 figure window in which we must choose the tables and graphs of the regression that we want. The *Output Variables* button allows you to choose the output variables specified in Figure 6-58. Buttons *Parametric Curves* (Figure 6-59) and *Nonparametric Curves VCG* (Figure 6-60) allow to draw parametric and non-parametric curves in the diagram of dispersion that occurs when there is a single explanatory variable.The window for curves not parametric *Nonparametric Curves (GCV)* includes a smoothing or sections (*Smoothing Spline*), *kernel*adjustment, adjustment and adjustment by local polynomials. Also in the latter method, the type of regression and weights for adjusting function must be specified. When there are only two explanatory variables in the model by default, trace the parametric diagram surface and even non-parametric diagrams can be created. Once selected all the options of the regression and accepted with *OK*, clicked in *Apply* in Figure 6-55 and the results of the regression (Figure 6-61).

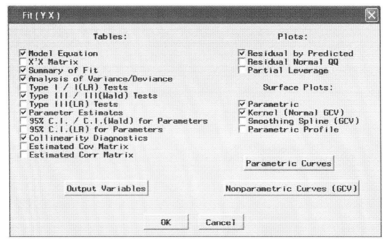

Figure 6-57

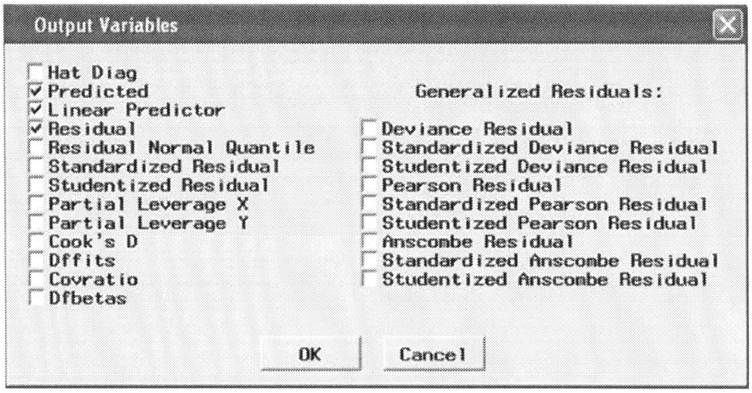

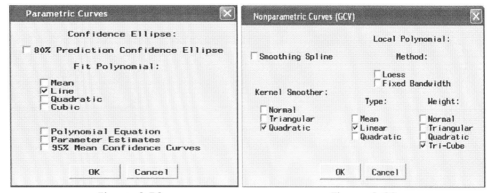

Figure 6-58

Figure 6-59   Figure 6-60

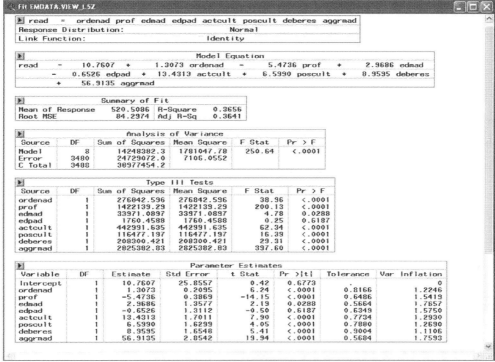

Figure 6-61

The tables and graphs that you have specified for the regression output in Figure 6-57 can be subsequently through the *Tables* (Figure 6-62) and *Graph* of the *Insight*menu bar options. Output variables specified in Figure 6-58 can be seen in the option *Vars* of the *Insight* (Figure 6-63) menu bar.

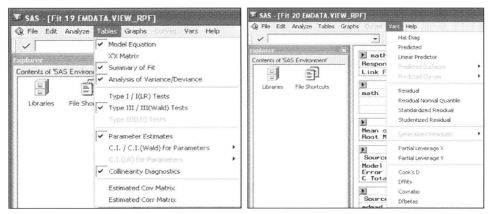

Figure 6-62   Figure 6-63

Multivariate (Y, X): enables procedures of multivariate analyses such as principal components, discriminant analysis and examination of relationships between one or two groups of variables. In the entry of *Multivariate(Y, X)* of the figure window 6-64 must enter at least one variable *and,* and if required by the method select box X independent or explanatory variables (case of the canonical discriminant analysis and maximum redundancy analysis). The option *Method* of Figure 6-64 leads us to screen Figure 6-65, which allows us to choose the method of multivariate analysis to use (main components, maximum redundancy analysis and canonical discriminant analysis).

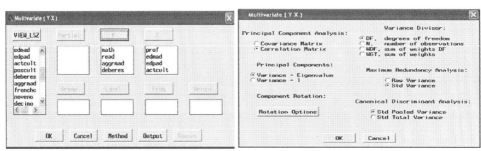

Figure 6-64   Figure 6-65

An analysis of main components must specify in Figure 6-65 if we will use the covariance matrix (if the variables are measured in comparable units) or correlations. The new components can have a variance equal to the eigenvalues with a mean equal to zero or a variance equal to one.

By pressing the button*Rotation Options*Figure 6-65 can rotate the components, if necessary, indicate in Figure 6-66 the method of rotation, the number of components that we represent and the value of the parameter *Gamma*, which is defined by default except for *Orthomax* rotation that needs that we may specify a certain value. Maximum redundancy or canonical correlation analysis is performed using the *Maximun Redundancy analysis* of Figure 6-65. Given two sets of variables, the maximum redundancy analysis is to find the linear combination of the explanatory variables that best predict the other set of variables. We must specify if we will use the sample variances (*Raw Variance*) or standardized variances (*Std Variance*). Canonical discriminant analysis must choose whether the variables that are created by means of linear combinations of the originals may have or variance equal to 1 intra-clase (*Std. Pooled Variance*) or the total sample variance equal to 1 (*Std. Total Variance*). Once selected the analysis method that we are going to carry out, in the option *Output* of Figure 6-64 chose outcomes pursued on Figure 6-67.

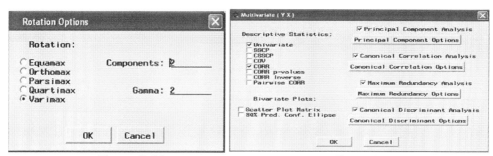

Figure 6-66   Figure 6-67

Figure 6-67 buttons*Main Component Options, Canonical CorrelationOption, Maximun Redundancy Options* and *Canonical Discriminant Options* you get as output options specified in the figures 8-68 to 8-71.

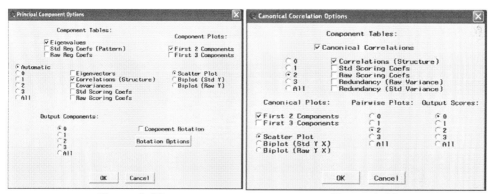

Figure 6-68   Figure 6-69

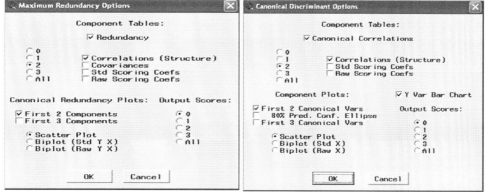

Figure 6-70   Figure 6-71

When you click *OK* in the figure 6-64 Gets the output of the procedure (Figure 6-72). *Tables, Graphs, Curves* and *Vars* of the *Insight* menu bar options contain information that we have chosen in the *Output*screen.

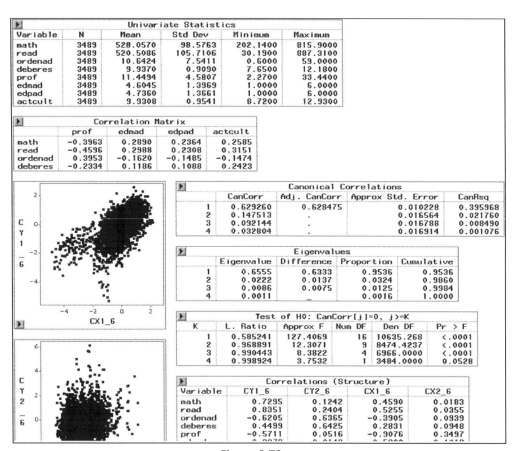

Figure 6-72

Chapter 7

PHASES OF CLEANING AND TRANSFORMATION OF DATA

7.1 CLEANING AND DATA TRANSFORMATION IN THE PROCESS OF EXTRACTION OF KNOWLEDGE

After the exploration phase, the process of extraction of knowledge includes the cleaning of data (*data clining*) mode. The information may contain outliers, missing values and incorrect values. This phase analyzes the influence of atypical data, attributed the missing information and disposed of or correct the incorrect data. The presence of atypical data andvalues missing(*data missing*) can lead us to use robust algorithms to atypical and missing data (e.g., decision trees) to filter information, replaced by values *imputation techniques* to transform continuous in using discrete data *Discretization techniques*.

Then, if necessary, takes place the *transformation* of data, usually by means of techniques of reduction or increase in the size and scaling simple and multi-dimensional, among others. The four early stages studied hitherto (selection, scanning, cleaning and transformation) are usually included under the name of *data preparation*. Between the advanced techniques of transformation have the reduction and increase in dimension.

7.2 VALUES ATYPICAL (OUTLIERS)

A value *outlier* or atypical is an extreme score within a variable. This type of values strongly affects the analysis in which intervene the above variable, especially if we work with small samples.

For example, if we are working with a linear regression model in which the variable is involved, the distortion produced normally is "espurea" increase the degree of linear relationship.

More specifically, we can define outliers as isolated observations whose behaviour clearly differs from half of the rest of the observations behavior. There is a first category of atypical cases formed by those remarks coming from a procedural error, as for example an error in coding, error of data entry, etc. These atypical data, if they are not detected by filtering, should be removed or re-encoded as missing data. Another category of atypical cases includes those observations that occur as a result of an extraordinary event remain an explanation for his presence in the sample. This type of atypical cases are normally retained in the sample, except that its significance is only anecdotal. Another additional category of atypical data includes extraordinary observations for which the researcher has no explanation. Normally these atypical data are removed from the analysis. A last category of atypical data are observations that are outside the ordinary range of values of the variable. They are often referred to as outliers and are removed from the analysis if you notice that they are not significant elements for the population. Characteristics of atypical case, as well as the objectives of the analysis that is performed, determine the atypical cases to eliminate. However, atypical cases must be considered in the set of all the variables considered. Therefore, should analyse them from a multivariate perspective. It can occur that a variable have removable extreme values to, but considering one sufficient number of other variables in the analysis, the researcher may decide to not remove them.

Exploratory data analysis tools are used to *detect outliers in a univariate context*. For example, on the box and whiskers chart outliers are presented as isolated at the ends of the whiskers points. The outliers often appear crossed out with an *x*. The usual *software* indicates the number of outliers for observation. In Figure 7-1 shows the graph of box and whiskers for a variable *V1*. There are two outliers prior to the moustache left and right mustache after two. The last one is an extreme value (symbol appears).

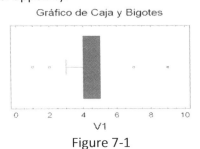

Gráfico de Caja y Bigotes

V1

Figure 7-1

Another way to detect outliers is to use a *chart control*, consisting of a graphic representation with a central line that denotes the average value of the variable and other two horizontal lines, called *Upper Control limit* (LSC) and *Lower Control limit* (SCI). These limits are chosen so that almost all the points of the variable is present among them. While the values of the variable are within the limits of control, is considered that there are no outliers. However, a point that is outside the bounds of control is interpreted as an outlier, and actions are needed for research and correction in order to find and eliminate the or assignable causes this behavior. It is customary to join different checkpoints in the diagram by using straight line segments in order to better visualize the evolution of the sequence of the values of the variable. Regardless of the distribution of the variable, is standard practice to place the control limits as a multiple of the standard deviation. In general choose multiple 3, i.e., it is customary to use the *control of three Sigma limits* in diagrams of control.Below is the chart control three sigmas for a variable with 25 values between 1238 and following 1295 (Figure 7-2). It is noted that the 22nd observation is an outlier to fall outside the limits of control.

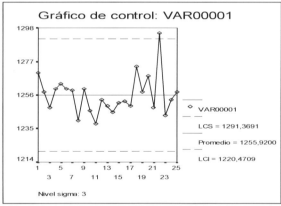

Figure 7-2

Used limits three sigmas because Imajority of the distributions that we find in practice are approaching the form of Gauss (density function of the normal distribution) campaign. As shown in Figure 7-3, the probability of finding a value within $\mu \pm \sigma$ is approximately 68%. Similarly, the probability that the values fall outside the limits $\mu \pm 2\sigma$ is approximately 4.5%, while the probability that the values fall outside the limits $\mu \pm 3\sigma$ is negligible (only 0.3% or three per thousand). For this reason, limits three sigmas are used.

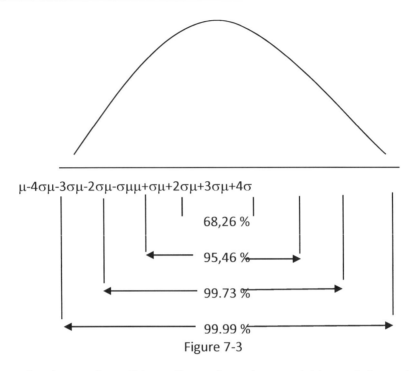

μ-4σμ-3σμ-2σμ-σμμ+σμ+2σμ+3σμ+4σ

68,26 %

95,46 %

99.73 %

99.99 %

Figure 7-3

Also detected possible outliers using *robust variable statistics* and see the difference with respect to the non-robust statistics. They tend to be regarded as robust centralization (location) the median statistics, the truncated average and the average winsorizada. The truncated mean dispenses with 15% of the values of the variable at each end and the Middle winsorizada replaces that 15% of values with values from the distribution center. As robust statistical dispersion (scale) of the average with respect to median variation, the truncated standard deviation and standard deviation winsorizada used respectively. When there are no outliers, robust statistics and the normal statistics do not differ much. Also for the normal average and the average winsorizada confidence intervals can be calculated. If its width is similar there are no outliers. However, it is more effective to use a *contrast formal statistics to detect outliers*, for example the *Dixon test* or the *test of Grubs*, whose p- values to detect outliers. For p-values less than 0.05 there are outliers to the 95% confidence.

When it comes to *detect outliers in a bivariate context, exploratory data analysis tools*, for example, the graph box and whiskers multiple (Figure 7-4) representing different graphics of a variable (power cars) can be used for different levels of the other (country of origin). There are outliers for three sources (3 for the one source, 4 for two and 1 for three).

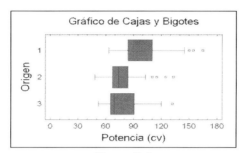

Figure 7-4

Another way of detecting outliers in a bivariate context consists of jointly evaluate pairs of variables using a scatter chart. In Figure 7-5, representing the cars according to their power consumption, 5 outliers above the band of foreign confidence and 3 appear below. Cases which clearly fall outside the range of the rest of the observations can be identified as isolated in the scatter chart points.

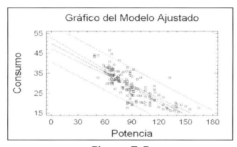

Figure 7-5

To *detect outliers in a multivariate context, statistics based on distances*, they can be used to detect the influential points. The *distance D^2 Mahalanobis* is a measure of the distance of each observation in a multi-dimensional space with respect to the Center half of the observations. The *statistical DFITS* measured the influence of each observation should be eliminated from the analysis. The *influence (Leverage)* measured the influence of each observation.

7.3 INFORMATION MISSING (MISSING DATA)

The treatment of missing information is one of the tasks prior to any analysis. When applies a method of multivariate analysis of the available data it can be that information for certain observations and variables there is no. We are then to absent or *missing*values. The presence of this missing information may be due to a defective registry information, the natural absence of the information requested or to a lack of response (full or partial).

The first test to be carried out when there is *missing* data is to check if they are randomly distributed in the whole set of data. It is vital that the researcher find out if the absence of data process occurs randomly. A first test to assess the missing data for a single variable *and* consists of two groups of values for, *and*those who have missing data and those who do not. Then, for each variable *X* other than *and*, performs a test to determine if there are significant differences between the two groups of values determined by the variable *and* (absent and not absent) on *X*. If we will considered *and* every one of the variables from the analysis and repeating the above process is that all differences are not significant, it can be concluded that the missing data are due to a *completely random process* and therefore reliable statistical analysis with our variable *accusing the missing data* may be performed by the methods that will be later. If a fairly high percentage of the differences are not significant, may be deemed absent data are due to a (not fully random) *random process* that also will allow to perform a reliable statistical analysis with our previous *imputation of missing information*variables, although with less reliability than in the previous case.

It is also usual to check the random distribution of the data *missing* by *test dicotomizadas correlations*. To perform this test, for each variable *and* the analysis is built a dichotomized variable by assigning the value zero to the missing values and value one to the present values. Then all variables in the analysis are dichotomize and the matrix of correlations accompanied by the contrasts of significance of each correlation coefficient of the matrix is. Correlations indicate the degree of association between the values lost on each pair of variables, so it can be concluded that if the elements of the matrix of correlations are not significant, missing data are completely random. If there is any significant correlation and most are not significant, the missing data can be considered random. Once checked the randomness of the data *missing* throughout the total data it is possible to impute the missing information and accurate statistical analysis.

Formal tests of the randomness of the data there are *missing* such as the *set of Little randomness test*, formal contrast based on the Chi-square, whose *p*-value indicates whether the missing values are or not a set of random numbers.

Then shown previous concepts with an example based on the data collected in a questionnaire with 6 questions on purchase of 20 respondents attitudes and behaviors. The answers to the 6 questions are collected in 6 variables (*V*1, *V*2, *V*3, 4 *V*, 5 *V*and *V*6) whose range varies between 1 and 10 reflecting valuation that the respondent gives to the feature that reflects the question.

The first question valued the importance which the respondent gives the impression that others have on it. The second question reflects the assessment that the respondent gives the guarantee of brands. The third question provides information on the frequency with which the respondent buy on the fly. The fourth question measures the preference that the respondent gives to buy on save and live better. The fifth question measures the respondent for wearing fashionable taste and the fifth question measures the tendency of the respondent to know new stores. The 6 questionnaires 20 variables data is collected in the table of the 7-6 figure.

Questionnaire	V1	V2	V3	V4	V5	V6
1	5	6	2	1	.	5
2	7	.	4	5	5	7
3	.	1	5	8	5	8
4	3	5	1	.	7	5
5	5	5	8	3	7	8
6	5	1	.	1	2	8
7	4	.	2	8	9	8
8	5	1	9	1	1	9
9	7	5	1	1	1	.
10	2	2	1	4	6	6
11	9	1	1	.	7	5
12	5	5	8	9	9	5
13	.	9	1	9	7	9
14	5	6	2	1	1	5
15	7	7	4	5	4	7
16	1	1	5	8	5	.
17	3	5	1	7	.	5
18	5	5	.	3	7	8
19	5	1	1	1	2	8
20	5	1	9	1	1	9

Figure 7-6

Once tabbed information, the first task would be to see the table of frequencies of the lost values for variables to get an idea of its magnitude. Below is the information (Figure 7-7), noting that for all the variables percentage of missing values is 10%, while that of valid values is 90%.

Overview of the processing of cases

	Cases					
	Valid		Lost		Total	
	N	Percentage	N	Percentage	N	Percentage
V1	18	90.0 %	2	10.0 %	20	100.0 %
V2	18	90.0 %	2	10.0 %	20	100.0 %
V3	18	90.0 %	2	10.0 %	20	100.0 %
V4	18	90.0 %	2	10.0 %	20	100.0 %
V5	18	90.0 %	2	10.0 %	20	100.0 %
V6	18	90.0 %	2	10.0 %	20	100.0 %

Figure 7-7

The next step is to determine if missing data are distributed randomly. To do this we compared the observations with and without missing data for each variable as a function of the other variables. The first task will be to generate new variables 11 *V*, *V*21, *V*31, 41 *V*, *V*51 and *V*-61 (one for each existing variable) by assigning it the value one for valid data and the value zero for missing data. We will have the table of Figure 7-8.

Cuest.	V1	V2	V3	V4	V5	V6	V11	V21	V31	V41	V51	VOLTAG
1	5	6	2	1	.	5	1	1	1	1	0	1
2	7	.	4	5	5	7	1	0	1	1	1	1
3	.	1	5	8	5	8	0	1	1	1	1	1
4	3	5	1	.	7	5	1	1	1	0	1	1
5	5	5	8	3	7	8	1	1	1	1	1	1
6	5	1	.	1	2	8	1	1	0	1	1	1
7	4	.	2	8	9	8	1	0	1	1	1	1
8	5	1	9	1	1	9	1	1	1	1	1	1
9	7	5	1	1	1	.	1	1	1	1	1	0
10	2	2	1	4	6	6	1	1	1	1	1	1
11	9	1	1	.	7	5	1	1	1	0	1	1
12	5	5	8	9	9	5	1	1	1	1	1	1
13	.	9	1	9	7	9	0	1	1	1	1	1
14	5	6	2	1	1	5	1	1	1	1	1	1
15	7	7	4	5	4	7	1	1	1	1	1	1
16	1	1	5	8	5	.	1	1	1	1	1	0
17	3	5	1	7	.	5	1	1	1	1	0	1
18	5	5	.	3	7	8	1	1	0	1	1	1
19	5	1	1	1	2	8	1	1	1	1	1	1
20	5	1	9	1	1	9	1	1	1	1	1	1

Figure 7-8

Now consider the two groups formed in the variable *V*1 (valid values and missing values) that are defined by the variable *V*11 and make a contrast of equality of means for the two groups of values defined in each of the remaining variables (2*V* to 6 *V*) values *V*11. We have the result in Figure 7-9.

V1	Levene test (for equal variances)		T-test for the equality of means							
	F	GIS.	t	GL	GIS. (bilat.)	Mean difference	Error tip. of the difference	95% Confidence for the difference interval		
									Lower	Superior
V2	14,050	002	668	14	515	1.36	2.033		-3,002	5,716
			335	1,048	792	1.36	4,047		-44,817	47,532
V3	435	520	-, 321	14	753	-, 79	2,444		-6,028	4,456
			-, 360	1,412	765	-, 79	2,182		-15,118	13,546
V4	3,168	097	2,370	14	033	4.93	2,079		469	9,388
			5,412	7,787	001	4.93	911		2,819	7,039

V5	2,865	113	521	14	610	1.14	2,192	-3,558	5,844
			894	2,595	447	1.14	1,279	-3,311	5.597
V6	4,359	053	1.524	16	147	1.75	1,148	-, 684	4.184
			2,753	2,549	085	1.75	636	-, 492	3,992

Figure 7-9

He is noted that you except for the variable *V4*, there are no significant differences between the means of two groups defined by absent vvalues 1 in the variables *V2*, 3 *V*and 5 *V*and *V6* (confidence intervals contain the value zero). The contrast of equality of means is done assuming equal variances (first line of the table for each variable) and unequal (second line for each variable).

Now consider the two groups formed in the variable *V2* (valid values and missing values) that are defined by the variable *V21* and make a contrast of equality of means for the two groups of values defined in each of the remaining variables (*V1* and 3 *V*to 6 *V*) values *V21*. We have the result in Figure 7-10.

V2	Levene		T-test for the equality of means						
	F	GIS.	t	GL	GIS. (bilateral)	Mean difference	Error tip. difference	95% Confidence for the difference interval	
								Lower	Top
V1	290	599	439	14	667	57	1,300	-2,218	3,360
			365	1,188	769	57	1,566	-13,239	14,382
V3	3,295	091	-, 321	14	753	-, 79	2,444	-6,028	4,456
			-, 587	3,067	598	-, 79	1,339	-4,995	3,424
V4	1,160	300	1,121	14	281	2.64	2,358	-2,414	7,700
			1,533	1,733	283	2.64	1,724	-5,988	11,273
V5	309	587	1,075	14	301	2.29	2,127	-2,277	6,848
			1,070	1,301	444	2.29	2,137	-13,729	18,300
V6	5,873	028	513	16	615	63	1,219	-1,959	3,209
			960	2,786	413	63	651	-1,540	2,790

Figure 7-10

Be observed that you for all the variables, there are no significant differences between the means of two groups defined values *V2* absent in each of them (confidence intervals contain the value zero). Repeating the contrasts of equality of means for groups that determine the values valid and absent of the variables *V3*, 4 *V*, 5 *V*and *V6* in the rest of the variables, we have results from Figure 7-11 to 10-14.

V3	Levene		T-test for the equality of means						
	F	GIS.	t	GL	GIS. (bilateral)	Mean difference	Error tip. difference	95% Confidence for the difference interval	
								Lower	Top
V1	1,956	181	-, 085	16	933	-, 13	1,473	-3,248	2,998
			-, 246	15,000	809	-, 13	507	-1,206	956

	F	GIS.	t	GL	GIS. (bilateral)	Mean difference	Error tip. difference	Lower	Top
V2	187	671	409	16	688	81	1,988	-3,402	5,027
			386	1,228	756	81	2,106	-16,631	18,256
V4	3,604	076	1,048	16	310	2.50	2,386	-2,559	7,559
			1,936	2,698	158	2.50	1,291	-1,882	6,882
V5	017	898	143	16	888	31	2,178	-4,305	4,930
			120	1,169	922	31	2,600	-23,309	23,934
V6	9,655	007	-,996	16	334	-1.19	1,192	-3715	1,340
			-2,893	15,000	011	-1.19	410	-2,062	-,313

Figure 7-11

V4	Levene test (variances)		T-test for the equality of means						
	F	GIS.	t	GL	GIS. (bilateral)	Mean difference	Error tip. difference	95% Confidence for the difference interval	
								Lower	Top
V1	4,819	043	-,868	16	398	-1.25	1,440	-4,303	1,803
			-,413	1,038	749	-1.25	3,028	-36,532	34,032
V2	187	671	409	16	688	81	1,988	-3,402	5,027
			386	1,228	756	81	2,106	-16,631	18,256
V3	5,206	037	1,320	16	206	2.94	2,226	-1,781	7,656
			3,833	15,000	002	2.94	766	1,304	4,571
V5	5,840	028	-1,197	16	249	-2.50	2,088	-6,926	1,926
			-3,478	15,000	003	-2.50	719	-4,032	-,968
V6	6,021	026	1,988	16	064	2.19	1,100	-,145	4,520
			5,775	15,000	000	2.19	379	1,380	2,995

Figure 7-12

V5	Levene test (variances)		T-test for the equality of means						
	F	GIS.	t	GL	GIS. (bilateral)	Mean difference	Error tip. difference	95% Confidence for the difference interval	
								Lower	Top
V1	054	819	689	16	501	1.00	1,452	-2,079	4,079
			897	1,536	488	1.00	1,114	-5,490	7,490
V2	6,349	023	-1,034	16	317	-2.00	1,935	-6,102	2,102
			-2,405	6,336	051	-2.00	832	-4,009	009
V3	3,618	075	1,047	16	310	2.38	2,268	-2,432	7,182
			2,565	8,439	032	2.38	926	259	4,491
V4	044	837	101	16	921	25	2,466	-4,978	5,478
			080	1,148	948	25	3,106	-28,992	29,492
V6	6,021	026	1,988	16	064	2.19	1,100	-,145	4,520
			5,775	15,000	000	2.19	379	1,380	2,995

Figure 7-13

V6	Levene test (variances)		T-test for the equality of means						
	F	GIS.	t	GL	GIS. (bilateral)	Mean difference	Error tip. difference	95% Confidence for the difference interval	
								Lower	Top

V1	4,376	053	689	16	501	1.00	1,452	-2,079	4,079
			330	1,039	795	1.00	3,029	-34,218	36,218
V2	187	671	409	16	688	81	1,988	-3,402	5,027
			386	1,228	756	81	2,106	-16,631	18,256
V3	340	568	294	16	772	69	2,338	-4,268	5,643
			320	1,329	792	69	2,148	-14,850	16,225
V4	574	460	-, 127	16	901	-, 31	2,466	-5,540	4,915
			-, 087	1,103	944	-, 31	3,587	-36,945	36,320
V5	134	719	943	16	360	2.00	2,121	-2,497	6,497
			943	1,264	491	2.00	2,121	-14,691	18,691

Figure 7-14

Be observed that you for virtually all of the variables, there are no significant differences between the means of two groups defined by absent from every one of these values (confidence intervals contain the value zero). Therefore one can conclude fairly reliably the random distribution of the lost data, conclusion that will perform statistical analysis using data by applying various methods of imputation of the missing information.

Dicotomizadas correlation matrix can be used to verify the randomness of the absent data also. It is calculating the matrix of correlations of the resulting variables by substituting values lost the initial variables by zeros, and valid values for a few. In our case would be finding the matrix of correlations of variables $V12$ $V62$. We have the results in Figure 7-15.

		V11	V21	V31	V41	V51	VOLTAG
V11	Pearson's correlation	1	-, 111	-, 111	-, 111	-, 111	-, 111
	GIS. (bilateral)	.	641	641	641	641	641
V21	Pearson's correlation	-, 111	1	-, 111	-, 111	-, 111	-, 111
	GIS. (bilateral)	641	.	641	641	641	641
V31	Pearson's correlation	-, 111	-, 111	1	-, 111	-, 111	-, 111
	GIS. (bilateral)	641	641	.	641	641	641
V41	Pearson's correlation	-, 111	-, 111	-, 111	1	-, 111	-, 111
	GIS. (bilateral)	641	641	641	.	641	641
V51	Pearson's correlation	-, 111	-, 111	-, 111	-, 111	1	-, 111
	GIS. (bilateral)	641	641	641	641	.	641
VOLTAG	Pearson's correlation	-, 111	-, 111	-, 111	-, 111	-, 111	1
	GIS. (bilateral)	641	641	641	641	641	.

Figure 7-15

The resulting correlations between dichotomous variables indicate the extent to which the missing data are related between pairs of variables. Low correlations indicate a low association between processes in absence of data for these two variables. In our case all the correlations are low and significant, which corroborates the presence of randomness of the missing data.

7.4 SOLUTIONS FOR MISSING DATA: DELETION OF DATA OR INFORMATION MISSING IMPUTATION

Once the existence of randomness in the missing data has contrasted already you can take a decision for such data before any statistical analysis with them.

We can begin by including only the analysis observations (cases) with complete data (rows whose values for all variables are valid), i.e., any row that has some missing data is removed from the data set prior to performing the assay. This method is called *approximation of complete cases* or *deletion of cases according to list* and usually the default method in most statistical *software* . This method is appropriate when there are too many missing values, because its abolition would lead to a representative sample of the total information. Otherwise the sample size would be reduced much to consider for the analysis and would not be representative of the complete information.

Another method consists of the *deletion of data according to partner*, i.e., works with all cases possible to have valid values for each pair of variables that are considered in the analysis regardless of what happens in the rest of the variables (rows). This method eliminates less information and is always used in any convertible or bivariate analysis at bivariante.

Another additional method is to *suppress the cases (rows) or variables (columns)* that behave worse regarding the missing data. Again, it is necessary to weigh the amount of data to delete. You should always be considered what is won by eliminating a source of missing data and what is lost by not having a specific variable or set of cases in the statistical analysis.

The alternative methods of suppression of data is the *imputation of the missing information*. Imputation is the process of estimation of missing values based on valid values of other variables or cases of the sample. Then different allocation methodologies are studied.

A first method of allocation does not replace missing data but that imputes the characteristics of the distribution (for example, the standard deviation) or the relationships of all the available valid values (for example, correlations).

The process of imputation is not to replace missing data for the rest of the cases, but to use the features of the distribution or the relations of all possible valid values, as representatives for all the entire sample. This method is called *complete availability approach*.

A second group of imputation methods are methods of replacement of missing data by values estimated on the basis of other information that exists in the sample. We will consider in this group substitution method of the case, the method of substituting the medium or median, substitution by a constant value method, method of imputation by linear interpolation, regression imputation method and multiple imputation method.

In the *method of allocation by replacement of the case* (cases) observations with missing data are replaced with other observations not master. For example, in a survey of households, sometimes a home of the sample which do not answer by another home that is not in the sample and that will probably answer is replaced. This method of imputation is often used when there are cases with all observations absent or most of them.

On the *method of substituting the average allocation* absent data shall be replaced by the average of all valid values of its corresponding variable. This method has the advantage that is easily deployed and provides comprehensive information for all cases, but has the disadvantage that modifies the correlations and invalidate the variance estimates derived from the standard formulas for the variance for the true variance of the data.

When there are outliers in the variables, replacing missing values for median (instead of by the media), since the median is a more robust statistical summary of the data. Thus is the *method of imputation of substitution by the median*.

Sometimes, when there is too much variability in the data, is usually replaced every absent value by the average or median of a certain number of adjacent to the observations. This type of allocation tend to also include the *imputation by interpolation method* in which each absent of a variable value for the resulting value to a Tween with the adjacent values is replaced.

Substituting constant value imputation method missing data shall be replaced by an appropriate constant value derived from external sources or from a previous investigation. In this case the researcher must ensure that the replacement of missing values for the constant value from an external source is more valid than the replacement by the average (value generated internally).

By regression imputation method uses regression analysis to predict the absent of a variable values based on their relationship with other variables in the data set from the regression equation linking them. Disadvantage of this method we would highlight that it reinforces already existing relations in the data as its use increases the resulting data are less generalisable and most characteristic of the sample. In addition, with this method underestimated the variance of the distribution. And let's not forget as a disadvantage to this method assumes that the variable with missing data has significant correlations with other variables.

Multiple imputation method is a combination of several methods from the already mentioned.

7.5 TRANSFORMATION DATA

When the exploratory analysis otherwise it, the original data (not the standardized or previously modified) may need to be transformed. They tend to consider four types of transformations:

Logical transformations: Categories of field of definition of variables come together to reduce its amplitude. Categories without answers can be removed in this way. They can also convert interval variables into ordinal or nominal and create fictitious variables (*dummy*).

Linear transformations: They get to the add, subtract, multiply or divide the original ob-be-holidays by a constant to improve his performance. These transformations do not change the shape of the distribution, or the distances between the values or the order, and therefore do not cause considerable changes in the variables.

Algebraic transformations: They get to apply monotonic nonlinear transformations to the original observations (square root, logarithms, etc.) by a constant to improve his performance. These transformations change the shape of the distribution by changing the distance between the values, but maintain the order.

Not monotonic nonlinear transformations: Change the distances and the order of the values. You cannot change the original information too.

Problems in the data are arranged with these transformations. For example: a negative asymmetry can lower with a parabolic or cubic transformation, a strong positive asymmetry may soften through a hyperbolic or hyperbolic quadratic transformation (with a negative sign) and a weak positive asymmetry may soften through a transformation of logarithmic or reciprocal square root of the square (with a negative sign) root. The logarithmic transformation can get seasonal average and variance for data. It is often chosen as a transformation that best solve the problem, once. If any fixes the problem, we carry out analysis of the original data without transforming. By combining linear and algebraic transformations can be extreme values distribution.

7.6 TRANSPOSE, MERGE, ADD, SEGMENT AND SORT FILES

Transpose creates a new data file which will transpose the rows the columns of the original data file so that the cases (rows) become variables and variables (columns) become cases.

Normally, if the data file contains a variable ID or name with unique values, you can use it as variable name: their values will be used as variable names in the transposed data file.

The merging of files is in the formation of a new file *with the same variables and different cases.* It's *Add (Append) cases* by merging the data file work with another data file that contains the same variable but different cases.

It is also possible *merge files with the same cases but different variables.* In this case it is necessary that there are key variables in the working file and the external file that merges with the. Both files must be sorted in ascending order of the key variables.

Add data combines groups of cases where unique overview and create a new data file added. The cases are added based on the value of one or more grouping variables. The new data file contains a case for each group. For example, you can add data regions by State and create a new file in which the State is the unit of analysis.

Segmenting a file is to divide datafile into different groups for the analysis based on the values of one or more grouping variables. If you select various grouping variables, cases are grouped by variable within the categories of the previous variable from the list.

7.7 CONSIDER CASES AND CATEGORIZE AND NUMERIZAR VARIABLES

Is common to also use weighting.*Weighted cases* provides different cases weightings (using a simulated replica) for statistical analysis. The values of the weighting variable must indicate the number of observations represented by cases in the data file. Cases with missing, negative values or zero for the weighting variable is excluded from the analysis. Fractional values are valid and are used exactly where acquire meaning and, most likely, where cases are tabulated.

Categorized variables consists in create a categorical variable from a variable scale, i.e., it is of convert continuous numeric data into a discrete number of categories. This procedure creates new variables that contain categorical data. It is also possible to create a numeric variable from a categorical by assigning numerical values to the categories (*digitisation*).

7.8 MATCHING

Matching to matching techniques pursue the comparability of groups using common features of all of them. Although the groups differ with respect to some of its variables, it is possible to compare them by a process of adjustment or standardization. This procedure is to match both groups with respect to some (s) characteristic (s), making it uniform in both groups (such as sex, age, their place of dwelling or the number of children for example). An important effect of the *matching* is the increase in the efficiency of the study, since it allows to limit the population to study than that in which the exposure is more representative. For example, in the study of vascular accidents and use of oral contraceptives, *matching* by age could restrict entry control of advanced age (65 years), in which the probability of exposure to oral contraceptives is low or zero.

-The *matching* corresponds to a procedure used a priori, in the design phase of the study. Occasionally can be matching a posteriori, when the researcher decides to match observations once collected the data from a set of individuals controls which were not previously subject to *matching*. He is however preferred to reserve the term *matching* for cases in which the procedure is used a priori.

The *matching* is also used when working with variables confusing difficult definition or measurement, as for example, type genetic, psychosocial or related to human behaviour. In these cases, researchers often use "pairs" of subjects (brothers, twins, members of a family or specific social group), in order to study the effect of the variable of interest alone having controlled the influence of the variables subject to matching, which are assumed to be common. The types of variables subject to *matching* can be varied, and logically depend on the problem to investigate.

There are several types of matching or *matching*. Two of the most used, depending on whether this procedure is applied collectively or to specific observations, are the *matching* groups and frequency and the individual *matching* (Figure 7-16).

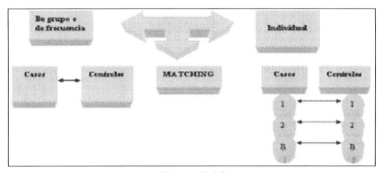

Figure 7-16

In *matching* group or frequency mode is restricted a priori the admission of subjects in both groups looking for study subjects that adequately represent the inclusion criteria. Thus, at study entry can be regulated by features such as sex, age, occupation, place of residence or modality of medical care. The contribution of the groups with regard to any factors confusing tends to be homogeneous in cases and controls, which increases the power of the study.

In the individual *matching* , the (s) characteristic (s) to match are defined specifically for each case and each control simultaneously. You will see that the effect of this procedure has direct implications in the form of analysis of the information: in this case the analysis is carried out by "peers" or "triplets" of comments, as opposed to *matching* by groups or frequency mode, in which groups are compared. It also has implications on the feasibility of finding appropriate subject inspections which comply with the requirements in the matching. To many variables to "match", greater difficulty in finding adequate controls. In both cases, the *matching* can be considered more than one control for each case.

The *matching* or matching also has disadvantages. This procedure involves technical and theoretical difficulties in the development of the study. The researcher is exposed to find difficulties to find adequate controls and in many cases must rule out controls with the consequent risk of skew measurements in the case of the (s) variable (s) to match other than epidemiological value. Researcher can be faced with the reality of finding *missing*at the base of a high frequency of values, and must dismiss these observations or procedures for the estimation of them using little epidemiological acceptance procedures. The study is also longer and therefore higher cost. Of *overmatching* or *matching* unnecessary (sobrepareamiento) refers to the use of this technique including variable innecesa-ences that may not necessarily be confusing variables.

7.9 TRANSFORMATION DATA DIMENSION REDUCTION TECHNIQUES

In the world of information today, it is common to have lots of variables measured or observed in a collection of individuals and pretend to study them together. Many variables on a sample is presumable that a part of the collected information may be redundant or be excessive, in which case the **multivariate dimension reduction methods** (analysis on principal components, factor, optimal scaling, etc.) try to eliminate it. These methods combine many observed variables to get few fictitious variables representing them with the minimum loss of information.

These dimension reduction methods are **the interdepedencia multivariate methods** in the sense that all its variables have an equivalent importance, i.e. If no variable highlights as dependent main in the objective of the research. You must also take into account the type of variables is handled. If they are quantitative variables, dimension reduction techniques can be the *principal component analysis* and *Factor analysis*. If they are qualitative variables, you can go to the *Correspondence analysis* and *Optimal scaling*.

Methods of interdependence are opposed to so-called **methods multivariate dependence** which is not acceptable equivalent variables importance, because any stands out as dependent main. In this case it be used multivariate analytical techniques or inferential whereas the dependent variable as explained by the other independent variables explanatory, and trying to relate all the variables by means of a possible equation or model that the link. The method chosen may then be linear regression, usually with all quantitative variables. Once configured the mathematical model you can reach to predict the value of the dependent variable known profile of all the others. If the dependent variable qualitative dichotomic (1.0; Yes or no) can be used as a sorting machine, studying its relationship with the rest of the Tableau variables through logistic regression. The observed qualitative dependent variable found the allocation of each individual to previously defined groups (two or more than two), can be used to classify new cases in which unknown group which probably belong to, in which case the discriminant analysis, which solves the problem of allocation on the basis of a quantitative profile of Tableau variables, Wissler. If the dependent variable is quantitative and the explanatory are qualitative we have models of the analysis of variance, which can extend to the loglinear analysis tables models contingency of high dimension. If the dependent variable can be qualitative or quantitative and qualitative independents, are facing segmentation.

On the other hand, the dimension reduction techniques play an important role within the data **emerging from multivariate analysis techniques** . The availability of large volumes of data and the widespread use of computer tools has transformed the multivariate analysis orienting it towards certain specialized techniques included in *data mining*.

7.10 PRINCIPAL COMPONENTS

Principal components analysis is a technique of multivariate statistical analysis that ranks among the methods of interdependence. It is a multivariate method of simplification or reduction of the dimension and that applies when there is a large set of variables with quantitative data correlated each other chasing get fewer variables, linear combination of primitives and incorrelacionadas, that are called principal components or factors, which summarizes as well as possible to the variable initials with the minimum loss of information, and whose subsequent interpretation will allow a simpler analysis of the studied problem.

This reduction in many variables to few components can simplify application on the latter's other multivariate techniques (regression, *clusters*, etc.).The high number of initial variables x_1, x_2,..., x_p are summarized in a few variables, C_1, C_2,..., C_k (*main components*) *perfectly calculable* and to synthesize most of the information contained in their data. Initially we have as many components as variables:

$$C_1 = a_{11}x_1 + a_{12}x_2 + \cdots + a_{1p}x_p$$
$$\vdots$$
$$C_p = a_{n1}x_1 + a_{n2}x_2 + \cdots + a_{pp}x_p$$

But are only retained the k main components ($k \leq p$) that account for a high percentage of the variability of the initial variables ($C_1, C_2,..., C_k$).

Its variance is used as a measure of the amount of information in a component. The greater your higher variance i.e. information that carries the built-in component. For this reason is selected as the first component that have greater variance, while, on the contrary, the last is the minor variance.

In general, the extraction of principal components is carried out on variables *common* to avoid problems of scale, although it can also be applied on variables expressed in *deviations* from the average.

When the original variables are very correlated with each other, most of its variability can be explained with very few components. If the original variables were fully incorrelacionadas each other, then the principal components analysis would be full of interest, since in that case the main components would agree with the original variables.

Calculation of the principal components

Analysis on components main is available a sample size n about p variables $X_1, X_2..., X_p$, (typified or expressed in deviations from its average) initially correlated, to subsequently obtain a number from them $k \leq p$ variables incorrelacionadas $C_1, C_2,..., C_k$ that are combination linear variables initial and that explain most of their variability. *The first principal component*, like the others, He is expressed as a linear combination of the original variables as follows:

$$C_{1i} = u_{11}X_{1i} + u_{12}X_{2i} + \cdots + u_{1p}X_{pi}, i=1,.., n$$

For the whole of the n observations sampling and all the components are:

$$\begin{bmatrix} C_{11} \\ C_{12} \\ \vdots \\ C_{1n} \end{bmatrix} = \begin{bmatrix} X_{11} & X_{21} & \cdots & X_{p1} \\ X_{12} & X_{22} & \cdots & X_{p2} \\ & & \vdots & \\ X_{1n} & X_{2n} & \cdots & X_{pn} \end{bmatrix} \begin{bmatrix} u_{11} \\ u_{12} \\ \vdots \\ u_{1p} \end{bmatrix}$$

In shorthand notation: $C_1 = X u_1$ y:

$$V(C_1) = \frac{\sum_{i=1}^{n} C_{1i}^2}{n} = \frac{1}{n} C_1' C_1 = \frac{1}{n} u_1' X' X u_1 = u_1' \left[\frac{1}{n} X' X \right] u_1 = u_1' V u_1$$

The first component C_1 gets so its variance is maximum subject to the constraint that the sum of the weights or_{1j} squared is equal to unity, i.e., the variable weights or weightings $(u_{11}, or_{12},..., u_{1p})'$ takes standard. It then tries to find C_1 maximizing $V(C_1) = u_1'Vu_1$, subject to the constraint:

$$\sum_{j=1}^{p} u_{1i}^2 = u_1' u_1 = 1$$

Demonstrates that, to maximize $V(_1C)$, the largest eigenvalue is taken λ matrix V. It is λ_1 the largest eigenvalue of V and taking u_1 as its normalized associated eigenvector $(u_1'or_1= 1)$, we already have defined the vector of weights applied to the variables initial for the first principal component, component that will be defined as:

$$C_1 = u_1 X = u_{11} X_1 + u_{12} X_2 + \cdots + u_{1p} X_p$$

To maximize $V(C_2)$ have to take the second largest eigenvalue λ matrix V (the largest had already taken it to get the first main component).

Taking λ_2 as the second largest eigenvalue of V and taking u_2 as its standard associated eigenvector $(u_2'u_2= 1)$, we have defined the vector of weights applied to the variables initial for the second main component, component that will be defined as:

$$C_2 = u_2 X = u_{21} X_1 + u_{22} X_2 + \cdots + u_{2p} X_p$$

Similarly, the component main h-th is defined as $C_h = Xu_h$ where u_h is the eigenvector V associated with its h-th largest eigenvalue. It is often called also a u_h axis factor h-th.

It shows the proportion of the total variability collected by the component main h-th (*percentage of inertia explained by h-th principal component*) will be given by:

$$\frac{\lambda_h}{\sum_{h=1}^{p} \lambda_h} = \frac{\lambda_h}{traza(V)}$$

If the variables are typed, *trace (V)* = *p*, so the proportion of the component h-th in the total variability will be λ_h/p. Also defines the *percentage of inertia explained by the k first principal component (or factorial axes)* as:

$$\frac{\sum_{h=1}^{k} \lambda_h}{\sum_{h=1}^{p} \lambda_h} = \frac{\sum_{h=1}^{k} \lambda_h}{traza(V)}$$

Scores or measurement of the components

Principal components analysis is often a prelude to other analyses, which replaced the set of original variables by the obtained components. For example in the case of estimation models affected by multicollinearity or correlation serial (autocorrelation). For this reason, it is necessary to know the values that take the components at each observation.

Once calculated coefficients u_{hj} (components of the normalized eigenvector associated with the eigenvalue of the matrix h-th $V = X'X / n$ relative to the primary component Z_h), you can get scores Z_{hj}, i.e. the values of the components corresponding to each observation, from the following list:

$$Z_{hi} = u_{h1}X_{1i} + u_{h2}X_{2i} + \cdots + u_{hp}X_{pi} \quad h = 1,...,p \, i = 1,...,n$$

Number of principal components a retain

In general, the objective of the implementation of the main components is to reduce the dimensions of the original variables, passing *p* original variables to *k* < *p* main components.

The problem that arises is how to fix *k*, or, put another way, what number of components must be retained? Although it does not lack for the extraction of principal components raise a previous statistical model, some of the criteria for determining what should be the optimal number of components to retain required the previous formulation of statistical hypotheses.

Criterion of the average arithmetic

According to this criterion are selected those components whose feature λ_j root exceeds the average characteristic roots. Remember that the characteristic root associated with a component is its variance. Analytically, this criterion involves retaining all those components that verify that:

$$\lambda_h > \overline{\lambda} = \frac{\sum_{j=1}^{p} \lambda_h}{p}$$

Using typed variables, then, as it has been, it is verified that $\sum_{j=1}^{p} \lambda_h = p$, so for typed variables is retained those components such as $\lambda_h > 1$.

Criterion of the graph of sedimentation

Sedimentation graph gets to represent in order characteristics and roots in x-axis numbers from the main components run operating to each characteristic root in descending order. Connecting all the dots you get a figure that, in general, looks like the profile of a mountain with a slope strong until reaching the base, formed by a plateau with a slight tilt. Continuing with the simile of the mountain, on the plateau is where the Pebble dropped from the top, i.e., where sediment accumulates.

For this reason, this graph is known with the name of graph of sedimentation. Its name in English is *scree plot.*According to the graphic criteria are retained all those components prior to the sedimentation area.

Matrix loads factorials, commonality, and circles of correlation

The difficulty in the interpretation of the components is the need for meaningful and measure something useful in the context of the phenomenon under study. Therefore, it is essential to consider the weight that each original variable has within the chosen component, as well as correlations between variables and factors.

A component is a linear function of all the variables, but it can be very well correlated with some of them, and less with others. We have already seen that the correlation coefficient between a component and a variable is calculated by multiplying the weight of the variable in that component by the square root of its own value:

$$r_{jh} = u_{hj} \sqrt{\lambda_h}$$

It shows also that these coefficients r represent the part of variance in each variable that explains each factor. In this way, each variable can be represented as a linear function of k retained components, where the weights or loads of each component or factor (*load factor*) in the variable match correlation coefficients.

Matrix calculation allows to obtain immediately the table of correlation coefficients variables-componentes (*pxk*), which is called *load factor matrix*. The equations of the variables according to the components (factors), dazzled the initially raised, are most useful in the interpretation of the components, and are expressed as follows:

$$
\begin{aligned}
Z_1 &= r_{11}X_1 + \cdots + r_{1p}X_p & X_1 &= r_{11}Z_1 + \cdots + r_{k1}Z_k \\
Z_2 &= r_{21}X_1 + \cdots + r_{2p}X_p & X_2 &= r_{12}Z_1 + \cdots + r_{k2}Z_k \\
&\quad\vdots & \Rightarrow & \quad\vdots \\
Z_k &= r_{k1}X_1 + \cdots + r_{kp}X_p & X_p &= r_{1p}Z_1 + \cdots + r_{kp}Z_k
\end{aligned}
$$

The first variable, the commonality is $r^2_{11} + \ldots + r^2_{k1} = V(X_1) = h_1^2$. Therefore, the sum of the commonalities of all variables represents the part of global inertia of the original cloud explained by the k factors retained, and coincides with the sum of the eigenvalues of these components. The commonality provides a criterion of quality of representation of each variable, so completely represented variables have commonality of the unit.

Also shows that the sum of vertical squares of loads all variables in a component factor is its own value. For example, the value of the first component will be $r^2_{11} + \ldots + r^2_{1p}. = \lambda_1$. It is clear that, when loads factorial coefficients of correlation between variables and components, their employment makes comparable weights of each variable in the component and facilitates their interpretation.

In this sense, its graphical representation can be oriented to the researcher in a first approach to the interpretation of the components. Obviously, this representation on a plane can only contain factors of two by two, so that as many graphics as pairs of retained factors can be. These graphs are called *circles of correlation* andare formed by dots representing each variable by means of two coordinates measuring the coefficients of correlation of this variable with the two factors or components is considered (Figure 7-17). All variables will be contained within a circle of unit RADIUS.

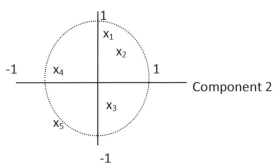

Figure 7-17

Rotation of the components

We often do not find credible interpretations to factors (components) obtained. It would be desirable, for an easier interpretation, which each component was related very well with few variables (correlation *r* ratios close to 1 or - 1) and evil with others (*r* close to 0). This optimization is obtained by a proper *rotation of the axes* that define the core components.

Rotate a set of components does not change the proportion of total inertia explained, how it changes neither the commonalities of each variable, which are not but the proportion of variance explained by all of them. The most commonly used rotations are VARIMAX and the (orthogonal) QUARTIMAX and PROMAX (oblique) rotation.

However, the coefficients, which are directly dependent on the position of the components with respect to the original variables (load factor and values), are altered by the rotation.

7.11 FACTORIAL ANALYSIS

The *factorial analysis* aims to simplify the multiple and complex relationships that may exist between a set of observed variables $X_1, X_2,..., X_p$. This tries to find common dimensions or *factors* that bind to the seemingly unrelated variables. Specifically, it is to find a set of *k < pnot directly observable factors*F_1, $F_2,..., F_k$ to sufficiently explain the observed variables losing the minimum of information, so they are easily interpretable (*beginning of interpretability*) and which are the least possible, i.e. *k* small (*principle of parsimony*). In addition, factors should be removed in such a way that they are independent, i.e., that they are orthogonal. Accordingly, factor analysis is a technique for data reduction that examines the interdependence of variables and provides knowledge of the underlying structure of the data.

Factor your data reduction capability is the most characteristic aspect of the analysis. The relationship between the observed variables X_1, X_2,..., X_p are given by the matrix of correlations, whose determinant must be small (there is relationship between them).

The principal component analysis and factor analysis have in common that they are technical reduction of its size to examine the interdependence of variables, but differ in their purpose, their characteristics and their degree of formalization.

The difference between analysis on principal components and factor analysis is that analysis in factorial tries to find latent, unobservable and yet measures synthetic variables whose existence is suspected in the variables original and they are waiting to be found, while in the analysis in main components are obtained synthetic variables combination of originals and whose calculation is possible based on independent mathematical aspects of your practical interpretability.

Analysis on principal components the variance of each original variable is explained fully by variables whose linear combination determine the (components). But this does not happen in the factor analysis.

Analysis factor only part of the variance of each original variable explains fully by the variables whose linear combination it determine (*factors common* $F_1 F_2$,..., F_p). This part of the variability of each original variable explained by common factors is called *communality*, while the portion of variance not explained by common factors is called *oneness* (*commonality + uniqueness* = 1) and represents the part of own variability f_i of each variable x_i.

$$x_1 = r_{11} F_1 + r_{12} x_2 + \cdots + r_{1p} F_p + f_1$$
$$\vdots$$
$$x_n = r_{n1} F_1 + r_{n2} F_2 + \cdots + r_{np} F_p + f_n$$

When the commonality is unitary (*uniqueness, null*) in principal components analysis coincide with the factorial. I.e., principal components analysis is a particular case of factor analysis in which the common factors account for 100% of the total variance.

The methods to get the factors include the following:

- *Method of the main components.*
- *MINRES (waste minimisation), ULS (not weighted least squares) and GLS (generalized least squares) methods.*
- *Maximum likelihood method.*
- *Method of iterated principal components or major axes.*
- *The main factor method.*
- *Alpha method .*
- *Method of factoring image.*
- *The centroid method .*
- *Turstone method .*

Below are the characteristics of the most important methods of factor extraction.

- **Method of the main components**. Method of extraction of factors used to form non-correlated linear combinations of the observed variables. The first component is the maximum variance. The successive components explain progressively lower variance proportions and are not correlated with the other. The principal component analysis is used to obtain the initial factor solution. It can be used when a correlation matrix is singular.

- **Not weighted least-squares method**. Extraction method of factor that minimizes the sum of the squares of the differences between the matrices of correlations observed and reproduced, ignoring the diagonals.

- **Generalized least-squares method**. Method of extraction of factors that minimizes the sum of the squares of the differences between observed and reproduced correlation matrices. The correlations are weighted by the inverse of its uniqueness, so the variables that have a high value of uniqueness receive less than those that have a value of·uniqueness.

- **Maximum likelihood method**. Extraction method of factor that provides estimates of the parameters which most likely have produced the matrix of correlations observed, if the sample comes from a multivariate normal distribution. The correlations are weighted by the inverse of the uniqueness of the variables and using an iterative algorithm.

- *Principal axis factoring*. Extraction method of factors as part of the original matrix of correlations with squares of multiple correlation coefficients inserted in the main diagonal as initial estimates of the commonalities. Overruns resulting factorials are used to estimate again the commonalities and replace previous estimates in the diagonal of the matrix. The iterations continue until changes in the commonalities from one iteration to the next, meet the criteria of convergence for the extraction.

- *Alpha*. Method of extraction factor considers the variables included in the analysis as a sample of the universe of possible variables. This method maximizes the Cronbach's Alpha for the factors.

- *Factorization image*. Method of extraction of factors, developed by Guttman and based on the theory of images. The common part of a variable, called the partial image, is defined as its linear regression on the remaining variables, rather than being a function of the hypothetical factors.

7.12 CONTRASTS IN FACTORIAL MODEL

In the model factorial can perform various types of contrasts. These contrasts are usually grouped into two blocks, as previously applied to the extraction of factors or that are applied later. With contrasts previously applied to the extraction of factors tries to analyze the relevance of the application of the factor analysis to a set of observable variables. With contrasts applied after obtaining the factors to assess model factor once estimated.

Within the Group of *contrasts that previously applied to the extraction of factors* we have the contrast of sphericity of Barlett and the extent of sampling adequacy of Kaiser, Meyer and Olkin.

Obviously, before performing a factor analysis we'll we if the original variable p are correlated with each other or are not. If they weren't there would be no common factors and, therefore, it would make no sense applying factor analysis. This issue tends to be tested using the contrast of sphericity of Barlett, based on which the population correlation Rmatrix$_p$collects the relationship between each pair of variables using its elements ρ_{ij} located outside the main diagonal. The elements of the main diagonal are ones, since all variable is completely related to itself. Where did not exist no relationship between the variables p study, the Rmatrix$_p$would be identity, whose determinant is a unit.

Therefore, to determine the absence or non-relationship between the variable p can arise the following contrast:

$$H_0 : |R_p| = 1$$
$$H_1 : |R_p| \neq 1$$

Barlett introduced a statistician to this contrast based on the matrix of sample correlation R, under the hypothesis H_0 has a *Chi-square* distribution with $p(p-1)/2$ degrees of freedom. The expression of this statistic is as follows:
$$-[n-11-(2p+5)/6]Ln|R|$$

On the other hand, Kaiser-Meyer and Olkin defined as KMO's global sample fitness model factor based on correlation coefficients observed for each pair of variables and their coefficients of partial correlation using the following expression:

$$KMO = \frac{\sum_j \sum_{h \neq j} r_{jh}^2}{\sum_j \sum_{h \neq j} r_{jh}^2 + \sum_j \sum_{h \neq j} a_{jh}^2}$$

r_{JH} **are the coefficients of correlation observed between the variables X_j and X_h**
a_{JH} **are the coefficients of the partial correlation between the variables X_j and X_h**

In the event that there is adequacy of the data to a model of factor analysis, the term of the denominator, collecting the ajh coefficients, will be small and therefore measure KMO will be next to the unit. KMO values below 0.5 will not be acceptable, whereas inadequate data to a model of factor analysis. For values greater than 0.5 is considered acceptable the adequacy of the data to a model of factor analysis. While more fences are 1 the values of KMO best is the adequacy of the data to a model factor, whereas already excellent fitness for KMO values close to 0.9.

There is also a measure of sampling adequacy individually for each of the variables as KMO-based. This measure is called MSA (*Measure of Sampling Adequacy*), defined in the following way:

$$MSA_j = \frac{\sum_{h \neq j} r_{jh}^2}{\sum_{h \neq j} r_{jh}^2 + \sum_{h \neq j} a_{jh}^2}$$

If the MSAj value is near the unit, variable Xj will be suitable for your treatment in the analysis of factorial with the rest of the variables.

Also in the model factorial can be *contrasts after the factors with which to assess the estimated factor once model*. Among them we have the contrast for the goodness of fit of the maximum likelihood method and the contrast to the goodness of fit of the MINRES method.

7.13 ROTATION OF THE FACTORS

The work in the factor analysis pursues common factors have a clear interpretation, because that way are better analyzed existing interrelations between the original variables. However, very rarely it is easy to find a proper interpretation of the initial factors regardless of the method used for its extraction. Precisely the procedures of **rotation of factors**have been devised to obtain, from the initial solution, a few factors that are easily interpretable.

Ortogonal Rotations

- *Method Varimax.*
- *Method Quartimax.*
- *Methods Ortomax: General Ortomax, Biquartimax, and Equamax.*

Below are the most important methods of orthogonal rotation features.

- **Method Varimax**. Method of orthogonal rotation which minimizes the number of variables that have high saturations in each factor. It simplifies the interpretation of factors.

- **Method Quartimax**. Rotation method that minimizes the number of factors necessary to explain each variable. It simplifies the interpretation of the observed variables.

- ***Method Equamax***. Rotation method which is combination of the Varimax method, which simplifies the factors, and the Quartimax method, which simplifies the variables. Minimizing both the number of variables that saturate high by a factor as the number of factors necessary to explain a variable.

Oblique Rotations

- *Method Oblimax and method Quartimin.*
- *Methods Oblimin: Covarimin and Oblimin direct (or general) and Biquartimin.*
- *Method Direct Oblimin: rotation Promax.*

Below are the most important methods of oblique rotation features.

- ***Direct Oblimin criterion***. Method for oblique rotation (not orthogonal). When delta is equal to zero (the default) solutions are the most oblique. As delta is becoming more negative, the factors are less oblique. To override the value by default 0 for delta, enter a number less than or equal to 0.8.

- ***Rotation Promax***. Oblique rotation that allows that the factors are correlated. You can calculate more quickly that a direct oblimin rotation, so it is useful for large data sets.

7.14 GRAPHICAL INTERPRETATION OF THE FACTORS

Below is a graph (Figure 7-18) concerning four variables X_1, X_2, X_3 and X_4 represented by two factors F_1 and F_2.

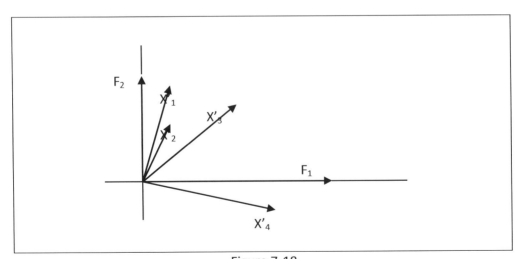

Figure 7-18

As overruns, weights or load factor of each variable in each factor (the parent factor elements), are represented by orthogonal projections of each variable in each factor, the fourth variable is explained strongly and positively by the first factor (projection positive large x'_4 on F_1), while it represents little and in the negative by the second factor (small negative projection of X'_4 on F_2).

In the same way, the first and second variable are explained strongly and positively by the second factor, and are explained shortly and positively by the first factor. The third variable is explained in the same way by the first and second factor.

If the geometric representation is diffuse, can be a rotation of factors that clarify the projections of the variables on them. With a rotation factor becomes a solution initial factor preferred solution otherwise. Such a transformation is aimed to show the way more convincing and clear for its scientific interpretation solution.

7.15 SCORES OR MEASURING THE FACTORS

Factor analysis is often a prelude to other analyses, which replaced the set of original variables by the factors obtained. For example, in the case of estimation of affected models of multicollinearity. Therefore, it is necessary to know the values taking the factors in each observation (factorial scores). However, it is important to note that, except the case that has been applied to the analysis of major components for the extraction of factors, some exact scores for factors are not obtained.

Instead, it is necessary to make estimates to obtain them. These estimates may be made by different methods. The best-known procedures, and which are implemented in software packages are the *least squares,regression, Anderson-Rubin and Barlett.*

The characteristics of the most important methods for obtaining of the components given below.

- *Regression method*. Method of estimation of the coefficients of the factor scores. The resulting scores have mean 0 and variance equal to the square of the multiple correlation between scores estimated factorials and the true factor values. Scores can be correlated even when factors are orthogonal.

- ***Bartlett's scores***. Method of estimation of the coefficients for factor scores. The resulting scores have a mean of 0. Minimizing the sum of squares of the unique factors about the range of variables.

- ***Anderson-Rubin method***. Method of estimation of the coefficients for factor scores. It is a modification of the method of Bartlett, which ensures the orthogonality of the estimated factors. The resulting scores have a mean of 0, a standard deviation of 1 and not are correlated.

Chapter 8.

PHASES OF CLEANING AND TRANSFORMING DATA WITH SAS ENTERPRISE MINER

8.1 THE PHASES OF CLEANING AND TRANSFORMING DATA IN ENTERPRISEMINER

Remember that SAS Institute considered within the process of *Data Mining* phase change (*Modify*), which takes a place after the scan (*scan*). Initially the exploration phase takes partners indicated nodes in Figure 11-1, but they are generally considered the assignment of attributes (*Data Set Attributes Node*), transformation of variables (*Transform Variables*), atypical data (*Filter Outliers*) filtering and nodes imputation of missing values (*Replacement*) usually belong to this phase.

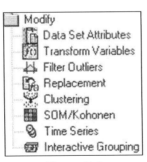

Figure 8-1

8.2 THE NODE VARIABLE TRANSFORMATION

Working with data mining, it is very common to create new variables from existing ones. These transformations tend to be done after having previously tried the lost data.

Once we already have our work in SAS (*educa.sas7bdat*file) format data in a specific library (library *work* representing the subdirectory *c:\libros\miningt*), open the project P1 (*File → Open*) and using *File → New → Diagram* create diagram D10. Then the *variable Transform* node is obtained through the button *Tools* from the browser's project of Enterprise Miner as a sub-option of the category *Modify* (Figure 8-1) or by dragging the node itself on the area next to the *Input Data Source* node to which the data set has been assigned previously *educa.sas7bdat* of the library work. Then will be the union of the two (Figure 8-2).

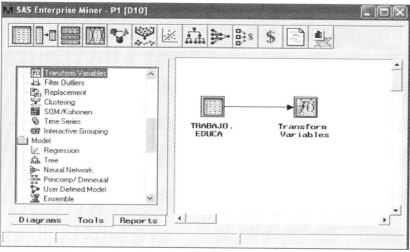

Figure 8-2

Then double click on the *variable Transform* node and choose tab *Variables* (Figure 8-3) which shows the variables of the model next to certain descriptive statistics in this node entry screen. In the *Keep* column, we specify if you want to use the variable on subsequent nodes.

To transform a variable, click with the right button of the mouse on the variable transform (*STUD*) and choose *Transform* (Figure 8-4) in the resulting pop-up menu. Then select one of the possible predefined processing options (Figure 8-5).

In our case we choose the function logarithm (*log*) and obtain a new variable in the DataSet SAS (logSTUD) which is the logarithm of the variable *STUD* (Figure 8-6).

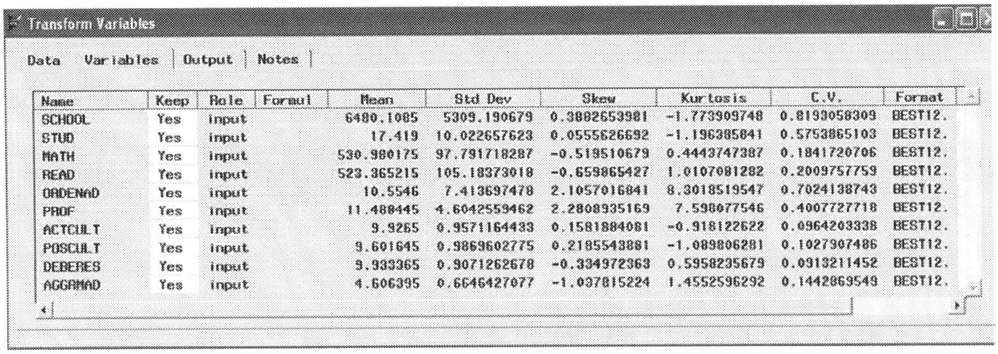

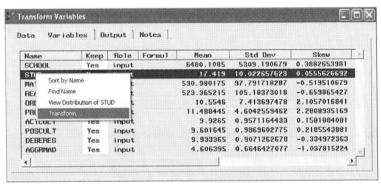

Figure 8-3

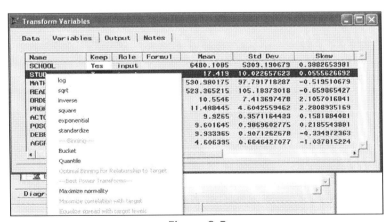

Figure 8-4

Figure 8-5

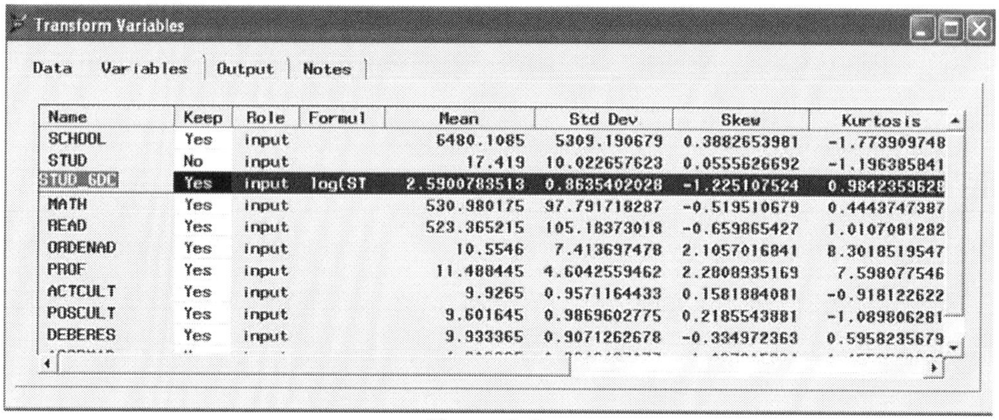

Name	Keep	Role	Formul	Mean	Std Dev	Skew	Kurtosis
SCHOOL	Yes	input		6480.1085	5309.190679	0.3882653981	-1.773909748
STUD	No	input		17.419	10.022657623	0.0555626692	-1.196385841
STUD_GDC	Yes	input	log(ST	2.5900783513	0.8635402028	-1.225107524	0.984235962
MATH	Yes	input		530.980175	97.791718287	-0.519510679	0.4443747387
READ	Yes	input		523.365215	105.18373018	-0.659865427	1.0107081282
ORDENAD	Yes	input		10.5546	7.413697478	2.1057016841	8.3018519547
PROF	Yes	input		11.488445	4.6042559462	2.2808935169	7.598077546
ACTCULT	Yes	input		9.9265	0.9571164433	0.1581884081	-0.918122622
POSCULT	Yes	input		9.601645	0.9869602775	0.2185543881	-1.089806281
DEBERES	Yes	input		9.933365	0.9071262678	-0.334972363	0.5958235679

Figure 8-6

In Figure 8-5 there are three groups of transformations, which are as follows:

- *: Simple transformations*
  - *Log:* calculates the napierian logarithm.
  - *Sqrt:* calculates the square root.
  - *Inverse:* calculates the inverse.
  - *Square:* calculates square.
  - *Exponential:* calculates the exponential value.
  - *Standardize:* standardizes the value.
- ***Binning**:*
  - *Bucket:* creates categories of the variable
  - *Quantile:* creates quantiles of the variable
  - *Optimal Binning for relationship to target:* creates an optimal number of partitions of the explanatory variable in relation to a binary response. This division is based on the calculation of contingency tables.

- ***Best Power Transformations****:*

  o   *Maximize normality:* choose a transformation of quantiles that is closest to the value of a normal distribution. It is useful for asymmetric distributions. These transformations are:

  - The same variable
  - Log (x)
  - $x^{1/4}$
  - $x^{1/2}$
  - x^2
  - x^4
  - e^x

  o   *Maximize correlation with target*: Select previous transformations which have a greater correlation with the result. It is useful for smoothing or make linear relationship between an explanatory variable and the response variable.

  o   *Equalize spread with target levels:* choose the transformation that has smaller variance of the variances between the levels of the target variable. It is useful to help correct the possible heteroscedasticity in the relationship between the explanatory variable and the explained.

To create a new variable according to the requirements of the user, in the toolbar select the *Create variable* (Figure 9-7) button, which opens the window of Figure 8-8 in which we will define the name type, and the variable new label.

To define the transformation, select the option *defines...,* which leads us to the figure 8-9 at which define the expression that generates the new variable. When you click *OK*, appears on the screen *variable Create* already the expression that generates the new variable (Figure 8-10). Pressing *OK* we already have the new variable incorporated into the DataSet (Figure 8-11).

Once transformed a variable, this can be modified by selecting the *mod. Definition* when you click with the right button on the transformed variable (Figure 8-12). We obtain again the screen *Create Variable* and with their button *sets* we return to define the new changes in the *Customize*screen.

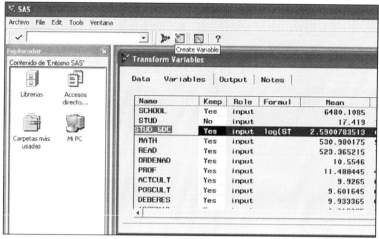

Figure 8-7

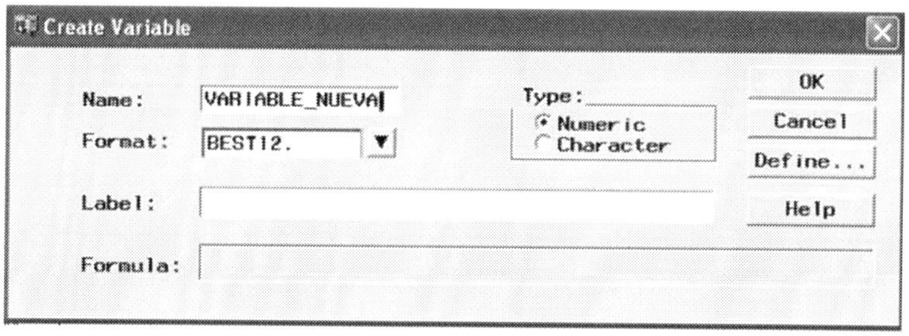

Figure 8-8

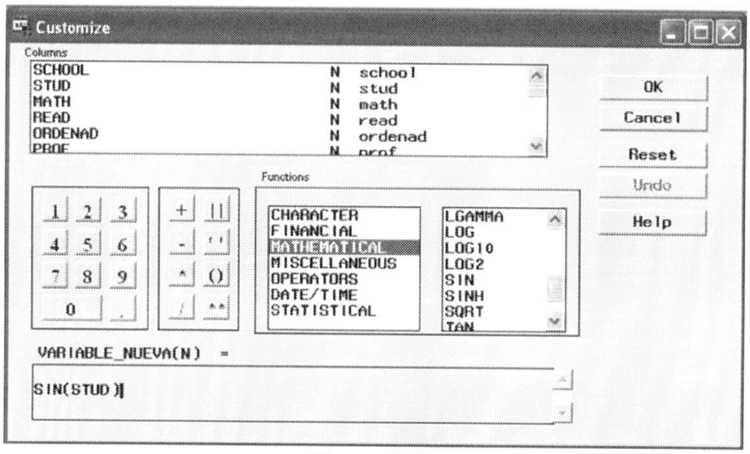

Figure 8-9

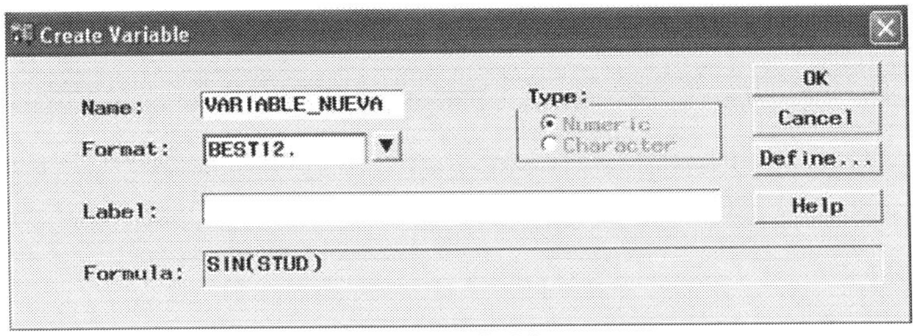

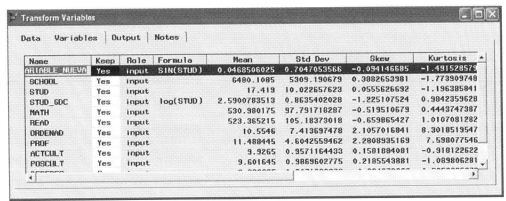

Figure 8-10

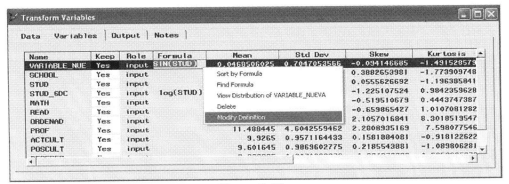

Figure 8-11

Figure 8-12

8.3 THE NODE ALLOCATION OF ATTRIBUTES

The *assignment of attributes* node offers the possibility of changes in the type of variables, their role and their measurement. It also also allows to modify the name of the data files, its description or its objective in the analysis. Therefore, it is a node that affects metadata in the *Data Mining*process.

The *Data Set Attributes* node is obtained through the button *Tools* from the browser's project of Enterprise Miner as a sub-option of the *Modify* category or dragging the node itself on the area next to the *Input Data Source* node has been that previously assigned the data set *educa.sas7bdat* of the library work. Then will be the union of the two (Figure 8-13).

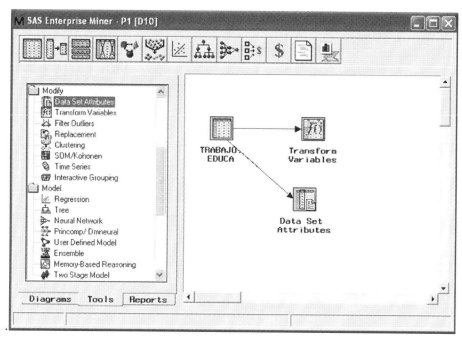

Figure 8-13

When you double click on the *Data Set Attributes* node gets the node whose tab *Data* entry screen contains information about the file (Figure 8-14).

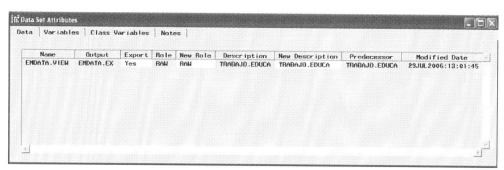

Figure 8-14

8.3.1 Modification of the characteristics of the file

The *Data* tab allows you to select the status of each file and the description of the modifications carried out. The *Export* column indicates if you want a certain base can be exported to successive nodes. Default set to "Yes" but we can change this status by clicking with the right button on the *Export* of the file whose status you want to change cell and selecting *set export → not* (figures 11-15 and 11-16).

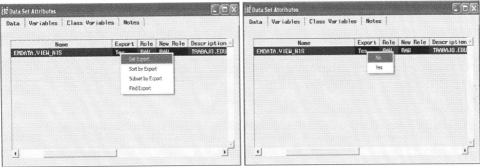

Figure 8-15 8-16

By default the new role (*New Role*) of each database is which had on the node that preceded. To assign a new role, we'll click with the right button of the mouse over the cell the *New Role* of the file that you want to change, choose *Set New role* (Figure 8-17) and then select one of the options in Figure 8-18.

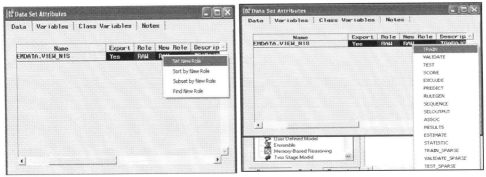

Figure 8-15   Figure 8-16

The options have the following meaning:

Train: data to fit the model.

Validate: data to model a model or to adjust the parameters of a model without this deteriorate by an "override" (*overfitting*) excessive.
Test: data never seen by the useful model to assess its results.

Score: objective data to another data file.

Predict: data contain values predicted by another model.

Rulegen: data generated rules.

Sequence: data corresponding to sequences of rules.

Seloutput: data contains the *output* (rules) Association node results window.

Assoc: data contain associations.

Result: results data file.

Estimate: data contains the parameters estimated by a model already built.

Statistic: the data contains statistics of a model already built.

Train_Sparse: data contain information from the file of an application of *text mining*training.

Validate_Sparse: data contain information from the file of an application of *text mining*training.

Test_Sparse: data contain information from the file of an application of *text mining*training.

You can also change the description of the data file in the *New Description* column and modify the date in the *Date Modified*column.

8.3.2 Modification of the characteristics of the variables

The *Variables* (Figure 8-19) tab allows you to modify the parameters of the variables. *Keep* field defines whether we want to or not to use this variable in successive nodes. The field *Role Model* assigned the role of variables. By default, each variable has the role he received in the initial data array. To change the role we click with the right button of the mouse over the cell *New Model Role* of the variable whose status you want to change and select *Set New model Roll →* *option* (figures 11-20 and 11-21).

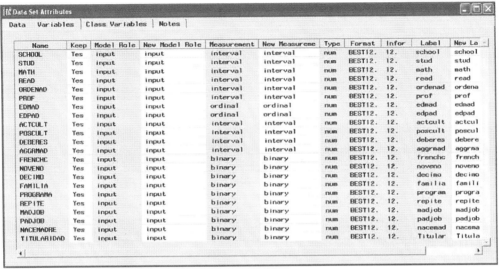

Figure 8-19

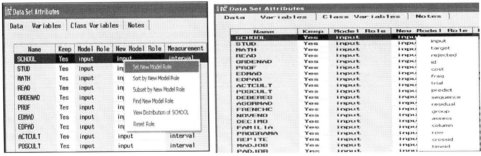

Figure 8-20   Figure 8-21

To change the role of a variable options (Figure 8-21) are the following:

- **Input**: variable used to predict a goal or for use in a type *cluster*analysis.

- **Target**: variable whose value we want to be able to predict.

- **Rejected**: removes a variable of successive assays.

- **ID**: variable tag. Rows with the same tag define a transaction. Association node requires at least one *Id* variable to discover associations, although they are normally excluded from the rest of the analysis.

- **Cost**: variable containing the cost of each unit. It is useful to define the matrix of costs for classification and prediction of objectives.

- **Freq**: variable that represents the frequency with which other values occur at each observation. It can also be used to assess other variables.

- **Trial**: represents objectives binomials, e.g. the number of people who respond to an offer advertising on the number of people who received the information. This information is used by artificial neural networks node when a target range with a binomial error function is available.

- **Predict**: variable that contains values predicted for a purpose.

- **Sequence**: variable that represents the amount of time between observation and observation.

- **Residual**: variable containing residues of a target.

- **Group**: variable group that can be used by successive nodes as node processing (*Group Processing Node*).

- **Assess**: created for the estimation of a model variable.

- **Row**: a variable that contains a number of rank of a matrix used in the specification of sparse matrices. The node's *text mining* using variable *row*.

- **Column**: a variable that contains a number of rank of a matrix used in the specification of sparse matrices. The node's *text mining* using variable *row*.

- **Crossid**: variable that contains groups or levels for cross-sectional analysis.

- **TimeID**: variable that contains a temporary as the day or date.

The field*New Measurement*allows you to change the level or type of measure variables.By default each variable will be measured as it was in the originating data node. To change the type of a variable measure we will click with the right button in the corresponding *New Measurement* cell and select *Set New Measurement* (Figure 8-22). It will then select one of the options in Figure 8-23. These options are as follows:

- **Binary**: contains two discrete values. For example Yes and NO.

- *Interval*: contains values that vary along a continuous range. For example distances in kilometers.

- *Nominal*: contains a set of values that do not have a logical order. For example, North, South, East, West.

- *Ordinal*: contain a discrete set of values that have a logical order. For example, outstanding, remarkable enough, suspense, very poor.

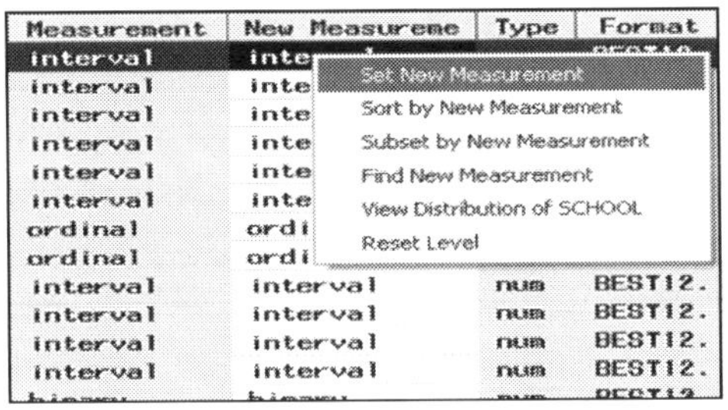

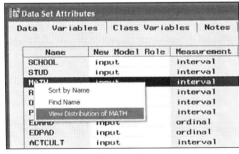

Figure 8-22

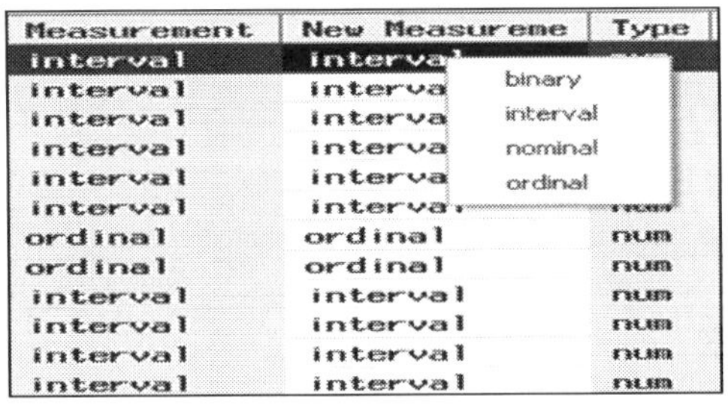

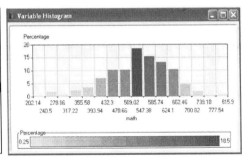

Figure 8-23

The *New Label* field allows you to change the original name of the variable with a new one. The *Name* field presents the possibility of viewing the distribution of a variable. So we will click with the right button on the name of the variable and select *View Distribution of* (Figure 8-24). Gets the distribution of frequencies of the variable (Figure 8-25).

Figure 8-24

Figure 8-25

8.3.3 Variables not continuous

The *variable Class* tab displays a table with information about all the variables that are not continuous (Figure 8-26). To establish the appropriate category it is necessary to click with the right mouse button in the column *New Order* in the cell of the variable target that we want to modify and select *Set New Order* (Figure 8-27). You then choose one of the following options (Figure 8-28):

- *Ascending:* the lowest level of the objective will be the modeling event.

- *Descending.* the highest level of the objective will be the modeling event.

- *Formatted ascending:* the lowest level with format ('No' receives the value 0 while "Yes" get the value 1) lens will be the modeling event.

- *Formatted descending:* the highest level with format ('No' receives the value 0 while "Yes" get the value 1) lens will be the modeling event.

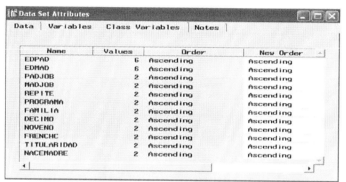

Figure 8-26

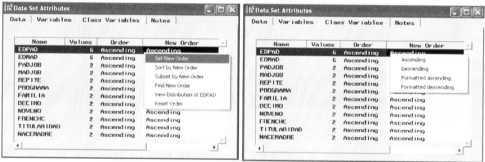

Figure 8-27   Figure 8-28

8.4 TREATMENT OF ATYPICAL DATA WITH THE NODE FILTER OUTLIERS

Extreme (*outliers*) and other observations do not you want to include in the process of *Data Mining*can be filtered through the node *Filter Outliers* . Filtering of these extreme values tends to produce better models since it tends to stabilize the estimation of parameters. Filtering is only done in the sample of training since validation and test samples are only used for their valuation.

El node *Filter Outliers* is obtained by pressing the button *Tools* from the browser's project of Enterprise Miner as a sub-option of the *Modify* category or by dragging the node itself on the working area next to the *Input Data Source* node that has been previously assigned the data set *educa.sas7bdat* of the library work. Then will be the union of the two (Figure 8-29). When you double click on node filtering *outliers* Gets the screen entry of Figure 8-30.

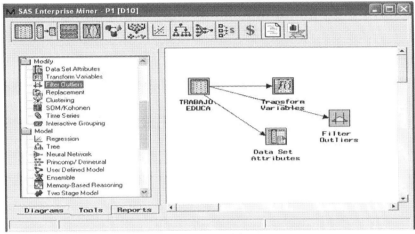

Figure 8-29

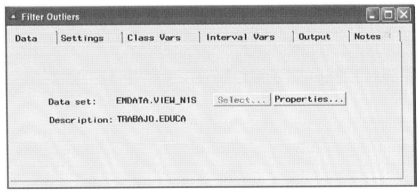

Figure 8-30

Filtering is normally executed by two steps:

1. On the *Settings*tab, set the automatic filtering options.

2. Examine and tune the results of filtering in the *Class Vars* and *Interval Vars*tabs.

8.4.1 Automatic filtering Options

The tab *Settings* (Figure 8-31) fields allow to establish automatic filtering of atypical data options.

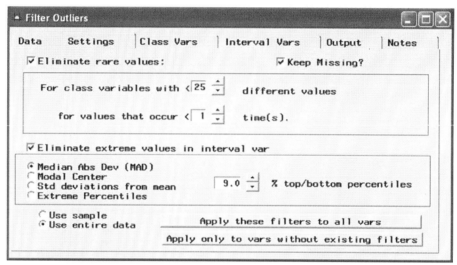

Figure 8-31

By default the options *Eliminate rare values* and *Eliminate extreme values in interval variables* are disabled. The option *keep missing?* is default activated, indicating that the deleted values are stored when you run the node. To apply the automatic filtering to all variables, according to the specified criteria, it is necessary to click on the option *Apply these filters to all bars*. If we however exclude certain variables filtering, make click in the option *Apply only to vars without existing filters*.

The option to *Eliminate extreme values for interval variables* allows you to choose one of the following methods:

- *Median Absolute Deviations:* removes the values with more than *n* typical deviations from the median.

- *Modal Center:* removes the values that deviate more than *n* spaces from the modal Center.

- *Std Deviations from mean:* removes the values that are more than *n* standard deviations of the mean.

- *Extreme percentiles:* removes the values that are in the extreme upper and lower percentiles.

The option *Eliminate rare values* allows to eliminate isolated values (occurring less *n* times in continuous variables and with less than *n* different classes in class variables). You can also use a sample (*Use single*) or the complete set of data (*Use entire data*).

8.4.2 Observation and adjustment of the results of the filtering

The *Class Vars* tab allows you to see a table with the variables of classification which shows the minimum value of the frequency and the excluded values (Figure 8-32).

If we stand on a variable and we click with the right button of the mouse gets the context menu of Figure 8-33 whose choice *View Distribution of* allows you to view the graphical distribution and the table of frequencies of the variable chosen (Figure 8-34).

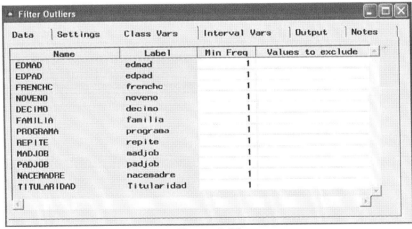

Figure 8-32

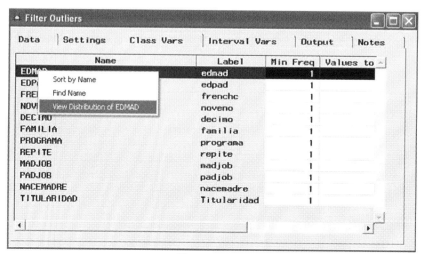

Figure 8-33

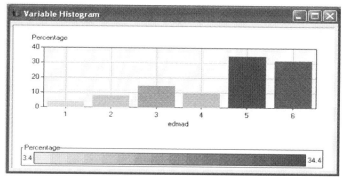

Figure 8-34

The *Interval Vars* tab presents the table of Figure 8-35 that allows to adjust the results of filtering. In this window you can change the option *Keep missing* view above (you click with the right button of the mouse over the variable to change, it is elected *Set Keep Missing* in the pop-up menu of Figure 9-36 and choose the appropriate option in Figure 8-37) and the interval of the range that you want to use in the analysis. With the context menu of the figure 8-38 can be minimum, maximum values and the distribution of the variable by clicking with the right button of the mouse on the column *Range to include* and selecting *Set range to include*. These findings limit the values that will be used in subsequent analysis. The minimum and maximum values can vary by selecting and moving the reference line of the minimum or maximum value while you hold down the left button of the mouse (Figure 8-39).

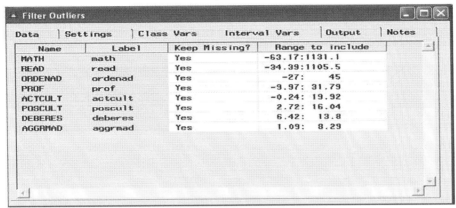

Figure 8-35

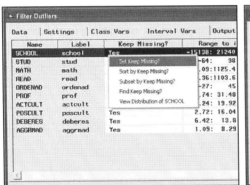

Figure 8-36

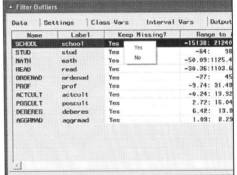

Figure 8-37

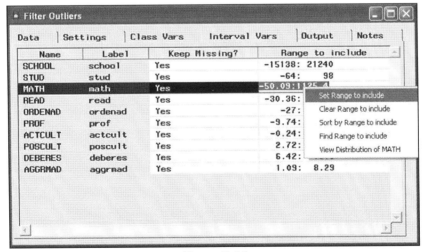

Figure 8-38

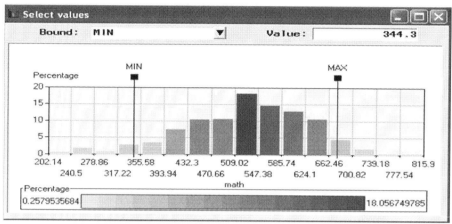

Figure 8-39

The *Output* tab leads to the figure 8-40, containing the name and description of the data with the values used (*Included observations*) and filtered data (*Excluded observations*). Once the node it is necessary to press *OK* and connect the results to the next node in the flowchart of the process of *Data Mining*.

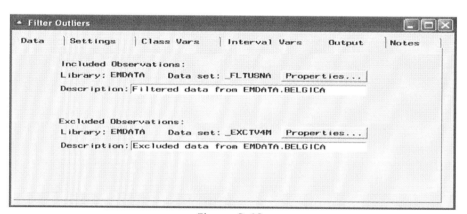

Figure 8-40

8.4.3 The node missing data imputation

Databases usually contain missing values due to errors, incomplete information, system or operator errors when entering data, union, or update databases, etc. When a comment contains a data lost in general this data is not used for the analysis. This rejection is not included in the analysis the rest of the information that may be relevant to the analysis. You can also skew the representativeness of the sample if the lost data are not distributed equally across the sample, but more affect some individuals than others. The replacement node function is to substitute appropriate lost and even values not lost prior to analysis. Any imputation method involves making a series of assumptions about the distribution of the variables, which makes that optimal method there is no.

I node *Replacement* is obtained by pressing the button *Tools* from the browser's project of Enterprise Miner as a sub-option of the *Modify* category or by dragging the node itself on the working area next to the *Input Data Source* node that has been previously assigned the data set *educa.sas7bdat* of the library work. Then will be the union of the two (Figure 8-41). When you double click on the imputation of missing values node gets the screen *Replacement* of Figure 8-42 with the *Default* tab that is enabled by default.

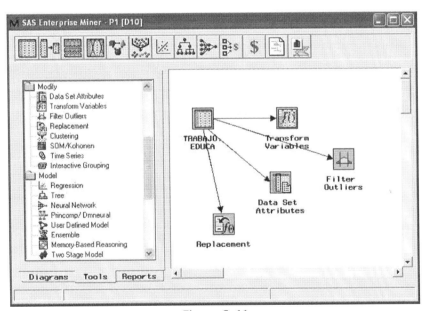

Figure 8-41

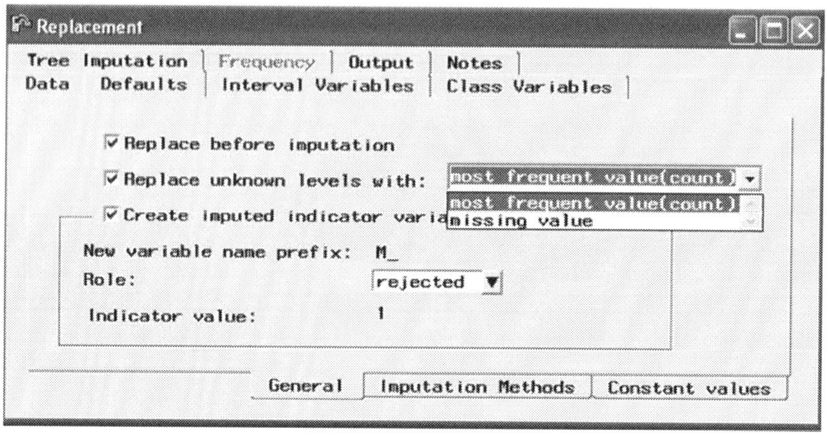

Figure 8-42

The tab*Default*allows you to configure the replacement methods that will be used by default. This tab contains three subwindows.

In the subwindow *General* (default) you can specify the following:

- Replace specific values not lost before attributing value to the lost data.
- Replace the unknown values of the class variables in the database for *scoring*. When this database contains values that are not present in the training data these values can be replaced by the most frequent value or missing values.

- Create variables with indicators for the imputed values to indicate the values replaced in each variable. The new variables are named using the *M_Nombre of the variable*expression. Each element contains a pointer with value 1 if the data was replaced and 0 if not. These variables are assigned the role of rejected (*rejected*) by default.

Default *Enterprise Miner* imputed missing values before proceeding to replace the values specified by the user.

In the subwindow*Imputation Methods* (Figure 8-43) can specify the type of allocation by default for continuous variables or interval and class (binary, nominal and ordinal).

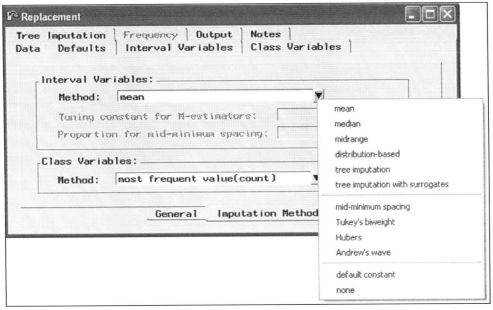

Figure 8-43

Continuous variables are the following allocation methods:

- *Mean*: the arithmetic mean. It is the preferred choice if the data are distributed symmetrically.

- *Median:* Median. It is the value that divides the sample above and below on exactly two halves. It is less sensitive to outliers than other measures of central tendency.

- *Midrange*: midrange. It is defined as the minimum value over the maximum divided by two.

- *Distribution-based*: the values are taken randomly from the distribution of the rest of sampling data. It has the advantage of leaving almost invariant distribution of the sample.

- *Tree imputation*: imputation using decision trees. It examines each input as an objective and the remaining inputs and rejected variables are used as predictors. It has the advantage of using information contained in other *inputs* to make the accusation.

- *Tree imputation with surrogates*: identical to the above but uses also Mediterrenean division rules where the predictor also contain missing values.

- *Mid-minimum spacing*: the fact is imputed using a proportion of master data (default 90%). Then add the minimum and maximum value of the restricted distribution and is divided by two.

- *Robust M Estimadores of location: Tukey's biweight, Hubers and Andrew's wave*: the estimators M reduced the effect of the extreme data samples using replacement functions. These estimators are robust efficiency in large outliers before signs or errors in the data. The value of the constant adjustment of these estimators can be changed in the option *Tuning constant for M-estimators*.

Class variables can be replaced by the following:

- *Most frequent value:* value or most frequent category (by default).

- *Distribution-based*: based on a distribution.

- *Tree imputation*: imputation in tree.

- *Tree imputation with surrogates*: imputation in tree with restrictions.

- *Default constant: constant*: constant by default.

- *None*: is left as the lost value.

In the subwindow*Constant values*(Figure 8-44) ef the possibility to define continuous variables (clear the extreme values of the tails of the distribution). In the *Trimming of variable interval* option will replace the values lower or higher than a value determined by the value in box *With value*. *Imputation* option allows you to specify the values to assign continuous variables or class. Both numerical values and characters can be attributed.

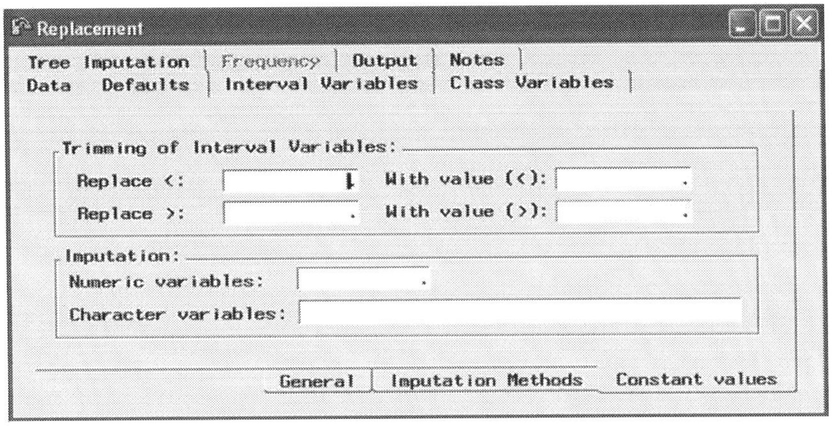

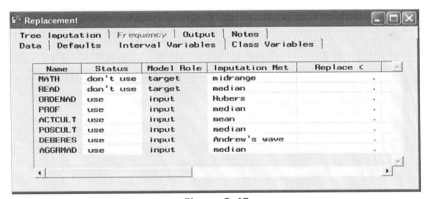

Figure 8-44

Interval Variables (Figure 8-45) tab allows you to specify in each variable allocation method via the context menu activated by right mouse button by selecting *Select Method...*(Figure 8-46). Then choose the method of imputation in Figure 8-47. You can also choose the *status* and values to replace as we saw in the subwindow *Constant values* earlier. For this you click on the variable to replace with the right button of the mouse and choose the appropriate option in the pop-up menu of Figure 8-46.

Figure 8-45

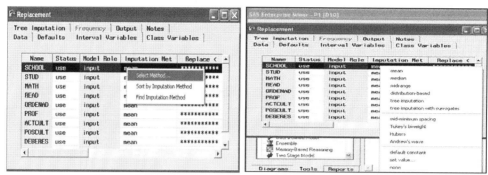

Figure 8-46   Figure 8-47

The tab*Class Variables*(Figure 8-48) allows you to specify in each class variable imputation method through the context menu that is activated by the right button of the mouse by selecting *Select Method...*(Figure 8-49). Then you choose the method of imputation in Figure 8-50. Possible imputation methods for class variables are those based on decision trees, distributions and the allegation by constant.

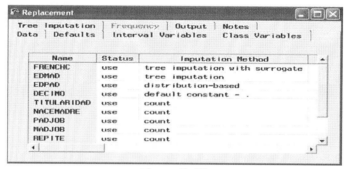

Figure 8-48

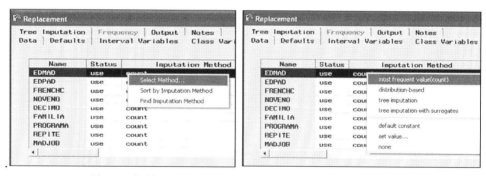

Figure 8-49   Figure 8-50

The tab*Tree Imputation*(Figure 8-51) allows selecting the variables that will be used as *input* in the imputation of data using decision trees. To do this we click with the right button of the mouse over a variable and choose *Set Status* from the resulting pop-up menu (Figure 8-52). We will assign the *status use* or *don't use* (Figure 8-53) according to which the variable is going to be used or not in the imputation of data using decision trees.

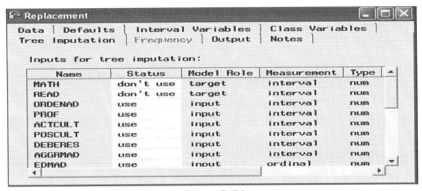

Figure 8-51

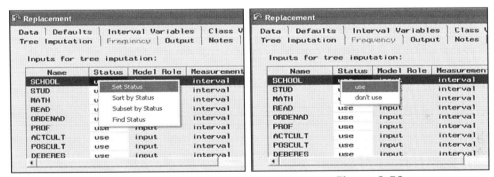

Figure 8-52   Figure 8-53

The tab *Frequency* is activated only if the *Input Data Source* node we assign the category of frequency to an *input*, in which case relative to the tab *Frequency* window provides the name of the variable frequency. Each observation would then represent *n* cases. If the value of the frequency is less than 1 or observation is lost, this observation is not used in the calculations. Lost in variable frequency values are not replaced by the node.

The tab*Output*it takes us to the window of Figure 8-54 ccontains information on data charged in previous databases. These data will be passed to successive nodes in the flowchart of the process of *Data Mining*.

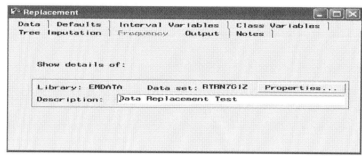

Figure 8-54

Once the node by clicking with the right button on it and *Run* eleigiendo from the resulting pop-up menu (Figure 8-55) access the display of results in Figure 8-56.

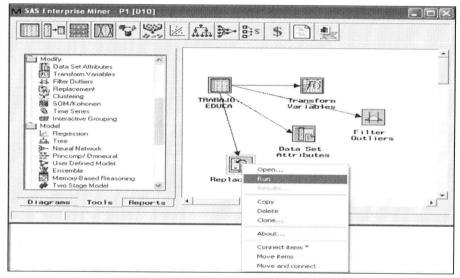

Figure 8-55

	school	stud	math	read	ordenad	prof
1	1001	2	560.43	569.51	29.3	5.32
2	1001	7	513.4	496.84	29.3	5.32
3	1001	8	429.46	535.13	29.3	5.32
4	1001	16	714.04	738.66	29.3	5.32
5	1001	17	448.67	584.35	29.3	5.32
6	1001	18	618.93	611.85	29.3	5.32
7	1001	22	657.83	563.42	29.3	5.32

Figure 8-56

The *Table View*tab shows the charged for training, validation, test and scoring (Figure 8-56).

The *Interval Variables*tab shows continuous variables, its role in the model, the imputation method followed, imputed values, number of imputed values, number values charged to both sides of the distribution and the labels of the training (Figure 8-57) data.

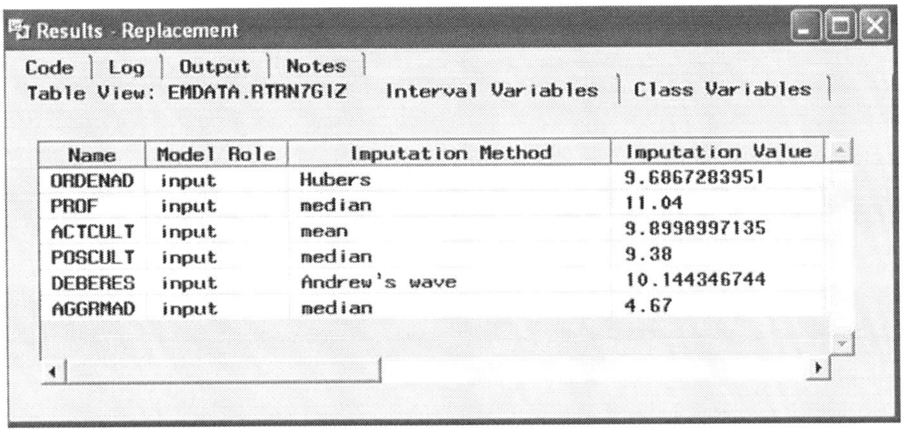

Name	Model Role	Imputation Method	Imputation Value
ORDENAD	input	Hubers	9.6867283951
PROF	input	median	11.04
ACTCULT	input	mean	9.8998997135
POSCULT	input	median	9.38
DEBERES	input	Andrew's wave	10.144346744
AGGRMAD	input	median	4.67

Figure 8-57

The *Class Variables* tab shows the variables of class, its role in the model, the imputation method followed, the imputed values, number of imputed values, number values charged to both sides of the distribution and training (Figure 8-58) data labels.

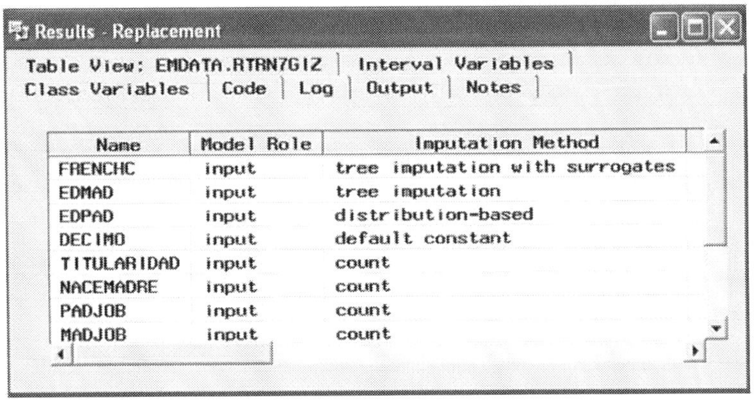

Name	Model Role	Imputation Method
FRENCHC	input	tree imputation with surrogates
EDMAD	input	tree imputation
EDPAD	input	distribution-based
DECIMO	input	default constant
TITULARIDAD	input	count
NACEMADRE	input	count
PADJOB	input	count
MADJOB	input	count

Figure 8-58

Tabs *Output, Log and Code* show respectively the SAS for the replaced data *output* , the result of the SAS Log window and the SAS code with details of how the imputation was carried out.

8.5 THE NODE SCANNING PATTERNS FOR PRINCIPAL COMPONENTS

The *exploration of patterns* (*Insight*) node allows you to explore and analyze data interactively including principal components analysis.

Once we already have our work data in SAS format (file *educa.sas7bdat*) in a certain library (library *work* that represents the subdirectory *c:\libros\miningt*), use the node*Insight*using the *Tools* of Enterprise Miner project browser button as a sub-option of the category *Explore* or dragging the node itself on the working area next to the *Input Data Source* node that will be assigned the data set *educa.sas7bdat* of the library work. Then will be the union of the two (Figure 8-59).

Then double click on the node is made*Insight*choose the tab*Data* y choose between using a sample of the data set or all data (Figure 8-60). To then run the node *Insight* by selecting it and clicking above the icon *Run* ☈ to obtain the general framework of *Insight* (Figure 8-61).The option *Edit* from the menu bar of *Insight* (Figure 8-61) allows you to govern the editing options (Windows Presentation and management variables, observations and formats, etc.).

The option*Analyze* menu bar of *Insight* displays the analysis that can be carried out (Figure 8-62).The first group of options of *Analyze* are used for univariate and multivariate data analysis. The following options are used for the analysis of the distribution of variables, the adjustment of models and multivariate data analysis.

The option*Multivariate (Y, X)*Figure 8-62**allows**as principal components multivariate analysis procedures, analysis discriminant and examination of relationships between one or two groups of variables. In the variable *and* the entry of *Multivariate(Y,X)* of the figure window 8-63 must introduce variables to reduce by principal components (*comp, prof, edmad, edpad, actcult, postcult, duties* and *aggrmad*) by selecting them in the field VIEW_RPF and clicking on the box *and*. The option *Method* of Figure 8-63 leads us to screen Figure 8-64, which allows us to choose the method of multivariate analysis to use (main components, maximum redundancy analysis and canonical discriminant analysis).

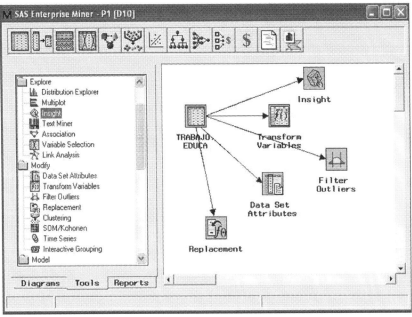

Figure 8-59

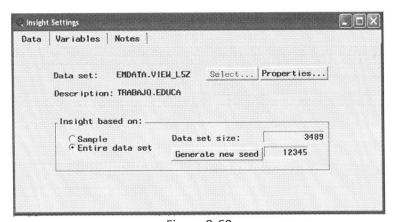

Figure 8-60

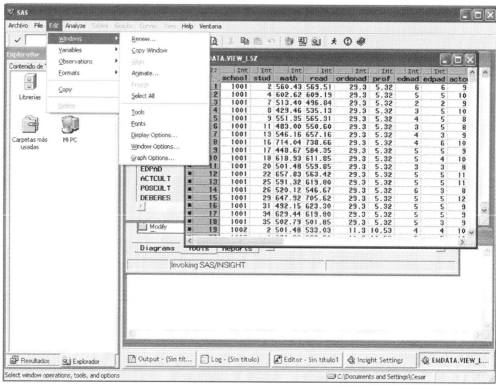

Figure 8-61

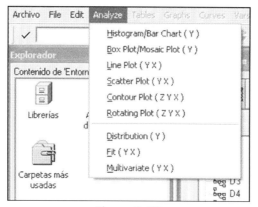

Figure 8-62

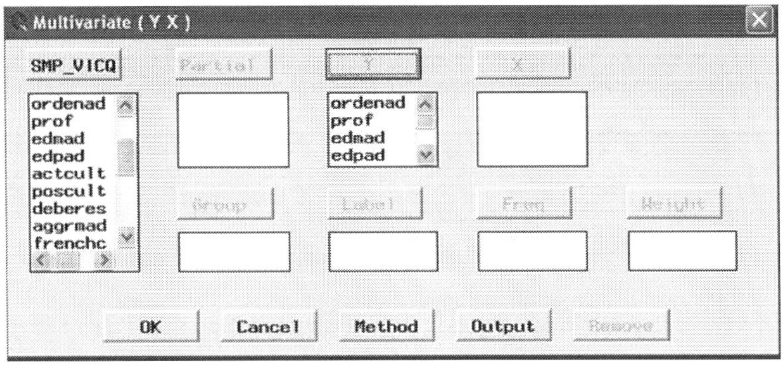

Figure 8-63

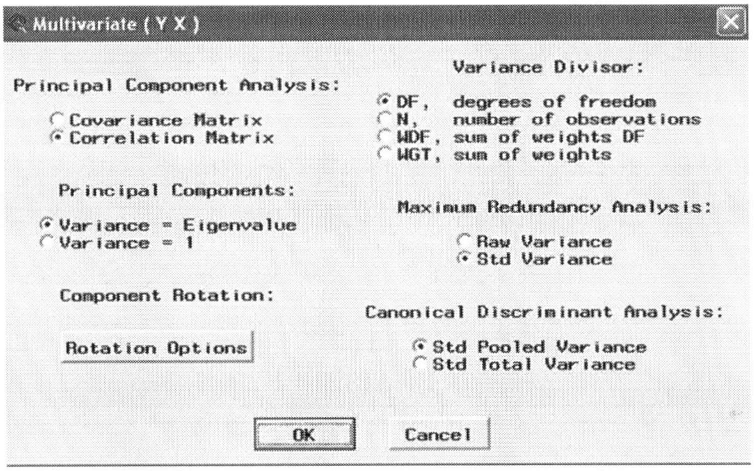

Figure 8-64

An analysis of main components must specify in Figure 8-64 if we will use the covariance matrix (if the variables are measured in comparable units) or correlations. The new components can have a variance equal to the eigenvalues with a mean equal to zero or a variance equal to one.

By pressing the button *Rotation Options* Figure 8-64 can rotate the components, if necessary, indicate in Figure 8-65 method of rotation, the number of components that we represent and the value of the parameter *Gamma*, which is defined by default except for *Orthomax* rotation that needs that we may specify a certain value. Once selected the analysis method that we are going to carry out, in the option *Output* of Figure 8-63 chose outcomes pursued over the figure 8-66.

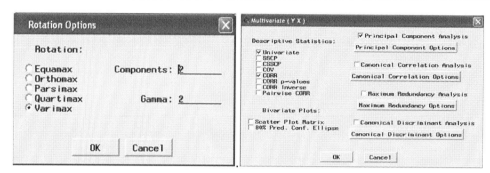

Figure 8-65   Figure 8-66

Figure 8-66 *Main Component Options* button allows you to get as output of the principal components analysis options Figure 8-67.

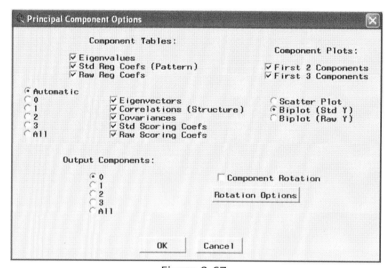

Figure 8-67

To press *OK* successive times gets the output of the procedure (figures 11-68-11-70). The options *Tables, Graphs, Curves* and *Vars* from the menu bar of *Insight* they contain the information that we have chosen in the display *Output*.

CHAPTER 8. PHASE OF CLEANING AND TRANSFORMING DATA WITH SAS...221

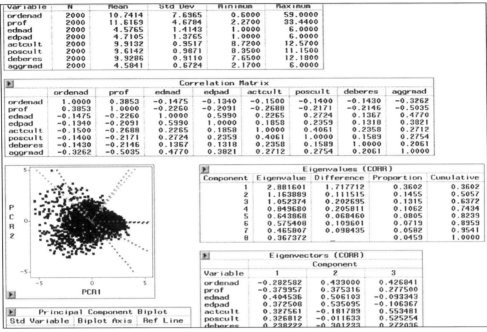

Variable	N	Mean	Std Dev	Minimum	Maximum
ordenad	2000	10.7414	7.6965	0.6000	59.0000
prof	2000	11.6169	4.6784	2.2700	33.4400
edmad	2000	4.5765	1.4143	1.0000	6.0000
edpad	2000	4.7105	1.3765	1.0000	6.0000
actcult	2000	9.9132	0.9517	8.7200	12.5700
poscult	2000	9.6142	0.9871	8.3500	11.1500
deberes	2000	9.9286	0.9110	7.6500	12.1800
aggraad	2000	4.5841	0.6724	2.1700	6.0000

Correlation Matrix

	ordenad	prof	edmad	edpad	actcult	poscult	deberes	aggrmad
ordenad	1.0000	0.3853	-0.1475	-0.1340	-0.1500	-0.1400	-0.1430	-0.3262
prof	0.3853	1.0000	-0.2260	-0.2091	-0.2688	-0.2171	-0.2146	-0.5035
edmad	-0.1475	-0.2260	1.0000	0.5990	0.2265	0.2724	0.1367	0.4770
edpad	-0.1340	-0.2091	0.5990	1.0000	0.1858	0.2359	0.1318	0.3821
actcult	-0.1500	-0.2688	0.2265	0.1858	1.0000	0.4061	0.2358	0.2712
poscult	-0.1400	-0.2171	0.2724	0.2359	0.4061	1.0000	0.1589	0.2754
deberes	-0.1430	-0.2146	0.1367	0.1318	0.2358	0.1589	1.0000	0.2061
aggrmad	-0.3262	-0.5035	0.4770	0.3821	0.2712	0.2754	0.2061	1.0000

Eigenvalues (CORR)

Component	Eigenvalue	Difference	Proportion	Cumulative
1	2.881601	1.717712	0.3602	0.3602
2	1.163889	0.111515	0.1455	0.5057
3	1.052374	0.202695	0.1315	0.6372
4	0.849680	0.205811	0.1062	0.7434
5	0.643868	0.068460	0.0805	0.8239
6	0.575408	0.109601	0.0719	0.8959
7	0.465807	0.098435	0.0582	0.9541
8	0.367372	---	0.0459	1.0000

Eigenvectors (CORR)

Variable	Component 1	2	3
ordenad	-0.282582	0.439000	0.426841
prof	-0.379957	0.375316	0.277500
edmad	0.404536	0.506103	-0.093343
edpad	0.372508	0.535095	-0.106367
actcult	0.327561	-0.181789	0.553481
poscult	0.326812	-0.011633	0.525254
deberes	0.238222	-0.301233	0.272036

Figure 8-68

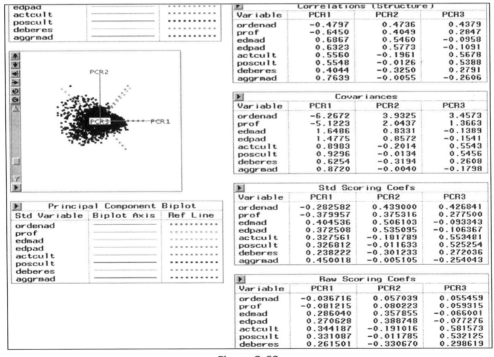

Correlations (Structure)

Variable	PCR1	PCR2	PCR3
ordenad	-0.4797	0.4736	0.4379
prof	-0.6450	0.4049	0.2847
edmad	0.6867	0.5460	-0.0958
edpad	0.6323	0.5773	-0.1091
actcult	0.5560	-0.1961	0.5678
poscult	0.5548	-0.0126	0.5388
deberes	0.4044	-0.3250	0.2791
aggrmad	0.7639	-0.0055	-0.2606

Covariances

Variable	PCR1	PCR2	PCR3
ordenad	-6.2672	3.9325	3.4573
prof	-5.1223	2.0437	1.3663
edmad	1.6486	0.8331	-0.1389
edpad	1.4775	0.8572	-0.1541
actcult	0.8983	-0.2014	0.5543
poscult	0.9296	-0.0134	0.5456
deberes	0.6254	-0.3194	0.2608
aggrmad	0.8720	-0.0040	-0.1798

Std Scoring Coefs

Variable	PCR1	PCR2	PCR3
ordenad	-0.282582	0.439000	0.426841
prof	-0.379957	0.375316	0.277500
edmad	0.404536	0.506103	-0.093343
edpad	0.372508	0.535095	-0.106367
actcult	0.327561	-0.181789	0.553481
poscult	0.326812	-0.011633	0.525254
deberes	0.238222	-0.301233	0.272036
aggrmad	0.450018	-0.005105	-0.254043

Raw Scoring Coefs

Variable	PCR1	PCR2	PCR3
ordenad	-0.036716	0.057039	0.055459
prof	-0.081215	0.080223	0.059315
edmad	0.286040	0.357855	-0.066001
edpad	0.270628	0.388748	-0.077276
actcult	0.344187	-0.191016	0.581573
poscult	0.331087	-0.011785	0.532125
deberes	0.261501	-0.330670	0.298619

Figure 8-69

Std Reg Coefs (Pattern)							
Component	ordenad	prof	edmad	edpad	actcult	poscult	deberes	aggrmad
PCR1	-0.282582	-0.379957	0.404536	0.372508	0.327561	0.326812	0.238222	0.450018
PCR2	0.439000	0.375316	0.506103	0.535095	-0.181789	-0.011633	-0.301233	-0.005105
PCR3	0.426841	0.277500	-0.093343	-0.106367	0.553481	0.525254	0.272036	-0.254043
PCR4	0.170643	0.088020	0.078675	0.133104	-0.198748	-0.393810	0.862552	-0.025377
PCR5	0.691895	-0.499392	-0.060972	-0.183698	0.141504	-0.253703	-0.124446	0.366811
PCR6	0.178030	-0.127503	-0.073937	-0.132982	-0.699732	0.628220	0.135415	0.162096
PCR7	-0.074725	0.539325	0.247638	-0.517678	0.050019	-0.055232	0.021206	0.606818
PCR8	0.010794	0.271102	-0.703419	0.475879	0.040803	0.002346	-0.015339	0.450802

Raw Reg Coefs							
Component	ordenad	prof	edmad	edpad	actcult	poscult	deberes	aggrmad
PCR1	-2.174902	-1.777599	0.572122	0.512741	0.311739	0.322591	0.217016	0.302598
PCR2	3.378773	1.755887	0.715764	0.736537	-0.173008	-0.011483	-0.274417	-0.003433
PCR3	3.285195	1.298261	-0.132011	-0.146409	0.526745	0.518471	0.247819	-0.170822
PCR4	1.313359	0.411793	0.111267	0.183211	-0.189148	-0.388724	0.785767	-0.017064
PCR5	5.325189	-2.336368	-0.086231	-0.252853	0.134668	-0.250427	-0.113368	0.246649
PCR6	1.370214	-0.596510	-0.104567	-0.183044	-0.665932	0.620107	0.123360	0.108996
PCR7	-0.575123	2.523187	0.350226	-0.712562	0.047603	-0.054519	0.019318	0.408032
PCR8	0.083078	1.268327	-0.994822	0.655027	0.038832	0.002316	-0.013973	0.303125

Figure 8-70

Then explains the different sections of the output of the analysis of principal components according to the choice made in Figure 8-67.

Eigenvalues: shows the table with the eigenvalues.

Std Reg Coefs (Pattern): shows the coefficients of scores factorials of standardized variables (*and*).

Raw Reg Coefs: shows scores coefficients factor of the variables (*and*) focused.

Eigenvectors: returns a table with the eigenvectors.

Correlations (Structure): returns the correlation between the variables used and the extracted components, i.e., the *load factor*.

Covariances: returns the covariance between the variables used and the extracted components.

Std Scoring Coefs: if obtained coefficients are those enabling the original variables by multiplying the principal components, standard coefficients are regarding the standardized original variables.

Raw Scoring Coefs: are the coefficients enabling focused original variables by multiplying the principal components.

Figure 8-67 *Automatic* button is used to show the principal components with eigenvalues greater than the average of eigenvalues. In this way where we have used the correlations matrix displays those eigenvalues greater than unity. By selecting 1, 2, 3, we will show only the selected eigenvalues. The *All* option will display all the eigenvalues. If you select 0, we will not obtain any table related to the eigenvalues of the analysis.

The structure of correlations *Correlations (Structure)* of the figure 8-69 presents loads factorial or correlations between variables and the components. This structure does not clearly delimit which variables are associated with each component, with what will be necessary to perform a rotation marking *Components rotation* in Figure 8-67, by clicking on *Rotation Options* and filling the resulting screen as in Figure 11-71. When you click OK Gets the result of Figure 8-72 with just two main components, but with already well defined factor loads. The variables *edmad* and *edpad* are associated with the second component (loads) and the rest of the variables are associated with the first component. Variables have been reduced to two components. One has to do with age and other cultural level.

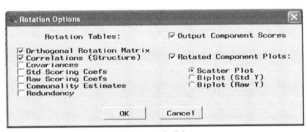

Figure 8-71

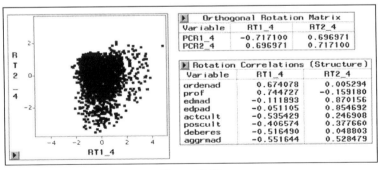

Figure 8-72

Chapter 9

DATA MINING PHASE. PREDICTIVE TECHNIQUES

9.1 TECHNIQUES PROPERLY SUCH DATA MINING

So far we have studied the first four phases of data mining, which are usually included under the name of *data preparation*. The next, or *actual data mining techniques*, phase includes *predictive techniques* focused on the *modelling and ad hoc classification*, and *descriptive techniques* usually focused on the *post-hoc classification* and other varied techniques.

Predictive techniques specify the model to the data based on theoretical knowledge. The model for data should contrast after the process of data mining before accepting it as valid. These techniques, we can include all types of regression, time series, analysis of variance and covariance, discriminant analysis, decision trees and neural networks. But, decision trees, neural networks and the discriminant analysis are in turn *classification techniques* that can take classes, or behavior profiles being order to build a model that allows to classify any new information. Decision trees allow you to classify data into groups based on the values of the variables. Base mechanism is to choose an attribute such as root and develop the tree according to the most significant variables.

Descriptive techniques no default role is assigned to the variables. Not assume the existence of dependent and independent variables and also assumes the existence of a prior model for data. Models are created automatically on the basis of the recognition of patterns. *Clustering* and segmentation techniques are included in this group (who are also technical classification in some way), techniques of Association and dependence, exploratory data analysis techniques and techniques of reduction of the dimension (factorial, principal components, correspondences, etc.) already seen in the phase of transformation.

9.2 PREDICTIVE TECHNIQUES

The classification of data mining techniques to discriminate between the existence or not of explained and explanatory variables. If there is a dependency between the explained variables and their corresponding explanatory variables, which can translate into a **model**, we have the *predictive techniques* or *explanatory methods*. This type of dependency analysis techniques can be classified depending on the metric or non-metric nature of independent and dependent variables.

The multiple regression analysis is a statistical technique used to analyze the relationship between a metric dependent (or endogenous) variable and several independent (or exogenous) also metric variables. The essential objective of the multiple regression analysis is to use independent variables, whose values are known, to predict the only criterion variable (dependent) selected by the researcher.

The functional expression of the multiple regression analysis is as follows:

$$y = F(x_1, x_2, \cdots, x_n)$$

where initially, the variable dependent *and* both the independent x_i are metric. Multiple regression also admits the possibility of working with independent variables not metric if dummy variables (*models of regression with dummy variables*) are used for conversion in metrics.

The *canonical analysis or the canonical correlation analysis* is a statistical technique used to analyze the relationship between multiple variables dependent (or endogenous) metrics and several independent (or exogenous) also metric variables. The essential objective of the canonical correlation analysis is to use independent variables, whose values are known, to predict the variables criterion (dependent) selected by the researcher.

The functional expression of the canonical correlation analysis is as follows:

$$G(y_1, y_2, \cdots, y_n) = F(x_1, x_2, \cdots, x_n)$$

where initially, both the independent and dependent variables $and_i x_i$ are metric. Shown that this model is an extension of the multiple regression model to the case of multiple dependent variables. The canonical correlation analysis can also extend to the case of non-metric dependent variables and the case of nonmetric independent variables.

Discriminant analysis is a statistical technique used to analyze the relationship between a variable dependent (or endogenous) not metric (categorical), and several independent (or exogenous) metric variables. The essential objective of the discriminant analysis is the known values of the independent variables can be used to predict with what category of the dependent variable correspond. We can thus predict in which category of credit risk is a person, the success of a product on the market, etc.

The functional expression of discriminant analysis is as follows:

$$y = F(x_1, x_2, \cdots, x_n)$$

where the variable dependent *and* is not metric and the independent variables are metric. It is therefore a special case of multiple regression analysis. Formally, we could say that the discriminant analysis is a classification technique which allows to group the elements of a sample in two or more different categories, predefined in a variable dependent not metric, based on a series of independent metric variables linearly combined.

In the discriminant analysis, for given values of the independent variables we must predict the probability of belonging to a category or class of the dependent variable (for example, probability that an individual buy a product or return a credit according to some variables measured in it). They *discrete choice models* have the same nature as the discriminant model, but now what is predicted is the probability of belonging to a category (class) for given values of the dependent variables. Therefore, discrete choice models directly predict the probability of occurrence of an event that is defined by the values of the independent variables. As a probability values are between zero and one, predictions made with discrete choice models must be limited so that they fall in the range between zero and one. The general model that meets this condition is a particular case of the multiple regression model is called a **linear probability model**, which has the functional form:

$$P_i = F(x_i, \beta) + u_i$$

It is observed that if F is the function of a random variable distribution, then P varies between zero and one.

In the particular case where the function F is the logistic function, we will be with the **Logit or logistic regression model**, whose functional form will be as follows:

$$P_i = F(x_i, \beta) + u_i = \frac{e^{x_i\beta}}{1 + e^{x_i\beta}} + u_i$$

In the particular case where the function F is the function of a unit normal distribution we facing the **Probit model**, whose functional form will be as follows:

$$P_i = F(x_i, \beta) + u_i = \left(2\pi\right)^{-\frac{1}{2}} \int_{-\infty}^{x_i\beta} e^{-\frac{t^2}{2}} dt + u_i$$

The simple variance analysis is a statistical technique used to analyze the relationship between a metric dependent (or endogenous) variable and several independent (or exogenous) not metric variables. The essential goal of the analysis of variance models is to determine whether different samples come from populations with equal average. The non-metric values of the independent variables will determine a number of groups in the dependent variable. So the ANOVA model measures the statistical significance of the differences between the means of the groups determined by the values of the independent variables on the dependent variable.

The functional expression of simple variance ANOVA analysis model is as follows:

$$y = F(x_1, x_2, \cdots, x_n)$$

where the variable dependent *and* is metric and the independent variables are not metric. It is therefore another particular case of the multiple regression model.

The simple Covariance analysis is a statistical technique used to analyze the relationship between a variable dependent (or endogenous) metric and several variables independent (or exogenous), part of which are not metric, being it another part metric (*covariates*).

The functional expression of the simple covariance, ANCOVA analysis model is as follows:

$$y = F(x_1, x_2, \cdots, x_n)$$

where the variable dependent *and* is metric and the independent variables are some metrics and other non-metric. It is therefore another particular case of the multiple regression model.

Multiple variance analysis is a statistical technique used to analyze the relationship between several variables dependent (or endogenous) metrics and several independent (or exogenous) not metric variables. Essential models of multiple variance analysis aims to contrast if the non-metric values of the independent variables will determine the equality of vectors of means of a series of groups determined by them in the dependent variables. So the MANOVA model measures the statistical significance of the differences between the vectors of means of the groups determined by the values of the independent variables on the dependent variables.

The functional expression of multiple variance MANOVA analysis model is as follows:

$$G(y_1, y_2, \cdots, y_m) = F(x_1, x_2, \cdots, x_n)$$

where the dependent variables are metric, and the independent variables are not metric. We are still talking about a particular case of the multiple regression.

The multiple Covariance analysis is a statistical technique used to analyze the relationship between several variables dependent (or endogenous) metrics and several variables (or exogenous) independent mixture of metric and nonmetric variables.

The functional expression of MANCOVA multiple Covariance analysis model is as follows:

$$G(y_1, y_2, \cdots, y_m) = F(x_1, x_2, \cdots, x_n)$$

where the dependent variables are metric and the independent variables are a part metric metric and elsewhere.

In the analysis of covariance, both simple and multiple, independent variable metrics (*covariates*) aim to eliminate certain effects that may bias the results by increasing the variance within groups. The analysis of covariance usually start removing, using a linear regression, the variation experienced by the dependent variables produced by the covariate or covariates of unwanted effects, to continue with an ANOVA or MANOVA analysis of adjusted dependent variables (residues of the previous regression).

The multiple regression admits the possibility of working with independent variables not metrics using dummy variables for its transformation in metrics. Each class of the variable no metric is assigned a numeric value.

Multiple dummy variables regression model is similar to the analysis of the multiple regression with the difference that the independent variables can be also not metric. Therefore, it is a statistical technique used to analyze the relationship between a metric dependent (or endogenous) variable and several variables and independent (or exogenous) metric, no metric or mixture of both. The essential objective of the multiple regression analysis is to use independent variables, whose values are known, to predict the only criterion variable (dependent) selected by the researcher.

The functional expression of the analysis of the multiple regression with dummy variables is as follows:

$$y = F(x_1, x_2, \cdots, x_n)$$

As well as the multiple regression, discrete choice models support the possibility of working with independent variables not metrics using dummy variables for its transformation in metrics.

It is really very interesting to note that all predictive techniques for modelling exposed here are a particular case or an extension of multiple regression model.

We could tabulate the *methods of the multivariate analysis of dependence, according to the nature of their dependent and independent variables*, as follows:

TECHNIQUE	Dependent variables	Variables independent
ANOVA and MANOVA	Metric (metric)	Non-metric
ANCOVA and MANCOVA	Metric (metric)	Metric and non-metric
MULTIPLE REGRESSION	Metric	Metric
MULTIPLE REGRESSION (DUMMY VARIABLES)	Metric	Metric and non-metric
CANONICAL CORRELATION	Metric and non-metric	Metric and non-metric
DISCRETE CHOICE	Non-metric	Metric
DISCRETE CHOICE (DUMMY VARIABLES)	Non-metric	Metric and non-metric

Chapter 10

PREDICTIVE TECHNIQUES OF MODELLING WITH SAS ENTERPRISE MINER

10.1 TECHNIQUES PREDICTIVE MODELING WITH SAS ENTERPRISE MINER

Enterprise Miner of SAS Institute software implements the phase of modeling on the stage model (*Model*) SEMMA methodology. This stage contains the nodes (*Regression*) regression; Decision trees (*Tree*); Artificial neural networks (*Neural Network*); Neural networks and/or analysis of main components (*Princomp/Dmneural*); Model defined by the user (*User Defined Model*); Models Union (*Ensemble*); Memory-based reasoning (*Memory Based Reasoning*) and models in two stages (*Two Stage Model*). See Figure 10-1.

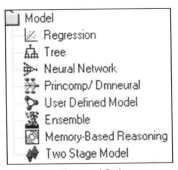

Figure 10-1

In this chapter we will take care of the *Regression*node, which allows you to adjust the most common types of regression models, such as multiple regression and logistic regression.

10.2 THE REGRESSION NODE: MULTIPLE REGRESSION MODEL

The *Regression* node can carry out multiple regressions and logistic regressions. Once we already have our work in SAS (*educa.sas7bdat*file) format data in a specific library (library *work* representing the subdirectory *c:\libros\miningt*), open the project P1 (*File → Open*) and using *File → New → Diagram* create diagram D11. Then the *regression* node is obtained through the button *Tools* from the browser's project of Enterprise Miner as a sub-option of the *Model* category or by dragging the node itself on the area next to the *Input Data Source* node has been that previously assigned the data set *educa.sas7bdat* of library work. Then will be the union of the two (Figure 10-2).

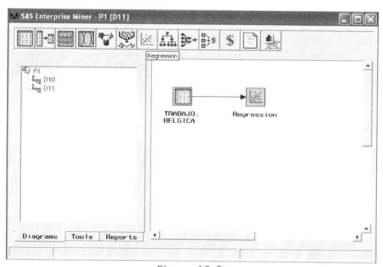

Figure 10-2

We consider a regression model that has variable *Math,* measuring the results of the math tests, such as dependent and the rest of the variables (except *Read* as independent). Therefore it is necessary to declare the *Math* and *Read* variables of type *Target* and the rest of type *Input*. This task is performed by double clicking on the *Input Data Source* node tagged as work.Belgium and choosing the *Variables*tab. Then you click with the right button of the mouse on the

*Math*variable, choose *Set Role Model* (Figure 10-3) and below *Target* (Figure 10-4). Repeat the process with the variable *Read* and already has two variables of type *Target* or dependent (Figure 10-5). The rest are of type *Input* or independent by default.

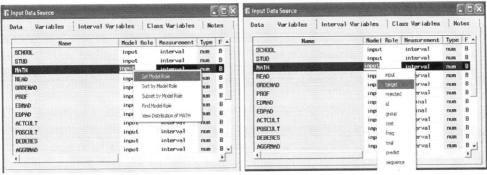

Figure 10-3 10-4

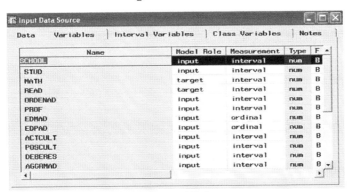

Figure 10-5

Then double click on the *Regression* node and gets the selection screen of the dependent variable which offers those variables defined *Target* type in the file's data (Figure 10-6). We chose *Math* as the model-dependent variable and click *OK*. Gets the display in Figure 10-7 in the *Variables*tabwill activate the explanatory variables or assigning *inputs Status → use*. If we do not want to include any of the variables, will change its *Status* to *don't use*. To do this you click with the right button of the mouse in the column *Status* on the variable to change the State, will choose *Set Status* (Figure 10-7) and then *use* or *don't use* (Figure 10-8) as needed.

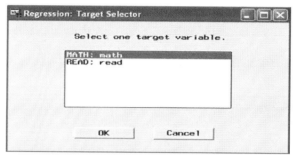

Figure 10-6

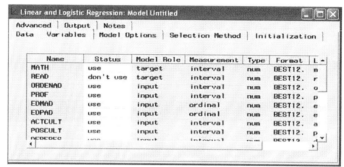

Figure 10-7

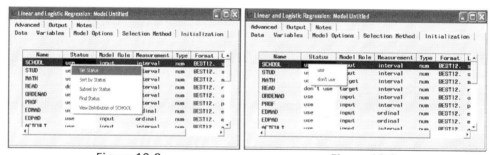

Figure 10-8   Figura 10-9

On the *Selection Method* tab select the method for the selection of explanatory variables (Figure 10-10). In this example, we have selected the *None*option, which implies that all the explanatory variables will be introduced in a single step in the analysis.

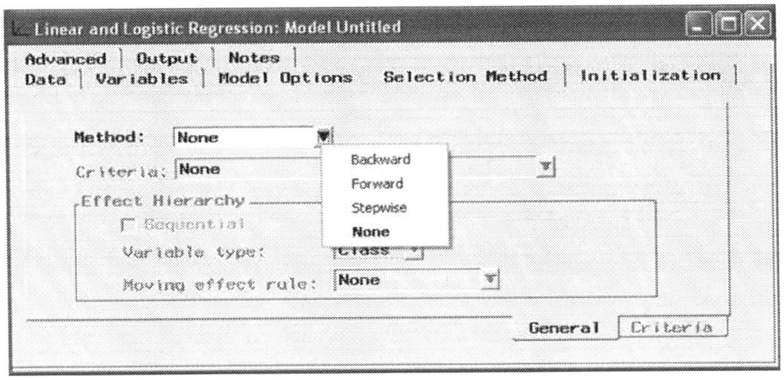

Figure 10-10

On the tab *Output* (Sub *Score Data Set*), we set specifications about where will be stored information with the predictions of the model (Figure 10-11). In this case predictions made on training, only available data, will be saved in the *EMDATA* library and within this in the *STRNHFST*file.

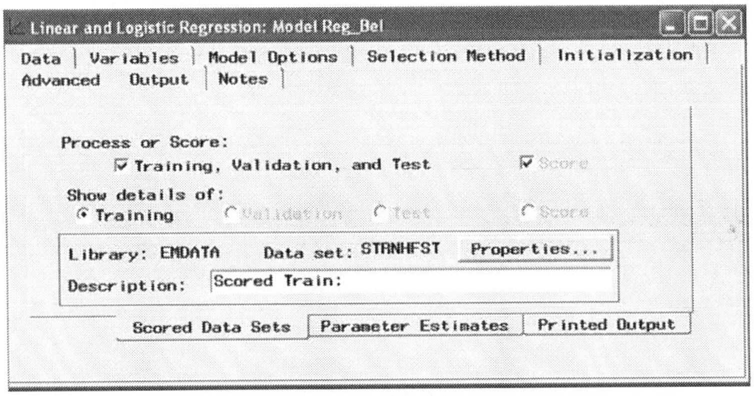

Figure 10-11

On the other hand, the tab *Output* (Sub *Parameter Estimates*) shows the file destination where it will be saved the estimated parameters (Figure 10-12).

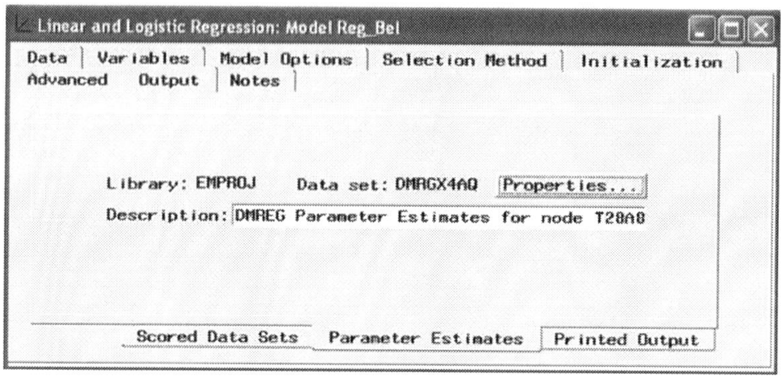

Figure 10-12

Finally in the window *Output* (Sub *Printed Output),* select the results we want (Figure 10-13).

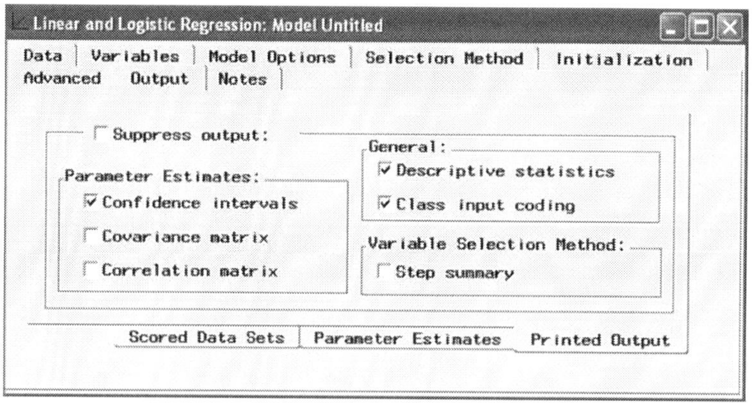

Figure 10-13

Once selected all these actions, we will be able to run the regression. Previously, when you close the node, prompted us that we assign a name to the built model (Figure 10-14). Once named and described click *OK* and run the node in the usual way.

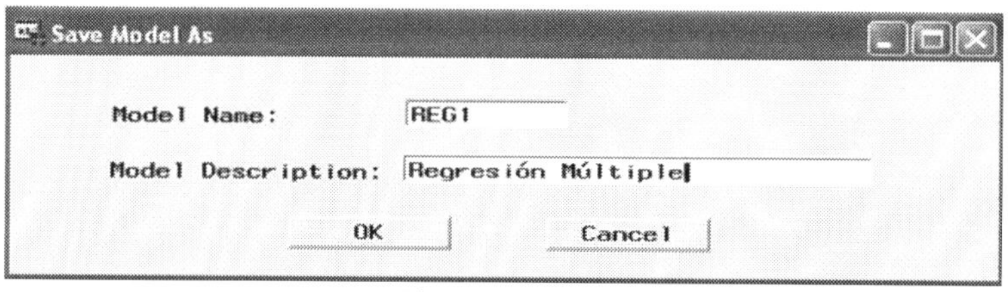

Figure 10-14

The regression by clicking with the right button of the mouse on the *Regression* node and choosing *Run* from the resulting pop-up menu (Figure 10-15) can also run. The figure below 10-16 whose *Yes* button allows you to see results (Figure 10-17).

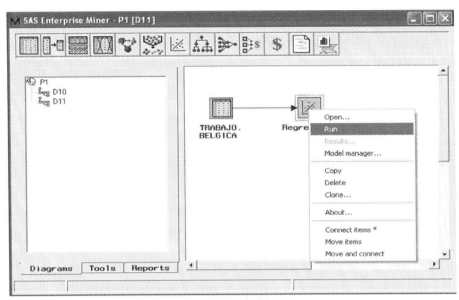

Figure 10-15

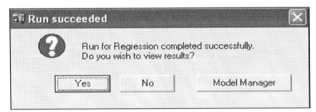

Figure 10-16

To **display the results in graphic form** , you can select the *Estimates* tab option *Effect T-scores* or importance of each regresor (Figure 10-17).

Another possibility is to select *Estimates* or size of the calculated coefficient (Figure 10-18).

Using the *Table* option, we can analyze the coefficients obtained for each regresor along with your statistic *T* of Student (Figure 10-19).

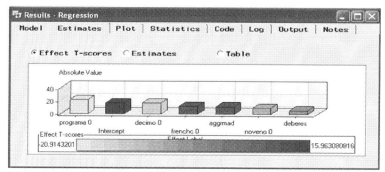

Figure 10-17

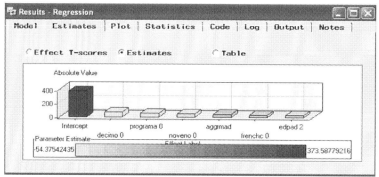

Figure 10-18

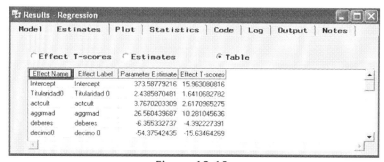

Figure 10-19

In the *Plot* window we can build different graphics between the variables and the estimated results (Figure 10-20).

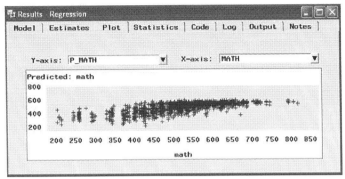

Figure 10-20

Some usual statistical adjustment of the executed model display in the window *Statistics* (Figure 10-21).

Fit Statistic	Label	Training
AIC	Akaike's Information Criterion	29701.193316
ASE	Average Squared Error	4901.6764782
AVERR	Average Error Function	4901.6764782
DFE	Degrees of Freedom for Error	3462
DFM	Model Degrees of Freedom	27
DFT	Total Degrees of Freedom	3489
DIV	Divisor for ASE	3489
ERR	Error Function	17101949.232
FPE	Final Prediction Error	4978.1324371

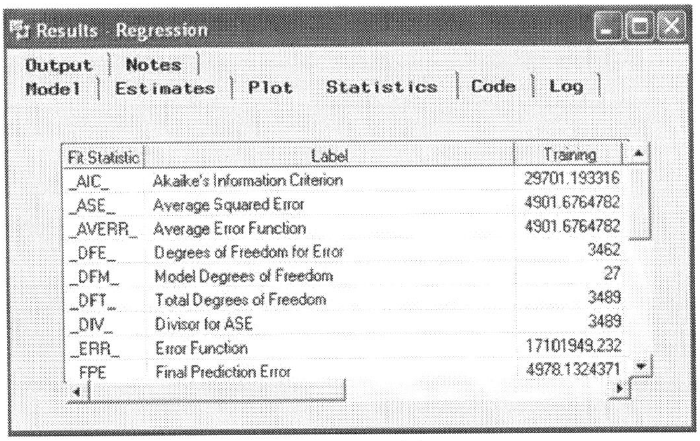

Figure 10-21

The *Code* window displays generated SAS code that allows you to run the analysis in the *Script Editor*.

Finally, of particular importance is the *Output*window. It shows all the results of the regression (Figure 10-22). This information includes the encoding of the nominal variables, descriptive statistics, analysis of variance or relevance of the model and coefficient of determination adjusted coefficient of determination and other statistical adjustment. Also includes estimates of the parameters with *p*-values and confidence (Figure 10-23) intervals.

Results - Regression

Model | Estimates | Plot | Statistics | Code | Log | Output | Notes

Summary Statistics for Interval Input Variables

Variable	Mean	Standard Deviation	Minimum	Maximum
actcult	9.930817	0.954110	8.720000	12.930000
aggrmad	4.604732	0.663290	2.000000	6.000000
deberes	9.936950	0.908977	7.650000	12.180000
ordenad	10.642448	7.541146	0.600000	59.000000
poscult	9.613838	0.986463	8.350000	11.150000
prof	11.449430	4.580730	2.270000	33.440000

Analysis of Variance

Source	DF	Sum of Squares	Mean Square	F Value	Pr>F
Model	26	16791963	645845	130.74	<.0001
Error	3462	17101949	4939.904458	.	.
Corrected Total	3488	33893912	.	.	.

Model Fitting Information

R-square	0.4954	Adj R-sq	0.4916
AIC	29701.1933	BIC	29703.6143
SBC	29867.4423	C(p)	27.0000

Figure 10-22

Results - Regression

Model | Estimates | Plot | Statistics | Code | Log | Output | Notes

Analysis of Parameter Estimates

Parameter		DF	Estimate	Standard Error	t Value	Pr>|t|	95% Confidence Intervals Lower	Upp
Intercept		1	373.6	23.4032	15.96	<.0001	327.7	419
actcult		1	3.7670	1.4394	2.62	0.0089	0.9459	6.58
aggrmad		1	26.5604	2.5834	10.28	<.0001	21.4970	31.62
deberes		1	-6.3553	1.4469	-4.39	<.0001	-9.1913	-3.51
decimo		1	-54.3754	3.4779	-15.63	<.0001	-61.1919	-47.55
edmad	1	1	-5.1482	7.6578	-0.67	0.5015	-20.1573	9.86
edmad	2	1	0.5627	4.4614	0.13	0.8996	-8.1815	9.30
edmad	3	1	-0.3062	3.4141	-0.09	0.9285	-6.9977	6.38
edmad	4	1	2.6655	4.0112	0.66	0.5064	-5.1963	10.52
edmad	5	1	1.5959	3.0400	0.52	0.5996	-4.3625	7.55
edpad	1	1	1.1240	8.0970	0.14	0.8896	-14.7459	16.99
edpad	2	1	-14.9532	4.6320	-3.23	0.0013	-24.0318	-5.87
edpad	3	1	4.9358	3.6190	1.36	0.1727	-2.1572	12.02
edpad	4	1	4.5454	4.2023	1.08	0.2795	-3.6910	12.78
edpad	5	1	7.6008	3.0679	2.48	0.0133	1.5878	13.61
familia		1	1.5242	1.4826	1.03	0.3040	-1.3815	4.43
frenchc		1	15.5749	1.4736	10.57	<.0001	12.6867	18.46
madjob		1	-1.0904	1.3279	-0.82	0.4116	-3.6931	1.51
nacemadre		1	-6.7677	1.9049	-3.55	0.0004	-10.5012	-3.03
noveno		1	-29.6289	3.7080	-7.99	<.0001	-36.8965	-22.36
ordenad		1	-0.4943	0.1908	-2.59	0.0096	-0.8682	-0.12

Figure 10-23

If you want to view or analyze the predictions and the obtained waste, these are available in the created file saved in the bookstore *EMDATA* and inside of this in the file *STRNHFST* (Figure 10-24).

VIEWTABLE: Scored Train:

	programa	repite	madjob	padjob	nacemadre	Titularidad	Warnings	Predicted math	Residual: math
1	1	0	1	1	1	1		559.52637919	0.9036208142
2	1	0	1	1	1	1		569.9228708	32.697129203
3	1	0	1	1	1	1		538.63763762	-25.23763762
4	1	0	1	1	1	1		570.87789484	-141.4178948
5	1	0	0	0	1	1		546.29092439	5.0590756148
6	1	0	0	1	1	1		568.12797625	-85.12797625
7	1	0	0	0	1	1		547.84503036	-1.685030359
8	1	0	0	1	1	1		553.66630233	160.37369767
9	1	0	1	1	1	1		577.0659721	-128.3959721
10	1	0	1	1	1	1		562.57588775	56.354112254
11	1	0	1	1	1	1		558.84071107	-57.36071107
12	1	0	0	0	1	1		558.62149589	99.208504108
13	1	0	1	1	1	1		585.6771188	5.6428811976

Figure 10-24

The parameters will be stored in the file that was designated in the regression node and the tab for this purpose output (Figure 10-25).

	Row Type	Row Name	Intercept	actcult	aggrmad	deberes	decimo 0	edmad 1	edmad 2
1	PARMS	math	373.58779216	3.7670203309	26.560439687	-6.355332737	-54.37542435	-5.148187506	0.5627388
2	T		15.963080816	2.6170965275	10.281045636	-4.392227391	-15.63464269	-0.672276178	0.1261342175
3	LCLPARMS		327.71828701	0.9458694486	21.496995069	-9.191302318	-61.19194555	-20.15729007	-8.181500464
4	UCLPARMS		419.45729732	6.5981712133	31.623884306	-3.519363156	-47.55890315	3.8609150534	9.3069780643

Figure 10-25

10.3 THE REGRESSION NODE: GENERAL LINEAR MODEL GLM

The different tabs display *Linear and Logistic Regression* of the node *Regression* (obtained when you double click on the *Regression* node) that is observed in Figure 10-26 options work with model linear General GLM which, as we all know, encompasses all categories of regression models including those relating to the analysis of variance and Covariance.

Name	Status	Model Role	Measurement	Type	Format	L
SCHOOL	use	input	interval	num	BEST12.	s
STUD	use	input	interval	num	BEST12.	s
MATH	use	target	interval	num	BEST12.	m
READ	don't use	target	interval	num	BEST12.	r
ORDENAD	use	input	interval	num	BEST12.	o
PROF	use	input	interval	num	BEST12.	p
EDMAD	use	input	ordinal	num	BEST12.	e
EDPAD	use	input	ordinal	num	BEST12.	e
ACTCULT	use	input	interval	num	BEST12	

Figure 10-26

Figure 10-26 tabs allow you to choose the data, variables, options, method, output and other features of the model.

The *Data* tab shows the data sources available that are predecessors to the node which can assign one of the usual roles:

- *Training*: to fit the model.

- *Validation*: to assess the model, or to control the process of regression by successive steps (*Stepwise*).

- *Test*: serves to evaluate the model.

- *Score*: used to predict values in a new database that does not contain the target. So in addition to assign to the data role *Score* in the sub-tab *Scored Data Set* from the *Output* tab will activate square *Score* (Figure 10-27).

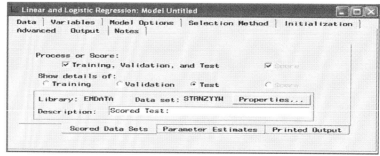

Figure 10-27

The *Variables* tab leads to the table of Figure 10-28, in which we can see the parameters such as *Status, Role Model* or *Measurement* already discussed in previous nodes. We can also change the status of a variable to make it or not considered in the analysis. This is particularly important if we have several *outputs* since you can only use one of them.

Name	Status	Model Role	Measurement	Type	Format	L
MATH	use	target	interval	num	BEST12.	a
READ	don't use	target	interval	num	BEST12.	r
ORDENAD	use	input	interval	num	BEST12.	o
PROF	use	input	interval	num	BEST12.	p
EDMAD	use	input	ordinal	num	BEST12.	e
EDPAD	use	input	ordinal	num	BEST12.	e
ACTCULT	use	input	interval	num	BEST12.	a
POSCULT	use	input	interval	num	BEST12.	p
DEREREES	use	input	interval	num	BEST12	d

Figure 10-28

One of the most interesting functions of this tab is the possibility to call the *Interaction Builder* function. When there is a valid theoretical model on all cases in the *Data Mining* process is interesting to investigate the possible influence of crossover effects of certain variables that we suspect they may have a relationship in the result in order to implement complete models of analysis of variance and covariance. To enable this option, select the icon to build interactions, which is third in the toolbar of the node ⁎⁎ . This will activate the options in Figure 10-29.

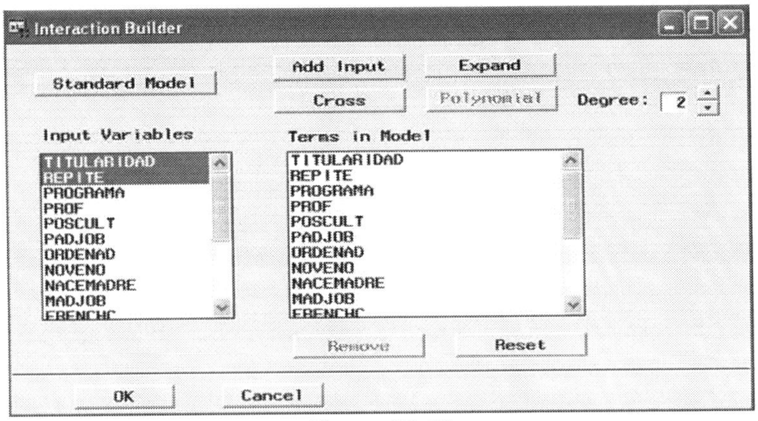

Figure 10-29

Standard Model: is the model by default which only considers each variable individually. To create interactions in the *Input Variables* window select the variables that you want to combine holding down *control*.

Cross: combines the selected variables.

Expand: carries out all the possible combinations 2 to 2, 3 to 3, etc., of the selected variables.

Polynomial: creates the squares, cubes, etc. of the selected variables.

To delete a variable once selected will click on *Remove*. To return to the model without interactions we may click on *Reset*.

In the *Model Options* tab we select the options of Figure 10-30.

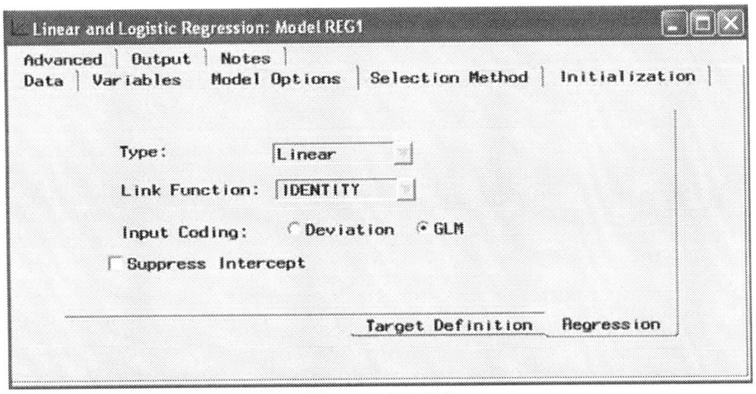

Figure 10-30

- *Regression type: linear or logistic*. By default if the continuous variable is dichotomous, activate the logistical option, while if it is continuous linear option will be activated.

- *The method of encoding a categorical input*:

  o **Deviation**: using this encoding the estimated parameter measures the difference between each level and the average throughout each level. Thus, the parameters for all levels are restricted to add zero. This encoding is also called *effects coding*. The following example shows how the three categories of the variable race can be encoded:

Code in deviations from the average		
Level	White race	Race black
White	1	0
Black	0	1
Hispanic	-1	-1

The parameter estimated for white and black measured the difference in the effect between being of that race and the average of all other levels (white, black, Hispanic). As the sum of the parameters of all levels is equal to zero, the estimate of the difference in the effects between the Hispanic category and the average of all levels by calculating the negative of the sum of the two parameter estimates value.

  o **GLM**: GLM General linear model, Wissler, where the estimated parameters measured the effect of the category with respect to a reference level which by default is the latest. This form of encoding also receives the name of *dummy*variables. The following table shows how a codification of this kind would be made.

Code in deviciones media		
Level	White race	Race black
White	1	0
Black	0	1
Hispanic	0	0

- **Supress Intercept**: allows you to delete the ordinate at the origin of the model.

The tab **Selection Method** (Figure 10-31) allows to build the model using different methods and criteria.

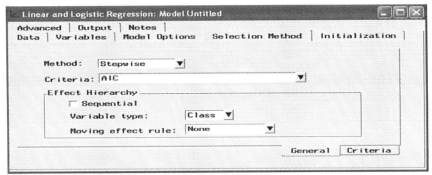

Figure 10-31

Then describes the fields of the figure 10-31 to the select *General* in the lower right of the figure.

■   **Method**: there are four options available.

○   **Backward**: part of a model with all the variables and effects that will eliminate those not significant until the exit criteria any variables.

○   **Forward**: part of a model without any variable and consistently add those more significant effects until any variables meet the entry criteria.

○   **Stepwise:** part of a model without any variables and systematically adds and deletes variables until the specified input and output criteria are met.

○   **None:** (default): the analyst defines variables that will be introduced in the model.

The choice of a method by successive steps involves selection of the criteria of input and output variables. To do this select the *Criteria* from the bottom right of the Figura.14-31. The figure is obtained 10-32.

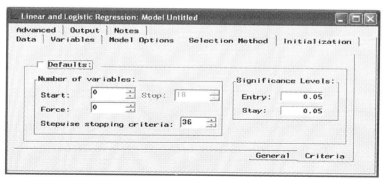

Figure 10-32

By default, the significance level is set at 95%. The choice *Number of variables* the number of variables can be varied to begin the method of successive steps (*Start*), the number of stop (*Stop*) or force that there is a minimum number of variables (*Force*). In the *Stepwise* option you can specify a number of maximum steps of selecting variables.

■   *Criteria:* allows you to choose the criteria for the selection of the model. The node has the following options.

o   *AIC(Completo Akaike Information Criterion):* the Akaike information criterion penalizes the number of parameters of the model.

o   *SBC(Completo Schwarz Bayesian Criterion):* Schwarz Bayesian criterion penalizes the number of parameters of the model. Choose the model with the value of smaller SBC.

o   *BIC(Bayes' Information Criterion):* Bayesian information criterion. It penalizes the number of parameters of the model. Choose the model with the value of smaller BIC.

o   *Validation Error:* choose the model with the lowest error in the validation sample. For logistic regression models the error is the negative value of the *loglikelihood*. In multiple regression error is the sum of squared errors.

o   *Validation Misclassification:* choose the model with the lowest classification error rate.

○ ***Cross- Validation Error:*** by this measure is chosen that model that has validation error in the matrix of cross-validation of the training data. In logistic regression error is the negative of the loglikelihood. For linear regressions error is the sum of squared errors.

○ ***Cross Validation Misclassification:*** choose the model with the error rate of lower classification in the matrix of cross-validation of the training data.

○ ***Profit/Loss****:* criterion by default if you define two or more decisions in the matrix of losses. The node choose the model that the error maximizes or minimizes the loss in cases of the validation sample. To use this approach, it is necessary to define an array of loss or profits for the goal. These values set the odds of belonging a priori that are specified.

○ ***Cross Validation Profit/Loss:*** this criterion to choose the model that maximizes benefits matrix or minimizes the matrix of losses in the matrix of cross-validation of the training data.

○ ***None:*** the final model will be produced according to the method of selection chosen.

■ ***Effect Hierarchy:*** controls if the model includes values crossed between two variables also include variables or main effects.

○ ***Sequential:*** force the sequential entry of hierarchical effects. I.e. first would enter the individual effects, then the Crusaders and squares and so on. Thus it is prevented that a model has effects of high grades while at the same time they are the individual effects.

■ ***Variable Type:*** determines if only the class variables or also the variables of interval or continuous subject hierarchy option.

■ ***Moving Effect Rule:*** determines if the hierarchy is maintained if all the individual and multiple effects come out and enter the model at the same time. There are two options:

○ ***Single:*** this option can only enter or leave an element model at the same time of the subjects to the hierarchy. The first step would be selected only the variable A or B. Then you could enter the second main effect. If both effects are maintained in the model as significant, could then enter A * B. B should be deleted before you can delete the effect or A * B.

o   **Multiple:** this option more of one effect can come in or out of the model at the same time.

o   **None** (default): the hierarchy of effects is not maintained and any effect can enter or exit at any time.

On the tab (Figure 10-33) **Initialization** the initialization values are established.

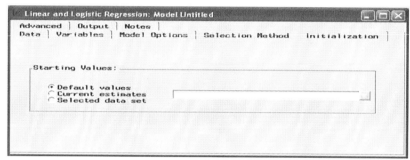

Figure 10-33

The initialization tab allows you to set the following values of start (*Starting Values*):

Default values: default values are assigned 0 both the slopes and the ordinate at the origin. These are the values for maximum likelihood estimates for the model with only a constant.

Current estimates: the estimated values of a previous regression can be used.

Selected data set: Specifies a file that contains the initial values to estimate the parameters. This file must be compatible with the data used or the analysis may not be performed correctly. Given that the node checks whether or not the data are compatible is important to make sure that is.

The tab **Advanced** (Figure 10-34) to specify the optimization algorithm, the time of maximum use of microprocessor computer and the criteria of convergence for the regression.

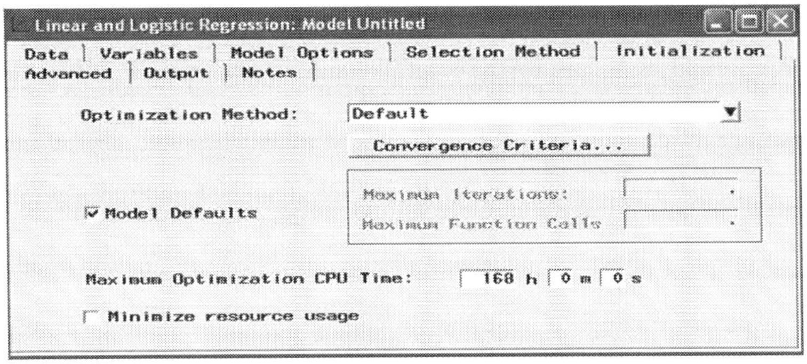

Figure 10-34

The following table provides a description of the algorithms of nonlinear optimization (*Optimization Method*), maximum number of iterations allowed (*Maximum Iterations*), and the maximum number of calls to the function (*Maximun Function Calls*).

Optimization methods available in the regression node.		
Optimization algorithm	*Number of maximum iterations*	*Nº Max. Calls to the function*
Conjugate Gradient	400	1000
Double Dogleg	200	500
Newton-Raphson with Line Search	50	125
Newton-Raphson with Ridging	50	125
Quasi-Newton	200	500
Trust-Region	50	125

In principle the algorithm should be chosen according to the type of *Data Mining* that we are carrying out problem. The type is as follows:

▪ *Small and medium-sized problems*: for issues of up to 40 parameters, where the Hessian is easy to calculate, the best methods are *Trust-Region, Newton-Raphson with line Search* and *Newton-Raphson Ridging with*.

▪ *Medium-sized problems*: for issues where the number of parameters is of about 400, the objective function and gradient are much easier to calculate than the Hessian. Therefore, *Double-Dogleg* and *Quasi-Newton* methods require more iterations than previous methods but its calculation is much faster.

- **Big problems**: we will consider that a problem with more than 400 parameters is large. In these cases *the Conjugate Gradient algorithm* is the most appropriate since this method is optimal in problems where it is necessary to make a rough calculation of the Hessian.

The default method depends on the number of parameters. If it is equal or less than 40, the method chosen is *Newton-Raphson Ridging with*. Between 41 and 400, the default method is the *Quasi-Newton,* while that if the number of parameters is greater than 400 regression node automatically selects the *Conjugate Gradient*method.

While each method presents to optimize numbers seen in the above table, these can be changed in the following way. Firstly, it is necessary to deselect the *Model Defaults*dialog box. Then the values that we consider to be appropriate are introduced. By default the time of optimization is set to 168 hours, value that we can change in the field specified for this task. In the regression by successive steps optimization time restarts whenever a model fits.

A list of the criteria of convergence (Figure 10-35) can be obtained by clicking on the button *Convergence Criteria* of the figure 10-34.

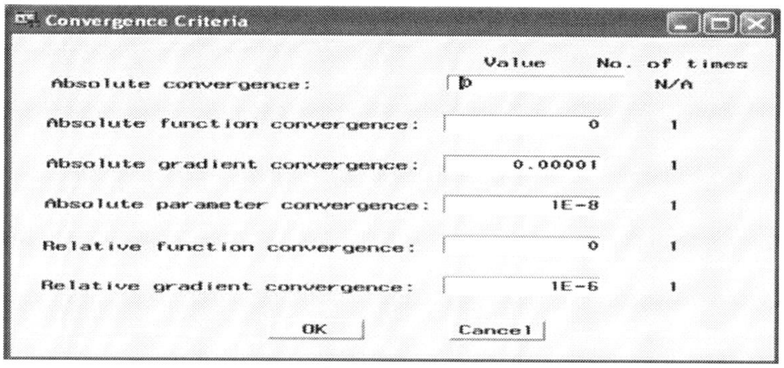

Figure 10-35

These defaults can be changed by entering new values in the corresponding cell.

The *Output* tab leads to a window in which, in addition to the usual options, we have one sub-tab called *Printed Output* in which you can select outputs which are not shown by default (Figure 10-36).

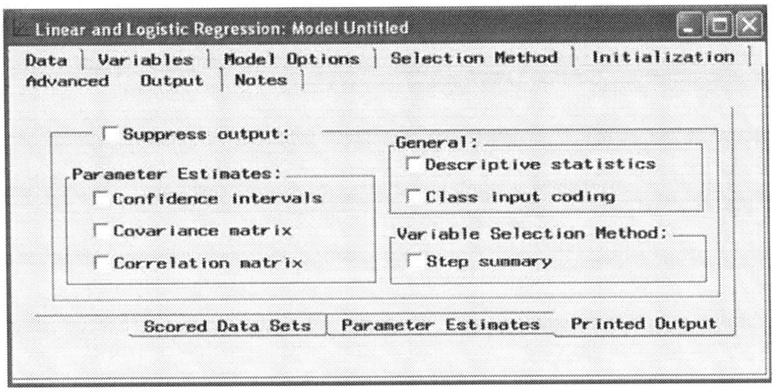

Figure 10-36

Once launched regression will obtain the *results window* of Figure 10-37 which is select the *Model* tab which shows all the characteristics of the executed model. The *Estimates* tab we can see both graphic and numerical value of the parameter estimates. The *Plot* window allows you to build different graphics between the variables and the estimated results.

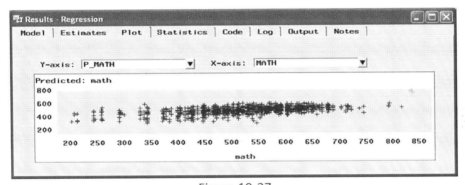

Figure 10-37

The *Statistics* (Figure 10-38) window shows the descriptive statistics of the stop and optimization criteria.

| Model | Estimates | Plot | Statistics | Code | Log | Output | Notes |

Fit Statistic	Label	Training	Validation	Test
AIC	Akaike's Information Criterion	12325.590377		
ASE	Average Squared Error	6801.6565596	7454.0989298	7310.1017717
AVERR	Average Error Function	6801.6565596	7454.0989298	7310.1017717
DFE	Degrees of Freedom for Error	1393		
DFM	Model Degrees of Freedom	3		
DFT	Total Degrees of Freedom	1396		
DIV	Divisor for ASE	1396	1047	1046
ERR	Error Function	9495112.5573	7804441.5795	7646366.4532
FPE	Final Prediction Error	6830.9529985		
MAX	Maximum Absolute Error	315.76557312	301.69511627	331.264445
MSE	Mean Square Error	6816.3047791	7454.0989298	7310.1017717
NOBS	Sum of Frequencies	1396	1047	1046
_NW_	Number of Estimate Weights	3		
RASE	Root Average Sum of Squares	82.472156269	86.337123706	85.499133163
RFPE	Root Final Prediction Error	82.649579542		
RMSE	Root Mean Squared Error	82.560915566	86.337123706	85.499133163
SBC	Schwarz's Bayesian Criterion	12341.314475		
SSE	Sum of Squared Errors	9495112.5573	7804441.5795	7646366.4532
SUMW	Sum of Case Weights Times Freq	1396	1047	1046

Figure 10-38

The *Output* (Figure 10-39) window shows the results obtained in the analysis.

| Model | Estimates | Plot | Statistics | Code | Log | Output | Notes |

```
                    Analysis of Variance
                         Sum of          Mean
               DF        Squares         Square      F Value      Pr >F

                2        3594201        1797101       263.65      <.0001
             1393        9495113     6816.304779        .           .
ed Total     1395       13089314          .            .           .

                   Model Fitting Information
             R-square       0.2746       Adj R-sq        0.2735
             AIC         12325.5904      BIC          12325.1403
             SBC         12341.3145      C(p)           805.4919

                   The SAS System       10:38 Monday, February 28, 2005
                   The DMREG Procedure

                 Type III Analysis of Effects
ect                         DF       Type III SS      F Value     Pr > F

cult                         1      129851.6363       19.0502     <.0001
rmad                         1     2919775.118       428.3516     <.0001

                 Analysis of Parameter Estimates
                                                             95% Confidence
                                                                Intervals
                         Standard
               DF  Estimate    Error    t Value  Pr>|t|     Lower     Upper

                1   97.7312   25.2110    3.88    0.0001    48.3186    147.1
                1   10.6062    2.4300    4.36    <.0001     5.8435   15.3690
                1   70.1082    3.3874   20.70    <.0001    63.4690   76.7474
```

Figure 10-39

The node of regression, as well as *Ensemble* (combination of models), *Tree* (decision trees), *Neural Networks* (neural networks) and *User Defined Model* (user-defined model) nodes, includes a utility called **Model Manager**, in which you can store and access different models to convenience. This utility allows to obtain the same results as the node of valuation, so it will be the detail of their options in discussion of this node (*Assessment node*). To open the *Model Manager* , there are two options:

- If the node is closed, click regression node and select *Model Manager*.

- If the node is open must be selected in the main menu *Tools* → *Model Manager*.

The input of the *Model Manager* display presents several tabs, which are described below.

Model Manager opens the models tab **Models** (Figure 10-40) that shows the created models. Each model displays information about when the model was created and generated statistics on training, validation, and test data.

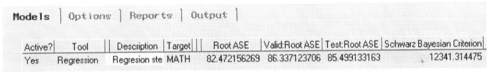

Figure 10-40

The **Options** tab is used to select partition of data that we will use to assess the model, to specify whether the data will be saved after the valuation and to indicate if we may on the DataSet or a sample assessment (Figure 10-41).

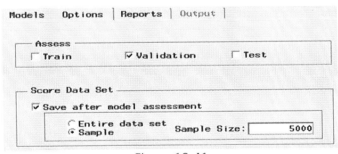

Figure 10-41

The **Reports** tab displays the current rating for the selected model (Figure 10-42).

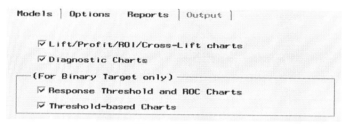

Figure 10-42

To view the charts (Figure 10-43) is necessary to use the *Tools* in the main menu option and choose one of the following options depending on the data: *Lift Chart, Response, Threshold, ROC Chart.*

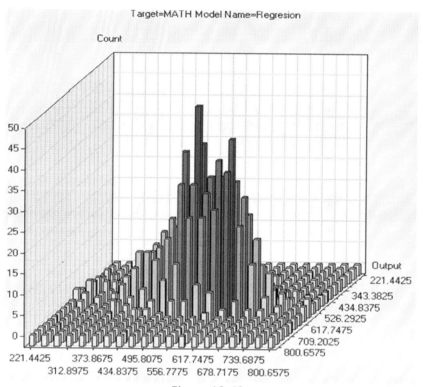

Figure 10-43

The **Output** tab only appears active node assessment to allow the results to other nodes.

10.4 THE REGRESSION NODE: PROBIT AND LOGIT DISCRETE CHOICE MODELS

We will then carry out an exercise of logistic regression and the execution with the regression node. We will use the data file *credits* where we'll look at the explanatory variables that influence a credit whether or not paid.

Firstly, we will connect the node that contains the data with regression (Figure 10-44).

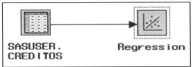

Figure 10-44

Similarly to the previous example, the *Variables* tab activate the explanatory variables or inputs by assigning them a *Status* → *use* (Figure 10-45).

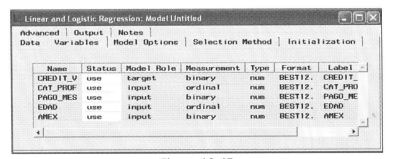

Figure 10-45

Model Options (Figure 10-46) tab select the option *Logistic* and in this case we will use as a function of transformation the logistic function (LOGIT). Note You can also choose the option PROBIT.

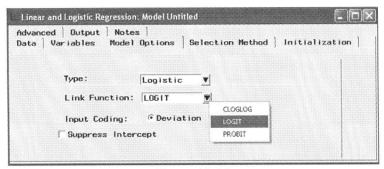

Figure 10-46

Once selected the remaining options, as in the previous example, (default settings) the model name and proceed to its implementation (Figure 10-47).

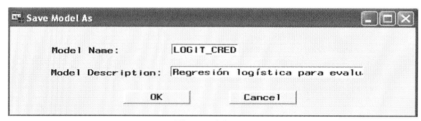

Figure 10-47

The results of the logistic regression model can be manipulated in a way analogous to the case of multiple regression. However, unlike the previous case, the dependent variable is in this dichotomous occasion. Therefore, that the PLOT tab now shows the confusion matrix in the form of histograms in three dimensions (Figure 10-48).

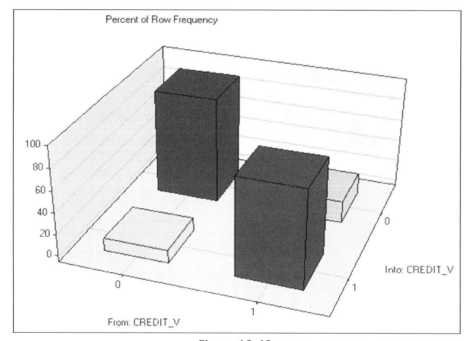

Figure 10-48

The *Output* tab displays all of the detail of the logistic regression results. A small part of these is shown as example below (Figure 10-49).

```
                         The SAS System              10:40 Monday, May 30, 200
                         The DMREG Procedure

                   Testing Global Null Hypothesis BETA=0

                                  Intercept
                       Intercept     and
        Criterion        Only     Covariates    Chi-Square for Covariates

        -2 LOG L        447.250     178.829      268.420 with 8 DF (p<.0001)

                       Type III Analysis of Effects

                                        Wald          Pr >
                   Effect      DF    Chi-Square    Chi-Square

                   AMEX         1       0.6579       0.4173
                   CAT_PROF     4       8.1145       0.0875
                   EDAD         2      35.2061       <.0001
                   PAGO_MES     1      39.7557       <.0001

                   Analysis of Maximum Likelihood Estimates

                                   Standard     Wald         Pr >
   Parameter       DF   Estimate    Error    Chi-square   Chi-square   exp(Est)

   Intercept        1     1.7727    0.5654       9.83       0.0017      5.887
   AMEX       0     1     0.1608    0.1982       0.66       0.4173      1.174
   CAT_PROF   1     1     2.7304    1.0681       6.53       0.0106     15.340
   CAT_PROF   2     1    -0.8562    0.5363       2.55       0.1104      0.425
   CAT_PROF   3     1    -0.2442    0.5360       0.21       0.6486      0.783
   CAT_PROF   4     1    -1.3739    0.8808       2.43       0.1188      0.253
   EDAD       1     1    -2.4410    0.4365      31.27       <.0001      0.087
   EDAD       2     1     0.0338    0.4789       0.00       0.3437      1.034
   PAGO_MES   1     1    -1.6550    0.2625      39.76       <.0001      0.191
```

Figure 10-49

If you want to view or analyze the predictions of the estimated probabilities of group membership and obtained waste, these are available in the created file saved in the *EMDATA* library and from within this file *Strnqz*29 (Figure 10-50).

Figure 10-50

PREDICTIVE AND DESCRIPTIVE TECHNIQUES OF CLASSIFICATION. DECISION TREES AND CLUSTER ANALYSIS

11.1 EL CLUSTER ANALYSIS AS TECHNICAL DESCRIPTIVE CLASSIFICATION

Analysis*cluster*is a technique of*Data Mining*of automatic classification of data.Its essential purpose is to reveal data (cases or variables) for its efficient grouping concentrations in*clusters*(or conglomerates) according to homogeneity.Grouping can be done for both cases and variables, qualitative or quantitative variables can be used. Groups of cases or variables are made based on the proximity or distance of each other, so it is essential to the proper use of the concept of distance.It is essential that the elements within a *cluster* are homogeneous and the different possible of the contained in other *cluster*s.

Analysis*cluster*is therefore a technique of classification, also known with the name of*numerical taxonomy*. Other names assigned to the same concept are analysis of *conglomerates, typological analysis, automatic classification* and others. The number of *cluster* is not known in advance and the groups are created according to the nature of the data. It is therefore a technique of classification *post hoc*.We could define the analysis *cluster* as a statistical method multivariate of automatic classification dealing from a table of data (casos-variables), place them into homogeneous groups, clusters or *clusters*, not known in advance but suggested by the very essence of the data, so that individuals that may be considered similar to be assigned to a same *cluster*, while different individuals (dissimilar) are located in *clusters* different. The essential difference with discriminant analysis is that in this last is necessary previously to specify groups on a target path (*ad hoc*classification technique), oblivious to the measurement of the variables in the sample cases.

The analysis *cluster* defines groups as diverse as possible based on the data without prior specification of the above groups (*post-hoc*classification technique). If the variables of agglomeration are on very different scales, it will be necessary to standardize the variables previously, or at least work with deviations from the average. It is necessary to also observe the atypical and missing values because hierarchical methods do not have solution with missing values and outliers deform distances and produce *clusters* unit. It is also harmful to the analysis *cluster* the presence of correlated variables, hence the importance of the preliminary analysis of multicollinearity. If necessary prior factorial analysis and post-above crowd factor scores. Analysis solution *cluster* does not have to be unique, but must not be contradictory solutions by different methods. The number of observations in each *cluster* should be relevant, since otherwise there may be outliers that blurring the construction of *clusters*. Conglomerates must have conceptual meaning and do not vary much by varying the sample or the agglomeration method. The final groups will be as different as they allow the data. Other analyses can be performed with these groups: descriptive, logistic regression, discriminant, difference...

11.2 TECHNIQUES IN THE CLUSTER ANALYSIS

We already know that the cluster analysis or *cluster* analysis is a set of methods and statistical techniques that allow to describe and recognize different groups underlying a dataset, i.e., allow sorting, or split into more or less homogeneous groups, a group of individuals who are defined by different variables. The main objective of the cluster analysis consists, therefore, get one or more partitions of a set of individuals on the basis of certain characteristics of the same. These features will be defined by scores that each of them has in relation to different variables.

Thus, one may say that two individuals are similar if they belong to the same class, group, cluster or *cluster*. If this goal is achieved, it will have to all individuals that are contained in the same conglomerate resemble each other, and will be different from the individuals who belong to another conglomerate. Therefore, members of a conglomerate have common characteristics that differentiate them from other cluster members. These features must, by the definition of the objective to achieve, be generic, and it is clear that hardly a single property can define a conglomerate.

The method to run a cluster analysis starts with the selection of the individuals under study, including in some cases their coding from the variables or characters that define them and their adequate transformation to undergo analysis if necessary (classification of variables, deviations from the average, etc.). Then determines the differences array defining gaps, similarities or differences of individuals. Once determined the differences of individuals, is to run the algorithm that will form the different groupings or clusters of individuals. Already determined the classification, the next step is to get a graphical representation of the clusters obtained, so that the results achieved are viewable. This process is carried out using a dendrogram. Achieved the purpose of the classification, the last phase to carry out is the interpretation of the results obtained.

The different methods of cluster analysis arise from the different ways to carry out the grouping of individuals, i.e., depending on the algorithm that is used to carry out the grouping of individuals or groups of individuals, are obtained with different methods of cluster analysis. A classification of methods of cluster analysis based on the algorithms of grouping of individuals could be the following:

- *Aglomerativos-Divisivos methods*: a method is Agglomerative if it considers as many groups as individuals and going on merging the two groups more similar, until you reach a certain ratings; While a method is divisive if part of a single group comprising all individuals, so that at each stage you are separating individuals from the groups stated above, forming thus new groups.

- *Hierarchical methods - hierarchical non*: a method is hierarchical if it consists of a sequence of $g+1$ *clusters*: $G_0,...,G_g$ where G_0 is disjoint from all individuals and Gpartition$_g$ is the partition set. The number of parties from each of the partitions decreases gradually, which makes these increasingly larger and less homogeneous. On the contrary, a method says non-hierarchical when homogeneous groups form without establishing relations of order or hierarchical among such groups.

- *Solapados-Exclusivos methods*: a method is overlapping if it supports that an individual can belong to two groups simultaneously in any of the stages of classification, while it is exclusive if any individual can simultaneously belong to two groups on the same stage.

- *Secuenciales-simultaneos* method: a method is sequential if each group applies the same algorithm recursively, while simultaneous methods are those in which the classification is achieved by a simple and not repeated operation on individuals.

- *Monoteticos-politeticos methods*: a method is said to be monotetico if it is based on a unique feature of the objects to be classified; While it is politetico if it relies on several features of them, without requiring that all objects possess them, even if the sufficient to be able to justify the analogy between members of the same class.

- *Directos-Iterativos methods*: a method is direct if you are using algorithms that once assigned an individual to a group already it is not removed, while the iterative methods to correct previous assignments returning to check on subsequent iterations if the assignment of an individual to a conglomerate is optimal, engaged in a new grouping of individuals if necessary.

- *Methods weighted weighted-No*: not weighted methods are those that establish the same weight to all the characteristics of the individuals to be classified; While the weighted make fall greater weight on certain characteristics.

- *Adaptive methods - Adaptive No*: non-adaptive methods are those for which the algorithm used is directed toward a solution in which the method of formation of conglomerates is fixed and is default, while the Adaptive (least used) are those who in some way learn during the process of formation of groups and modify the optimization criterion or the measure of similarity to use.

11.3 CLUSTERS HIERARCHICAL, SEQUENTIAL, AGGLOMERATE AND EXCLUSIVE (S.A.H.N)

The *methods of cluster analysis* that are most used are those who are at the same time sequential, agglomerate, hierarchical and exclusive, and receiving an acronym, in English-language, S.A.H.N. (*Sequential, Agglomerative Hierarchic and Nonoverlaping*). In all *methods of type S.A.H.N.* to follow two fundamental steps in the process of elaboration of the conglomerates. The first is that the coefficients of similarity or dissimilarity between the new conglomerates established and potential candidates to be admitted is recalculated at each stage, and the other is the criterion for admission of new members to an already established conglomerate. Among the different methods of cluster analysis of type S.A.H.N. we have the following:

- Method union simple (*Single Linkage Clustering*), environment or nearest neighbor (*Nearest Neighbour*) or minimum (*Minimum Method*) method

- Method of the maximum distance or maximum method (*Complete Linkage Clustering, Furthest Neighbour* or *Maximum Method*)

- Unweighted average or average distance method (*Weighted Pair Groups Method Using Arithmetic Averages* WPGMW)

- Method of weighted average or distance weighted average (*Unweighted Pair Groups Method Using Arithmetic Averages or Group Average* UPGMA)

- Method of the median or middle distance (*Weighted Pair Group Centroid Method* WPGMC)

- The centroid or method of the prototype distance (*Unweighted Pair Group Method Centroid* UPGMC)

- Ward or minimum variance method

11.4 THE DENDROGRAM IN THE CLUSTER ANALYSIS HIERARCHICAL

It is common in research the need to classify data into groups with tree structure of dependence, according to different levels of hierarchy. Based on so many early groups as individuals are studied, it's get successive including groups in such a way that they be progressively integrated in *clusters* which, in turn, will join each other in a top-level forming larger groups which will later meet up to the final *cluster* that contains all analyzed cases. The graphic representation of these stages of formation of groups, as an inverted tree, is called a *dendrogram* and is represented below:

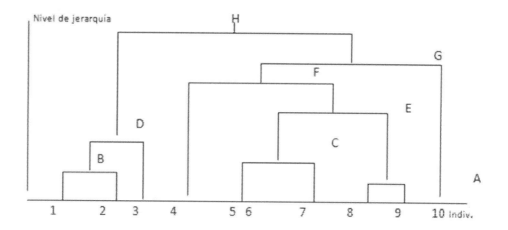

The figure, which corresponds to a study of individuals, demonstrates how the 8 and 9 are grouped into a first *cluster* (A). In a next higher level 1 and 2 individuals come together (*cluster* B); and then the 5, 6, and 7 (C). A next step includes the 3 individual *cluster* B (D); and so on until all of them are structured to achieve, at the highest level, the total *cluster* (H) which brings together the 10 cases.

11.5 CLUSTER ANALYSIS NON- HIERARCHICAL

The classification of all cases of a data table in separate groups that set up the own analysis provides no hierarchical *clusters* . This name alludes to the non-existence of a vertical structure of dependence among the groups formed, and therefore these do not arise at different levels of hierarchy. Analysis requires that the researcher set in advance the number of *clusters* you want to group your data. How it can there be a defined number of groups or, if it exists, usually not is known, the test should be repeated with different number in order to probe the classification that best fits the purpose of the problem, or the clearer interpretation.

Non-hierarchical methods, also known as *partitivos methods* or optimization, since, as we have seen, they are intended to make a single partition of individuals in *K* group. This means that the investigator must specify a priori groups which should be formed. This is, possibly, the main difference with regard to the hierarchical methods. The assignment of individuals to groups is made through a process that optimizes the selection criterion. Another difference is that these methods work with the original data matrix and do not require conversion into an array of nearby. Pedret gathers non-hierarchical methods in the following four families: *remapping, density, direct search and miniaturization.*

The *reallocation methods* allow an individual assigned to a group at a particular step in the process to be reassigned to another group in a later step if this optimizes the selection criterion. The process ends when there are no individuals whose remapping allows to optimize the result that has been achieved. Some of the best-known algorithms within these methods are MeQueen (1967), the *Quick Cluster Analysis K-means (or plots) method* and the *method ofForgy*, which are often grouped under the name of *centroids and centers of gravity methods*. On the other hand is the *method of thedynamic clouds*, due to Diday.

The *methods of the density* presented a typological approach and a probabilistic approach. In the first approach, groups are looking for areas in which a higher concentration of individuals is given. Among the best-known algorithms within these methods are *Wishart modal analysismethod of Taxmap of Carmichael and Sneath*and *Fortin method*. In the second approach, is based on the postulate that the variables follow a law of probability according to which parameters vary from one group to another. It tries to find the individuals who belong to the same distribution. The *method of combination of Wolf*stands out in this approach.

Direct methods allow to classify individuals and variables simultaneously. The grouped entities, are no longer individuals or variables, but are observations, i.e., the crosses that configured the data matrix.

Miniaturization methods, such as the type Q factor analysis, related analysis *cluster*. This method consists of search factors in space of individuals, with each factor to a group. The interpretation of the groups can be complex, given that each individual may correspond to several different factors.

It is very intuitive to assume that a correct classification should be one in which dispersion within each group is the smallest. This condition is called *variance criteria* and leads to select a configuration where the sum of the variances within each group (residual variance) is minimal.
We have proposed various non-hierarchical classification algorithms, based on progressively minimize this variance, which differ in the choice of temporary *clusters* you need the start of the process and the method of assignment of individuals to groups. The two most commonly used are described here.

The *algorithm of the H-medias* part of a first arbitrary setting of groups with their corresponding average, choosing a first individual of each boot and then assigning each case to the group whose average is closer. Once all cases have been located, calculates again the means or centroids, and you take them rather than the first individuals as a better approximation of the same, repeating the process while the residual variance will decline. The boot partition defines the number of *cluster*who, logically, can decrease if no case is assigned to any of them.

The *algorithm of the plots*,the most important from the conceptual and practical points of view part also some arbitrary mean and, through successive tests, contrasts the effect that has the assignment of each of the cases to each of the groups on the residual variance. The minimum value of variance determines a configuration of new groups with their respective averages. All cases are assigned again to these new centroids in a process that is repeated until no transfer can already reduce the residual variance; or other criteria of stop is reached: a limited number of iteration steps or, simply, the difference between the centroids of the two consecutive steps is less than a preset value. The procedure configures the groups, at the same time, maximizing the distance between their centers of gravity. As the total variance is fixed, minimize the residual makes maximum the factorial or intergroups. And since that minimize the residual variance is equivalent to ensure that there is a minimum for the sum of squared distances from the cases to the middle of the *cluster* that will be assigned, is this the squared Euclidean distance used by the method.

As cases are tested sequentially to see their individual influence, the calculation may be affected by the order in the table; Despite what the algorithm that best results it produces. Other variants to this method are very similar classifications.

As any other non-hierarchical classification method, provides a final solution for the number of*clusters*chosen, which will arrive with less number of iterations as closer are "averages" boot of that are going to be finally obtained. The automatic programs are usually selected these first values, as many as groups is intended to form, among the most separate points cloud.

Not hierarchical *clusters* are suitable for large tables of data, and are also useful for the detection of atypical cases: If you select a large number of groups, exceeding the desired previously, those containing a very small number of individuals would serve to detect extreme cases that could distort settings.

It is advisable to perform the final analysis without them, already with the desired number of groups then, optionally, assign the atypical to the appropriate *cluster* that will have been formed without distorting influence. A major problem that the investigator has to classify your data into groups is, as he has been said, the choice of an appropriate number of *clusters*. Since it will always be convenient to perform several scores, the selection of the most appropriate to the phenomenon that is studied should be based on criteria both mathematical and interpretability. Among the former, we have defined numerous indicators of suitability as the cubic of *clusters* criterion and the Pseudo F are described in the example of practical application. Intelligent use of these criteria, combined with the practical interpretability of the groups, is the art of the decision in multivariate data classification.

Mathematically, a not hierarchical classification method is to form a preset number *K* of homogeneous, mutually exclusive classes, but with maximum divergence between classes. The *K* classes or *clusters* form a single partition (*clustering*) and are not hierarchically organized or interrelated. Hierarchical grouping or classification has a mathematical structure that is less accurate than the hierarchical classification. Thenumber of existing methods has grown excessively in recent years and some problems arising from its use have not yet been resolved.

Suppose that *N* is the number of subjects to be classified as *K* groups, with respect to *n* variables $X_1,..., X_n$. Sean W, B and T arrays of dispersion within groups, between groups and total respectively. As T = B + W and T does not depend on the manner in which have been grouped subjects, a reasonable criterion of classification consists in building *K* groups in such a way that B either maximum or minimum, W following any proper criteria. Some of these criteria are:

a) Minimize *trace (W)*
b) Minimize*Determinate (W)*
c) Minimize*Det (W) /Det (T)*
d) Maximize *Traza(W⁻¹B)*
e) Minimize $\sum_{i=1}^{K}\sum_{h=1}^{N_i}(X_{ih} - \overline{X}_i)'S_i^{-1}(X_{ih} - \overline{X}_i)$

(Criteria a) and b) are justified because they try to minimize the magnitude of the W matrix. The criterion e) is called *Wilks criteria* and is equivalent to b) because *det (T)* is constant. (D) is called *Hottelling criterion* and criterion e) represents the sum of each subject Mahalanobis distances to the centroid of the group to which it is assigned.

As the number of ways of grouping subject *Nk* groups is in the order of $k^N*k!$, once chosen optimisation criterion, it is necessary to follow a suitable classification algorithmto avoid such a large number of groupings.

The ISODATA method, introduced by Ball and Hall (1967), is one of the best known. Essentially it consists in starting from K classes (for example randomly built) and reassign a subject of a class in a class ij if the chosen optimisation criterion is improved. For mathematical track of these methods see Gnanadesikan (1977) and Squire (1977).

11.6 THE DECISION TREES FOR CLASSIFICATION

This section continues to Picon, Varela and Levy (2004) exhibition richness and its excellent work of overview. Decision trees, also called classification trees, have in fact resemble the dendrograms for cluster analysis hierarchical, but they are constructed and interpreted completely differently. It is a series of very flexible methods, which can handle a large number of variables and complicated interactions between them, and whose results are easily interpretable to anyone. Classification trees are made sequential data set partitions to maximize the differences of the dependent variable or criterion base (Hair, Anderson, Tatham & Black, 1999, p. 718;)Roman and Levy, 2003); lead therefore observations division into groups that differ with respect to a variable of interest. These methods are further characterized by developing a process of division of arborescent form. Using different indices and statistical procedures determines the more discriminant division between the selected criteria; i.e. one that allows better differentiate groups of the base criterion, thus obtaining the first segmentation. Then new segmentation of each of the resulting segments are made, and so on until the process terminates with any statistical standard preset or voluntarily interrupted at any time by the researcher. In addition, descriptors criteria do not have to appear in the same order for all segments, and a criterion may appear more than once for a same segment. At the end, enumerating the criteria by which has reached a given segment are obtained profile of the same.

For example, suppose we want to know what passengers on the Titanic were more likely to survive its collapse, and what characteristics were associated with the shipwreck survival. In this case, the variable of interest (VD) is the degree of survival. We could then divide the passengers in groups of age, sex and class in which traveled and seen the proportion of survivors of each group.

An arborescent procedure automatically selects the homogeneous groups with the biggest difference in the proportion of survivors among them; in this case, the sex (men and women). The next step is to subdivide each of the groups on the basis of another feature, resulting that the men are divided in adults and children, while women are divided into groups based on the class in which travel by boat. Use different predictors in every level of the process of division is a simple and elegant way to handle interactions that often complicate the traditional linear models in excess. When the process of subdivision has been completed, the result is a set of rules that can be easily displayed through a tree. For example: If a passenger of the Titanic is male and is an adult, then has a chance to survive the 20 per cent. In addition, the proportion of survival in each of the subsections can be used for predictive purposes to predict the degree of survival of the members of that group. A tree of classification of the degree of survival of the passengers of the Titanic could be that seen in Figure 11-1.

Figure 11-1

11.7 CHARACTERISTICS OF DECISION TREES

The most important features in the work with decision trees are the specification of criteria to minimize costs, the selection of the method of division and the choice of the stretch of suitable tree or the overfitting problem.

As to the ***specification of the criteria to minimize costs***, any tree analysis aims to classify or predicted with the minimum cost. In the majority of situations, the costs refer simply to the proportion of cases poorly classified. However, is not always true, since at least two other factors may also influence the final costs of a classification: a priori probabilities and a misclassification costs.

The *a priori probabilities*, also known as weights of class, specify the probability, without having any prior knowledge of the values of the predoctores, a case that falls in each of the classes of the dependent variable. For example, an educational study, shows that in general in secondary education there are many fewer school dropouts than kids who continue to study; Therefore the probability a priori that a student leaves the school is less than the probability that remain in it. Probabilities a priori constitute core elements of any decision tree and virtually all current programs offer the option of using weights estimated according to the proportions of each class. But it is not always appropriate to use this type of weightings. Thus, if we have a data file with 400 people who answered and 9600 that was no answer, and presumably the two subsamples are representative, these trees automatically apply probabilities of the 0.04 to those who responded and the 0.96 for those who did not respond. The problem is that since the tree tries to maximize the number of cases classified correctly, she will spend most of their effort to classify those who did not respond. It would even, although the tree considering evil to all who responded, only be it wrong in 4 per cent of the cases. Similar model would be theoretically accurate, but practically useless! Why packages also offer the possibility to specify likely same for each class, trying all them as if they were the same size.

Another factor influencing the cost of a classification are the *costs of a misclassification*. Most of decision trees enable the researcher also specify variable costs of a misclassification. An example of variable costs for a Bank it is 10 times more expensive to not be able to detect a fraudulent transaction that stop a legal transaction; or to be 200 times more expensive for a hospital does not detect a contagious disease in a patient who diagnose how contagious a disease that it is not. Typically, these costs are computed when the tree has already been fully developed and therefore have no impact on its basic structure. Only some programs, like the CART of Salford Systems, allows you to also use active matrix of costs, which allow that the decision tree go adapting in each one of the nodes to avoid the higher costs. As a general rule, it should be noted that minimize the costs corresponds to minimize the proportion of cases poorly classified only when a priori probabilities are estimated in proportion to the size of each class and a misclassification costs are the same in each class.

In terms of the **selection of the method of division**, it is choosing the method you select, at each of the levels of the division process, best the best predictor possible division. Currently dominated by mainly two approaches (Loh and Shih, 1997):

Comprehensive methods: the best-known and conceptually simpler is to examine all possible divisions according to each predictor data and select the division that produces the purest classifications (noting the improvement in the goodness of fit). It is the method used, for example, CART or exhaustive CHAID. The goodness of fit is determined by a number of measures (Gini, entropy, χ2, *twoing, symgini, twoing* ordered, diversion of least squares, linear combinations), each of which uses different strategies and developed substantially different classification trees. There is a universally preferable measure for any problems, so it is convenient to have a wide range of coefficients to be able to select which is best suited to each specific problem. However, most of the current *software* covers a very limited number of indexes, and several of the main packages only include a single coefficient. Two of the main problems of the comprehensive methods are computational complexity (when we have a large number of predictors with many levels each, the total number of possible divisions that should be examined by the program becomes huge), and above all the bias showing when selecting variables, since these methods tend to first select the predictors with more categories. The following methods able to solve both problems.

Methods of discriminant type: this type of methods follow a different, computationally simpler process. Instead of looking at the same time the best variable and its best point of division, address these two issues separately. On each node, first calculate a Chi-square test (for each categorical predictor) or ANOVA (for each metric predictor), selecting from among all significant variables, which provides lower associated probabilities. In a second phase, a discriminant analysis on the predictor is applied in order to find the best possible variable division. These procedures are used in the QUEST trees.

With regard to the ***choice of the appropriate size or the overfitting problem***, we have that a characteristic of classification trees is that if not set no limit on the number of divisions to run, you get always a pure classification, in which each node contains only a single class of objects. Pure classifications present several disadvantages because they tend to be unrealistic, there is a risk of finding ourselves with very few elements in each class and, in addition, come to extract the information data, including information idiosyncratic (noise), own the particular sample that we are using. This lack of generalization, from replication to other samples, is known as overfitting (or overlearning within the framework of neural networks), and to combat it have been raised numerous strategies different and sometimes complementary (Murthy, 1998). Two of the main are the Rules stop and pruning, which are specified below:

Stop rules. A first strategy is to stop the generation of new divisions when they involve a very small improvement of the prediction. For example, if ten divisions we classify correctly to 90 per cent of the subjects and with 11 divisions the percentage rises to 90.1 percent, doesn't make much sense add more to the tree. There are many direct stop such rules to automatically stop the tree construction process. The main ones are the following:

- Maximum length of the tree, i.e., number of maximum levels allowed under the root node.

- Minimum number of cases in a node, specify that the nodes do not exceed a certain number of cases.

- Tiny fraction of objects, which consists of the nodes do not contain more cases than a certain fraction of the size of one or more classes.

The stop rule establishes a priori own researcher, according to past research, analysis before, or even according to your own experience-experience and intuition.

A source of diagnostic information to determine if the size of our tree is appropriate is to evaluate, once stopped the process of division, their predictive quality in samples other than those used for its calculation. At least three optional ways to carry out a cross-validation of this type have been described:

- Validation cross into two halves: consists of dividing the data into two parts, sample estimation and sample validation, develop a tree from the estimation sample and use it to predict the classification of the validation sample.

- Validation cross- v parts: available sample is drawn randomly v subsamples and are calculated v classification trees, each time leaving out one of the v subsamples to validate the analysis in such a way that each subsample is used v- 1 times to get the tree and once to validate it. Extremely useful option with small sample sizes.

- Global cross-validation: here, replicates the full analysis a number of times away a fraction of the cases (cases *holdout*) to validate the selected tree. It is particularly useful in combination with the automated techniques of selection of trees, which is linked to the second of the strategies to prevent the override: pruning.

Pruning. After analyzing different stop rules for years, Breiman, Friedman, Losen and Stone (1984) come to the conclusion that it is impossible to specify a rule that is totally reliable. There is always the risk of not discovering relevant structures in the data due to a premature end of the analysis. For this reason, they suggest an alternative approach in two phases. In a first phase develops an enormous tree that contains hundreds or even thousands of nodes. In a second phase, the tree is pruned, removing branches unnecessary until the size of the tree. This process automatic and retrospective, which simultaneously compares all possible hives result of pruning in varying degrees the original tree, is not to be confused with the option offered by some programs (particularly those of type CHAID) manually pruning the tree once it has reached the final solution, option that does not eliminate the problems of using rules stop.

The first and main pruning algorithm is precisely to Breiman et to the. (1984). Consists of two steps: first builds a sequence of increasingly smaller subtrees, all of them as a result of increasingly to prune the tree. Then each subtree of the sequence is validated in a new sample (using a cross-validation in *v*-sides), choosing which lower costs of cross-validation (VC) presents. To calculate the costs of validation uses a function which penalizes the progressive complexity of the tree as this will have more branches. This function enters operation when it reaches a critical value that exceeds the costs of the process of division (IPDS). At that time, costs let down and begin to climb slightly, and it is around the turning point where the ideal size of the tree is located. As it is often common that there are several trees with VC costs close to the minimum, Breiman et to the. (1984) suggest use 1ET rule: select tree reduced complexity among all the trees that do not exceed the minimum cost VC more 1 measure of its standard error. Other methods of pruning (deviance-complexity, reduced error and pessimistic pruning), have been proposed but none proved to be clearly superior to others (Murthy, 1998), by which the choice of one or the other is in the hands of the researcher (and the availability of the corresponding statistical package).

11.8 TOOLS FOR WORKING WITH DECISION TREES

Several companies have developed specific *software* for classification trees. A classification of some of the main programs could be the following:

CART family: CART, Tree (S), etc.Its original purpose is the statistical prediction. Performs only binary divisions. Use cross-validation and pruning to determine the correct size of the tree. The dependent variable can be quantitative or nominal. The predictive variables may be nominal or ordinal, though recent versions also support continuous variables.

Family CLS: CLS, ID3, C4.5, C5.0, etc. Its initial purpose is to detect complex statistical relationships. The number of branches that may cause varies between two and the number of categories of the predictor. To determine the size of the tree use tests of statistical significance (with adjustments for multiplicity in the latest versions). AID, MAID and XAID work with quantitative dependent variables. RHAID, CHAID and TREEDISC with nominal, although the CHAID version developed by Statistical Innovations and that it distributes the SPSS can handle quantitative dependent variables (categorizing them). FIRM comes with two algorithmic versions to work with VD categorical or continuous. The predictors may be nominal or ordinal and normally support a category of missing values or *missing*. The latest versions allow you to also work with continuous predictors.

Methods of discriminant type. FACT and cheese. Its initial purpose is to solve problems of comprehensive methods. In particular, try to eliminate the so-called selection bias of the variable, which present methods as CART and which consists in the trend to first select the variables with more categories. FACT eliminates this bias only when you use ordinal dependent variables. QUEST manages to overcome this bias, the VD nominal or ordinal. In first case, designed to work with categorical dependent variables as continuous. FACT divides the population into as many groups as categories has the variable chosen, QUEST provides binary divisions.

Linear combinations: OC1, trees SE, etc. Its initial purpose is to detect linear relationships combined with learning concepts. The number of branches varies between two and the number of categories of the predictor.

Hybrid models: IND, Knowledge Seeker, etc.Its initial purpose is to combine methods from other families. IND combines the CART and C4.5, as well as Bayesian methods with minimal coding. Knowledge Seeker combines CHAID and the ID3 with a novel set of multiplicity.

But there are three arborescent procedures which currently enjoy greater acceptance both in the fields as applied theoretical: trees CHAID (kass, 1980), CART (Breiman et al., 1984) and QUEST (Loh and Shih, 1997).

11.9 TREES CHAID

CHAID or *Chi-square Automatic Interaction Detector* (Kass, 1980;) Biggs, of Ville and Suen, 1991) represents the culmination of a series of methods based on the automatic detector of interact (AID) of Morgan & Sonquist (1963). CHAID is an exploratory method of analysis of data useful to identify important variables and their interactions for the purpose of segmentation, analysis descriptive or as a prelude to other subsequent analysis.

The dependent measure can be qualitative (nominal or ordinal) or quantitative. For qualitative variables, the analysis carried out a series of analyses $\chi 2$ between Predictor and dependent variables. In the case of quantitative dependent variables, methods of analysis of variance, in which intervals (divisions) are determined optimally for the independent variables in such a way that they maximize the capacity to explain the variance of the dependent measure is used.

To split each node, Kass (1980) begins locating the allowable categories pair of the predictor (the set of allowable pairs is determined by the type of predictor that is being analyzed) with the lowest value of $\chi 2$. If the significance level is less than a certain critical level, both categories are attached and the process is repeated. If it is larger, they become two candidates to the division of the variable. This process continues with each pair of categories until they stop producing joints and possible divisions. The last candidate to the division (which usually does not usually coincide with the most significant division) is that you choose to divide the predictor. The process is repeated recursively at each node until it engages any of the rules of the process stop. To mitigate the variable selection bias, Kass uses a Bonferroni adjustment.

This original approach of Kass saves enough time to computer. However it does not guarantee to be able to really find the best possible division in each mode. Only an exhaustive search on each node in all the sets of candidates to a division categories can accomplish this. The exhaustive CHAID, proposed by Biggs, of Ville and Suen (1991), always selects the most significant division of all. The authors also found that the Bonferroni adjustment that uses Kass penalized in excess of the varibles with many levels, and although he manages to handle the error type I, presents an error type II too high. Therefore, exhaustive CHAID treats all variables equally, regardless of the type of variable and the number of categories. It also allows to work both with categorical dependent variables as metrics. Categorical variables using the Chi-square statistical and give rise to a classification tree. The metric variables use the statistical F and give rise to what is known as regression trees. You can also use predictors of metric type, using his previous conversion on categorical variables. Both the classic CHAID and the exhaustive can produce the VD divisions in more than two groups (unlike CART, which produces only a binary divisions).

278 DATA MINING WITH SAS ENTERPRISE MINER

11.10 TREES CART

CART (*Classification And Regression Trees*), also called C & RT in some programs and texts of statistics, constitute an alternative to the exhaustive CHAID to develop classification trees. In fact, the algorithm was developed by Breiman, Friedman, Losen and Stone in the early 1980s (1984) to try to overcome some of the deficiencies and weaknesses which showed the original formulation of the CHAID.

Until the appearance of the comprehensive version, CHAID seemed limited to nominal VDs and VIs categorical, and yet there was the need for a method allowing to use criteria and predictors of any level of measurement. In addition, CHAID had some aura of method ad hoc and no-estadistico (CART was strengthened with a whole statistical structure of cross-validation) and was perceived as excessively linked to marketing and related sciences (CART was adopted in medical environments and research).

As its name suggests, CART is suitable for classification trees (qualitative VD) or regression (quantitative VD) and, as a characteristic differential generates binary trees. It is built by dividing the sample into subsets of data. In each division, each predictor is evaluated to find the best point of cutting (with quantitative predictors) or the best groupings of categories (with categorical predictors). Then also compare predictors, selecting the predictor and the division that produces the greater goodness of fit. Therefore, as rule of division, this program uses measures of goodness, also known as measures of node impurity (Breiman et al., 1984;) Murthy, 1998). For quantitative variables, some of the proposed measures have been the reduction of the mean square error or the absolute average deviation from the median.

With qualitative variables, one of the most commonly used measures is the Gini coefficient, which assesses the probability of misclassification in the event of a node and reaches a value of 0 when the classification is perfect. Other similar coefficients (and, therefore, they share essentially the same advantages and disadvantages) include Bartlett as $\chi 2$, and measure G-cuadrado, similar to the $\chi 2$ of maximum likelihood with which it will talk in the modeling of finite samples. Very different from the previous ones is the coefficient *twoing*. It is a measure based on the clustering of the VD in the best two subclasses and subsequent calculation of the variance. *Twoing* tends to produce completely different trees that are achieved using Gini. In particular, while trees *twoing* tend to balance the distribution of data in each of the two categories, more the Gini coefficients and the entropy measures tend to produce trees that divide the data into excessively unbalanced subgroups.

Which tree is best? From the point of view of its predictive accuracy, it may be that both have a similar behavior, although probably most of market researchers prefer tree *twoing*. In any case, it is essential that different programs offer a good selection of measures (which shouldn't be missing *twoing*) to make the researcher to decide which to use. CART was the first program which took into account this, offering up to nine different. It is worth emphasising that available in CART coefficients not include uses CHAID because, according to its creators, the trend that has been observed in the measured χ2 develop trees false positives, i.e., showing the data structures that do not exist in reality (Salford Systems, 2002).

Related to this, it should be noted also that although some authors consider that trees built from probability distributions are more reliable than the built directly from the values of the attributes (Shang and Breiman, 1996), other authors have described several problematic aspects of using tests of statistical significance as rulers of stop (Neville, 1999), which is used which CHAID or QUEST. Historically, the most significant contribution of CART to the universe of classification trees has been the overfitting of the data treatment. Other innovative features of CART that with the passage of time have been incorporated into other programs include; the incorporation to the analysis of a priori probabilities, the use of surrogate divisions for values *missing* (i.e. divisions based on a second variable that mimics the first when this fails), or a heuristic search (not optimal) of divisions based on linear combinations of variables.

11.11 TREES QUEST

The acronym QUEST comes *Quick, Unbiased, Efficient Statistical Tree* (Loh and Shih, 1997). It's a classification tree algorithm created specifically to solve two of the main problems posed by methods such as CART and exhaustive CHAID to divide a group of subjects on the basis of an independent variable. Firstly the *computational complexity*. An ordinal variable with *n* values on one node leads to (*n*- 1) divisions, by which the number of calculations on each node increases proportionally the number of values. In the case of categorical variables, the number of calculations increases exponentially the number of categories, being in general *(2 - 1-1)*for a variable with *m* values. Secondly, the *biases in the selection of variables*. But a more serious problem from an interpretive point of view and generalizability of results is that comprehensive methods tend to select those variables that have a greater number of categories. Doyle (1973) was the first to realize this in the context of the AID and THAID algorithms, and, more recently, Loh and Shih (1997) found empirical evidence of this bias in the exhaustive methods.

The QUEST algorithm employs an approach whose calculation is much simpler than the exhaustive methods. Rather than attempting to simultaneously select the best predictor and its best cutting point, QUEST addresses these two problems separately. On each node, it estimated the association between each predictor and the RV through the statistical ANOVA F or F of Levene (in the case of continuous and ordinal predictors) or a Pearson χ2 (in the case of nominal predictors). To ensure binary divisions of the VD, applies an conglomerativo algorithm that forces always create two superclasses in the predictor. Finally, you select the predictor which presented higher association with VD, i.e. the lowest value *p* within the significant (corrected according to Bonferroni to eliminate bias in the selection of variables).

In a second phase, to find the best cut-off point is it uses a quadratic discriminant analysis (whose advantage over the linear is that it allows to accommodate different variances). The process is repeated recursively until it skips some of the stop rules. Thanks to this calculation procedure, QUEST does not response bias, shows greater simplicity of calculation, lets include methods of validation through pruning and can incorporate linear combinations of variables.

Comparing QUEST with comprehensive methods, found that when using multi-variate divisions there a winner clear. However, the QUEST trees based on divisions resulting from linear combinations have proven to be faster and, above all, accurate thorough procedures, which typically use multi-variate divisions (Loh and Shih, 1997). A recent comparison of the main tree methods (Song and Yoon, 2000) has shown that QUEST is the only method that shows no bias-serious when selecting a variable or another. CHAID is a soft bias and CART is clearly biased towards continuous predoctores or many categories. For his part, Quinlan (1993) C5.0 is which presents the most serious problem of bias, resulting in very poor statistical power.

In General, QUEST seems to be superior to CART, and this, in turn, higher than CHAID. The results largely depend on the type of concrete problem is dealing with.

11.12 ANALYSIS CONGLOMERATES AND DECISION TREES AS METHODS OF SEGMENTATION

Cluster analysis, also called *cluster*analysis, today constitutes one of the most widely used statistical procedures for segmentation. The definition of the technique itself resembles, in fact, the generic objectives that pursues the segmentation: identifying groups of subjects heterogeneous and homogeneous within each group.

The analysis sets these groups based on the similarity, presenting a set of entities (e.g. tourists) with respect to a number of features that the researcher has previously specified (motivations, needs, sought benefits, etc). However, is the analysis, and not analyst, which finally draws groups of subjects and their defining characteristics: number of segments, number of members of each segment, etc. Cluster analysis is, therefore, the paradigmatic example of the *post hoc segmentation*approach. It is also a descriptive method of segementacion.

On the other hand, decision trees are predictive segmentation methods, and today are the most commonly used tool for segmenting.

Chapter 12

DECISION TREES AND CLUSTERS WITH SAS ENTERPRISE MINER

12.1 ANALYSIS CLUSTER WITH ENTERPRISE MINER. CLUSTERING NODE

The node *Clustering* of Enterprise Miner is specially used to segment databases by cluster or *cluster*analysis. This analysis is often helpful to segment database. It is intended that the elements of each *cluster* are similar (homogeneity within) while the elements in different *clusters* tend to be different (heterogeneity between). This method is based on the use of distance Euclidean method of grouping of non-hierarchical type is based on the model of the *K* stockings, which implies that we should define a range of number of *clusters*a priori. This name is because the centers of *clusters* are the observations that are assigned to each group. The algorithm will try to reduce the sum of the distances to each square on each iteration until convergence is reached. The node includes a method for detecting *outliers* to avoid groups of a single individual. It is convenient to work with more than 100 observations. The node*Clustering*it is located in SAS Enterprise Miner in the category*Modify*(Figure 12-1)

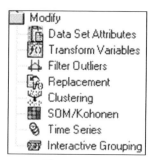

Figure 12-1

As an example, we will use data from the *World* file to group, from social and economic information, to various countries of the world in homogeneous groups. The objective is to know which countries are more or less similar according to the following variables: , *urban density, espvidaf, espvidam, alfabet, inc_pob, mortinf, tasa_nat, tasa_mort, tasasida* and *log_pib*. The rest of variables, except *country*, who has a paper label and they will be excluded from the analysis.

Once we already have our work in SAS (*mundo.sas7bdat*file) format data in a specific library (library *work* representing the subdirectory *c:\libros\miningt*), open the project P1 (*File → Open*) and using *File → New → Diagram* diagram D12 created. Then the node *Clustering* is obtained through the button *Tools* from the browser's project of Enterprise Miner as a sub-option of the category *Model* or dragging the node itself on the area next to the *Input Data Source* node has been that previously assigned the data set *mundo.sas7bdat* of the library work. Then will be the union of the two (Figure 12-2).

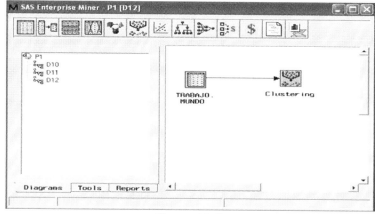

Figure 12-2

It will be necessary to declare variables , *urban density, espvidaf, espvidam, alfabet, inc_pob, mortinf, tasa_nat, tasa_mort, tasasida* and *log_pib* of type *input* and the *country* variable of type *id*, because that will be used as a label. This task is performed by double clicking on the *Input Data Source* node tagged as work.WORLD and choosing the *Variables*tab. Then you click with the right button of the mouse on each variable to be of type *input*Select *Set Model Role* and then *Input*. Repeat the process with the variables to exclude, that assigned type *rejected* and with the variable *country*which will be assigned type *id* (Figure 12-3).

Input Data Source

Data	Variables	Interval Variables			Class Variables		Notes	
Name		Model Role	Measurement	Type	Format	Informat	Variable	
PA_S		id	nominal	char	$16.	$16.	país	
POBLAC		rejected	interval	num	BEST12.	12.	poblac	
DENSIDAD		input	interval	num	BEST12.	12.	densidad	
URBANA		input	interval	num	BEST12.	12.	urbana	
RELIG		rejected	nominal	char	$8.	$8.	relig	
ESPVIDAF		input	interval	num	BEST12.	12.	espvidaf	
ESPVIDAM		input	interval	num	BEST12.	12.	espvidam	
ALFABET		input	interval	num	BEST12.	12.	alfabet	
INC_POB		input	interval	num	BEST12.	12.	inc_pob	
MORTINF		input	interval	num	BEST12.	12.	mortinf	
PIB_CAP		rejected	interval	num	BEST12.	12.	pib_cap	
REGI_N		rejected	ordinal	num	BEST12.	12.	región	
CALOR_AS		rejected	interval	num	BEST12.	12.	calorías	
SIDA		rejected	interval	num	BEST12.	12.	sida	
TASA_NAT		input	interval	num	BEST12.	12.	tasa_nat	
TASA_MOR		input	interval	num	BEST12.	12.	tasa_mor	
TASASIDA		input	interval	num	BEST12.	12.	tasasida	
LOG_PIB		input	interval	num	BEST12.	12.	log_pib	
LOGTSIDA		rejected	interval	num	BEST12.	12.	logtsida	
NAC_DEF		rejected	interval	num	BEST12.	12.	nac_def	
FERTILID		rejected	interval	num	BEST12.	12.	fertilid	
LOG_POB		rejected	interval	num	BEST12.	12.	log_pob	
ALFABMAS		rejected	interval	num	BEST12.	12.	alfabmas	
ALFABFEM		rejected	interval	num	BEST12.	12.	alfabfem	
CLIMA		rejected	ordinal	num	BEST12.	12.	clima	
REGION2		rejected	ordinal	num	BEST12.	12.	region2	

Figure 12-3

Once connected nodes *Input Data Source* and *Clustering* , and defined the role of each variable will keep the information of the data node and open the node *Clustering* by double clicking on it in the diagram. Gets the entry screen of the node in the *Variables* tab choose standardize data by the standard deviation (Figure 12-4).

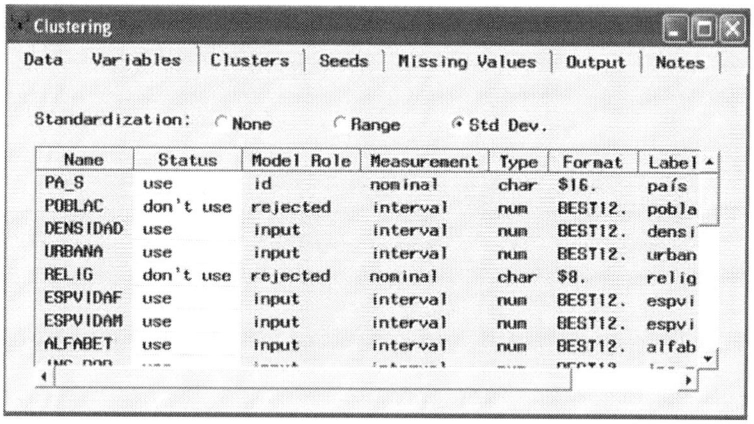

Figure 12-4

Then on the tab *Clusters*, we indicate that we want a solution that includes 6 groups of countries. We can define this parameter in the option *Number of Clusters* (Figure 12-5). *Missing Values* tab we chose as a method of imputation of missing values in the middle of the *cluster* or nearest Group (Figure 12-6). In the window *Output* (*Print*tab) ask results showing us the statistics of the *Cluster* and the Group of countries that makes up each group (Figure 12-7).

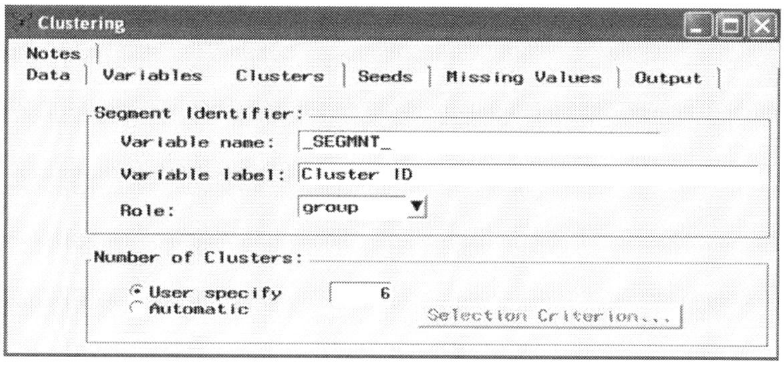

Figure 12-5

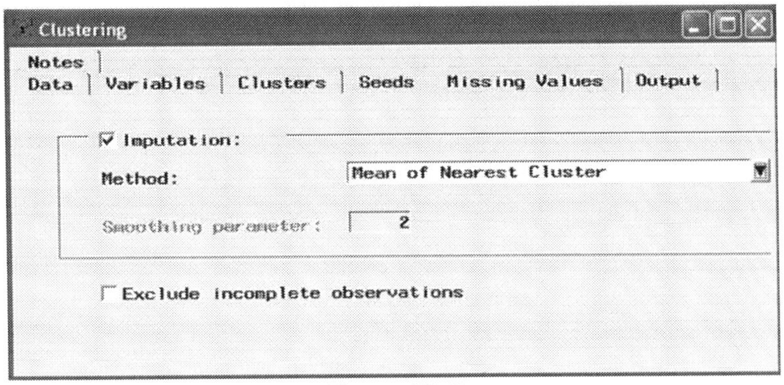

Figure 12-6

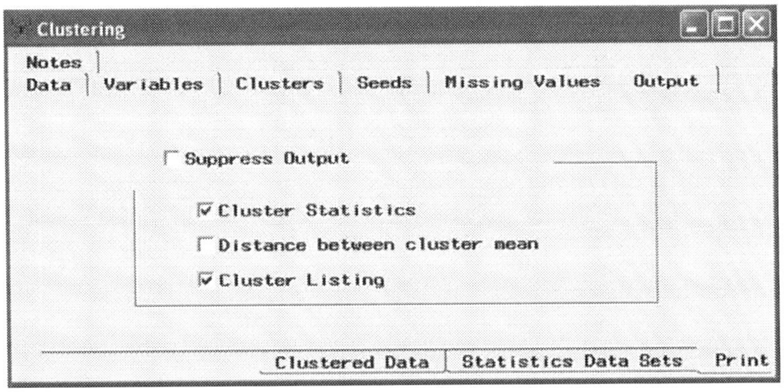

Figure 12-7

Then close the node (button 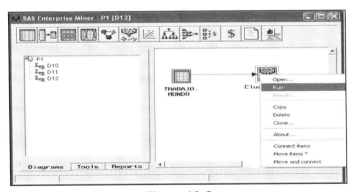) and then run it by clicking on it in the diagram with the right mouse button and choosing the option *Run* from the resulting pop-up menu (Figure 12-8). Completed execution the system asks if you want to view results (Figure 12-9). In accepting the *results Viewer*opens whose *Partition* tab (Figure 12-10) shows a graphic idea of *clusters*.

Figure 12-8

Figure 12-9

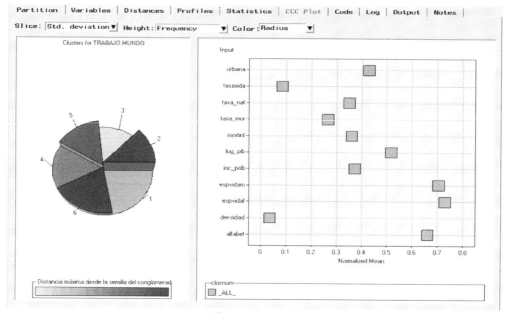

Figure 12-10

The *Variables* tab shows the relative importance of each of the variables used to make groups (Figure 12-11).

Name	Importance	Measurement	Type	Label
DENSIDAD	0	interval	num	densidad
URBANA	0	interval	num	urbana
ESPVIDAF	0.8988801851	interval	num	espvidaf
ESPVIDAM	0	interval	num	espvidam
ALFABET	0	interval	num	alfabet
INC_POB	0.5779027344	interval	num	inc_pob
MORTINF	0.4055080218	interval	num	mortinf
TASA_NAT	1	interval	num	tasa_nat
TASA_MOR	0	interval	num	tasa_mor
TASASIDA	0	interval	num	tasasida
LOG_PIB	0	interval	num	log_pib

Figure 12-11

The *Distances* tab shows that the groups are relatively close. Only the Group 3 appears to be much more distinct than the others.

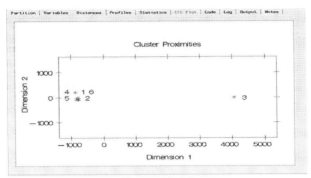

Figure 12-12

The *Statistics* tab shows the number of individuals in each *cluster*, the intra-group variance, the maximum distance of a country at the center of the *cluster* and the nearest *cluster* , etc. (fig. 12-13)

CLUSTER	Frecuencia del conglomerado	Desviación estándar de la raíz cuadrada	Distancia máxima desde la semilla del co	Conglomerado más cercano	Distancia hast
1	2	0.6847387476	1.6058547066	6	5.1022966981
2	45	0.4017126615	2.9602133874	5	2.87276929
3	2	0.4225281189	0.9909162738	2	7.3501779204
4	10	0.5073636452	2.0163182409	5	2.0450136549
5	30	0.4591475533	2.4785674593	4	2.0450136549
6	20	0.6364496464	2.8898787732	5	4.3315327218

Figure 12-13

The *Code* tab presents the SAS code of procedure (Figure 12-14).

```
00001 title;
00002 options nodate;
00003 proc fastclus data=_CLUSTMP maxc=6
00004 outseed=EMPROJ.CLS981WS(label="Clustered Seeds for EMDATA.VIEW_1M8")
00005 outstat=EMPROJ.CLS6NT9A(label="Clustered Statistics for EMDATA.VIEW_1M8")
00006 cluster=_SEGMNT_ radius=0 replace=Full maxiter=1 conv=0.0001 LIST std=std
00007 impute=NS
00008 ;
00009 var
00010 DENSIDAD
00011 URBANA
00012 ESPVIDAF
00013 ESPVIDAM
00014 ALFABET
00015 INC_POB
00016 MORTINF
00017 TASA_NAT
00018 TASA_MOR
00019 TASASIDA
00020 LOG_PIB
00021 ;
00022 id PA_S;
00023 run;
00024 quit;
00025 run;
00026 quit;
00027 *** END OF FILE ***
```

Figure 12-14

The *Output* tab lists the stockings in the variables used for each *cluster* as well as the group to which it belongs (Figure 12-15) country.

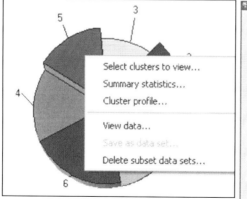

Figure 12-15

Yes in Figure 12-10 tab*Partition*you click with the right button of the mouse over the pie chart, we get the pop-up menu in Figure 12-16. The option *Cluster profile* this menu shows the decision tree that allows you to assign cases to a particular *cluster* (figures 17-17 and 17-18). Along with this chart, selecting the tab *Rules* we can see the logical rules that characterize the tree.

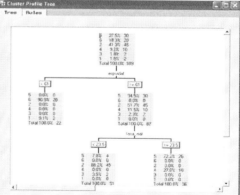

Figure 12-16   Figure 12-17

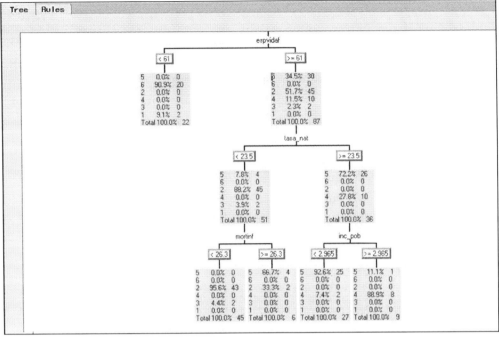

Figure 12-18

12.2 TREES DECISION-MAKING WITH ENTERPRISE MINER. TREE NODE

The node *Tree* Enterprise Miner allows implement different algorithms for the generation of logical rules of decision based on the information contained in the data. Its use requires a database in which we must specify a unique response, which can be rated, binary, ordinal or continuous, and at least one *input* or explanatory variables. The node *Tree* is located in SAS Enterprise Miner in the category *Model* (Figure 12-19)

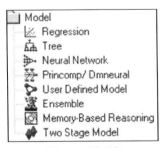

Figure 12-19

As an example, we will use the data from the file*Credits*to set the logical rules that will allow you to help make the decision on when you decide to assign or not credit. Once imported file, assign to the variable *customer* role ID in the model while the *CREDIT_V* variable will be the variable target (*Target*) and the other variables will be *inputs*.

Once we already have our work in SAS (*creditos.sas7bdat*file) format data in a specific library (library *work* representing the subdirectory *c:\libros\miningt*), open the project P1 (*File → Open*) and using *File → New → Diagram* create diagram D13. Then we put the *Input Data Source* node that is assigned the data set *creditos.sas7bdat* of the library work in the diagram. Then join the data with the partition node (*Data Partition*) and will randomly assign 80% data training, 10% to validation and 10% test. Once this task will connect the node's data partition with a decision trees node (*Tree*) as shown in Figure 12-20.

To assign to the variable*Customer*type*id*, the variable*CREDIT_V*type*Target*and the rest of the variables type*input*, double click on the *Input Data Source* node and choose the *Variables*tab. Then you click with the right button of the mouse on each variable to be of type *input*, choose *Set Role Model* and then *Input*. Repeat the process with the variables of type *id* and *target* (Figure 12-21).

To assign randomly 80% data training, 10% to validation and test 10% we double click on the *Data Partition* node and fill in the *Variables* tab as shown in Figure 12-22.

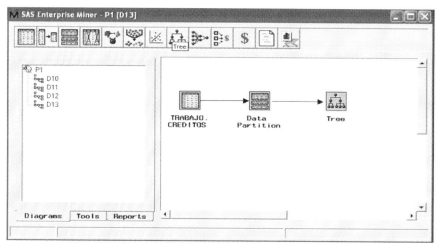

Figure 12-20

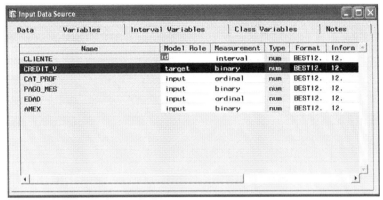

Figure 12-21

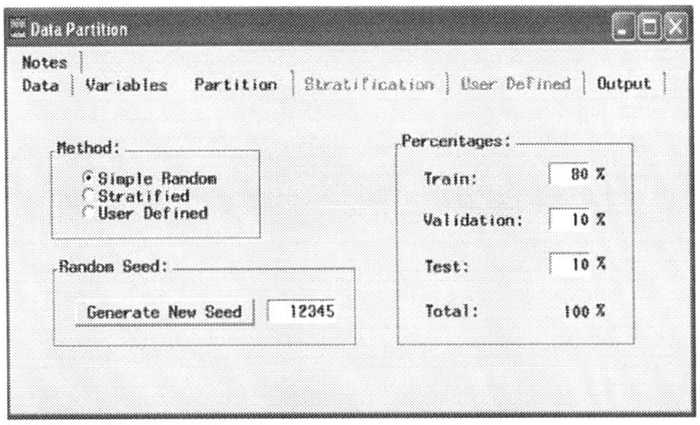

Figure 12-22

To set the specifications of the tree open the *Tree* node by double-clicking on it in the diagram. Gets the entry screen of the node whose *Variables* tab presents the variables involved in the tree and its properties (Figure 12-23).

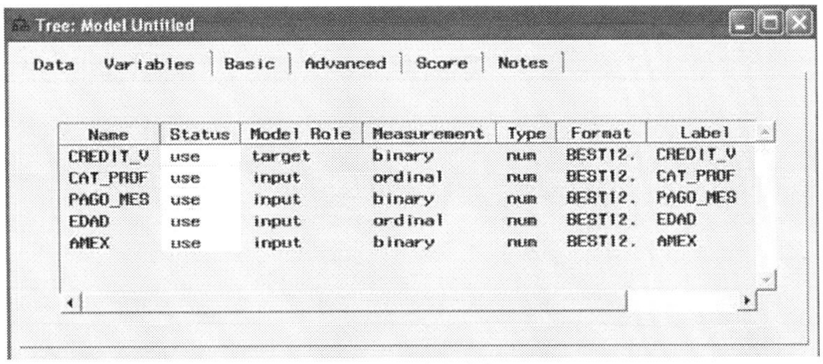

Figure 12-23

On the tab*Advanced*briefly as a measure for the assessment of the model the percentage of cases correctly classified. In addition we will define as enough observations to find a variable of division 25 (Figure 12-24).

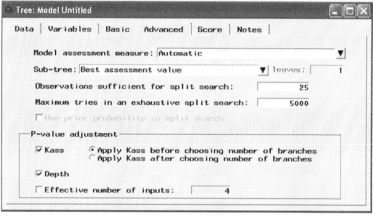

Figure 12-24

In the Advanced Options window obtained with the tab *Advanced* (Figure 12-24) in the Advanced Options window you can specify the following variables:

Model Assessment Measure: selects the best tree from the results in the validation sample. The list of measures of valuation depends on how the *output* is measured and if there is or not a matrix of costs or benefits for the goal.

For continuous variables, you can choose between several measures depending on whether or not there is an array of benefits. If there is no array of benefits we have:

- *Average Square Error:* measured by default.
- *Average in the top 10, 25 or 50%.*

If any parent's gain or loss we will have:

- *Average Square Error.*
- *Average profit/loss.*
- *Average profit/loss in the top 10, 25 or 50%.*

For categorical objectives we can choose from the following measures:

If there is no defined matrix of losses or profits:

- *Proportion of correctly classified:* proportion of cases classified correctly.
- *Ordinal proportion correctly classified*.
- *Proportion of event in top 10, 25 or 50%*
- *Total leaf Impurity (Fini index).*

If there is an array of losses or profits then valuation measures are:

- *Proportion of correctly classified.*
- *Average profit/loss.*
- *Average profit/loss in top 10, 25 or 50%.*
- *Total leaf impurity (Gini index).*

Specify the subtree method: this option specified as select a subtree within the main tree. If a tree tends to have too much depth and too many branches it will also tend to adjust the noise and will generate new data which are presented in a poor way. Each node can be evaluated in the following ways:

- ***Best value assessment****:* the smallest subtree with the best estimation is chosen by default.

- ***The most leaves****:* selects the entire tree. This option is appropriate when the tree is constructed interactively, or when other options are set to stop tree divisions.

- ***At most number of leaves indicated****:* select the subtree having as much *n* leaves. This number must be defined on the corresponding square to be activated by choosing this option (Figure 8-10).

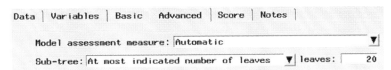

Figure 12-25

Split search criteria*:* this option sets an upper limit on the number of observations in the sample to make a partition. The algorithm for the creation of a decision tree search rules of partition branches that maximize the assigned criteria. Find the optimal partition is often evaluate each possible division of each variable and sometimes the number of possible divisions can become excessively large.

Maximum tries in an exhaustive search split: if the number of possible divisions is high this option uses a default algorithm of search (*stepwise, hill-climbing*) with a number of attempts.

P-value adjustment: this option is activated when you choose such as endpoint values of F or Chi-square statistics.

Kass: the search of optimal partition requires the calculation of various contingency tables. If we use the original table without changes in the categories, test χ^2 can be used. This test assumes that there is only a population of which we extract a single sample and calculate a single test. However to make the test repeatedly violates this assumption. This increases the possibility of finding some relationship simply by the fact of increasing the number of times the search which can lead to find spurious relationships or magnify found relations. That is why the *p-* value is corrected as described in the description made of decision trees.

To implement the algorithm, the first step is to create ordinal regressors rather than continuous dividing the distribution of continuous explanatory variables function into a number of categories containing approximately the same number of observations. For categorical variables, the categories are already defined. This would be the option ***Apply Kass before choosing number of branches***.

However, this option can lower further the significance of a partition as an alternative method called adjustment of Gabriel which applies if you select ***Apply Kass after choosing number of branches***.

Depth: this option performs a Bonferroni adjustment taking into account the number of sheets to correct the number of false rejections will tend to grow with the number of leaves.

Effective number of inputs: sets the p-values from the actual number of *inputs*. How many more likely inputs will be a spurious *input* gain to truly predictive *input* or *inputs* . How many more *inputs* incorrelacionados has more the risk will be high. *Inputs* adjustment multiplies the *p-* value for the declared number of *inputs* which are those that have the status of use in the variables window.

If now the display *Tree node* tree specifications we choose the tab *Score*, we can indicate that saved the response for data training, validation, and test (Figure 12-26).

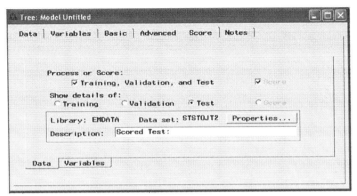

Figure 12-26

Shown that the *Score* tab has two subwindows:

Data: is used to select the data to evaluate (*score*) when the decision trees node is executed (Figure 12-26). By default neither training nor validation or test data are used to assess. So they are used for this purpose is necessary to activate the square of *Training, Validation and Test.*In this window you can also see details about training, validation and data test by selecting the *Properties*option.

Variables: in this window (Figure 12-27) are selected those variables that we want to be available for future analyses on other nodes.

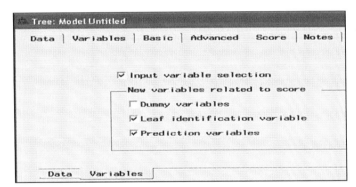

Figure 12-27

You can select the following variables:

Input variable selection: preselects the predictive variables important to reducing the dimensionality of the data. When you run the decision trees node assigned *input* status to those variables with a greater than 95% confidence level by assigning the status of rejected the rest. This will allow to include these variables in a rear as for example neural network node.

New variables related to score:

- **Dummy variables:** creates a variable *dummy* for each leaf of the tree. If each observation is assigned to a specific sheet then you must associate a value of 1 for this sheet and 0 for the rest.

- **Leaf identification variable:** this variable contains a numerical identification of the sheet on which the observation is assigned. It can be used to process a node processing groups groups or perform regressions for each of the groups found.

- **Variable prediction:** variables of prediction that can be used in subsequent analysis.

Once established all options of training the node can be executed in four ways:

If the node is closed:

- Select the node, right-click and select *Run*.
- Select *Actions* → *Run*.

If the node is open:

- Select *Tools* → *Train Model*
- Select the icon to run the tree 🏃 .

As we will later see the tree training also can be executed interactively.

Once defined prior assignment of a name for the model (Figure 12-28), and these options, run the node by clicking on it in the diagram with the right mouse button and choosing the option *Run* from the resulting pop-up menu (Figure 12-29). Completed execution the system asks if you want to view results (Figure 12-30). Accepting opens the *results Viewer* whose tab (Figure 12-31) *All* at the same time shows four tabs.

At the top left, the *Summary* tab shows statistics of adjusting the model both for training data and validation. In the top right, the tab it. *Ring* shows the proportion of cases occurring in each of the nodes in each of levels or rings of the tree. By selecting the *View Information About Point* icon on the toolbar 🔍 can see the rule that defines the node (Figure 12-32). In the bottom left, the *Table* tab displays the proportion of cases correctly classified, both training and validation, according to the number of leaves of each tree. In the bottom right, the *Plot* tab performs a graphical representation of the previous result. In a decision tree, we want to choose the point that presents a greater number of cases well classified in the validation sample. In this case us down with five-leaf tree because the vertical white line is 5. You can change point by clicking *n* the diamond of the figure.

Figure 12-28

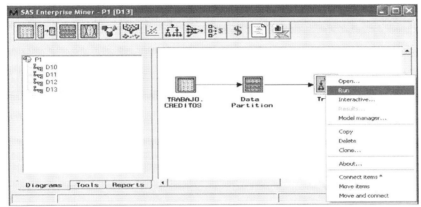

Figure 12-29

Figure 12-30

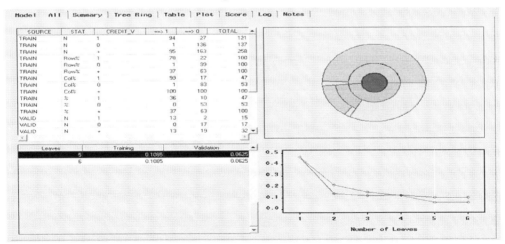

Figure 12-31

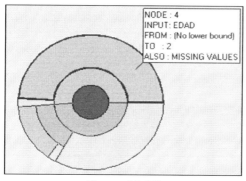
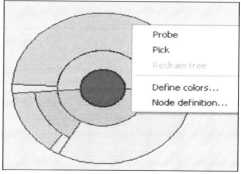

Figure 12-32   Figure 12-33

Within the window of the graphic of the tree *Tree Ring*ring, if we click with the right button of the mouse on the chart (Figure 12-33) you can select the following options:

- **Probe:** shows some information summarized in a text box to select a node or simply by moving the cursor over the graphic (Figure 12-32).

- **Pick:** select and highlight a node on the other (Figure 12-32).We a time selected will click on *Node Definition* to assess the logical rule that defines its properties.

- **Redraw tree:** redraws the diagram of the classical decision tree from the selected node. This option is especially useful to view details of the tree since normally the number of branches, nodes, and the depth of the tree will make impossible their full display in a single window. To print the entire tree on occasions it will be necessary to save the image and then change it in another program that will allow its manipulation.

- **Defines Colors:** choose the desired colors according to preferences to highlight certain results (Figure 12-34).

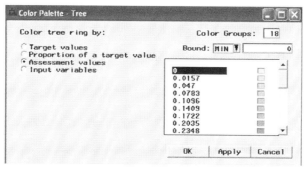

Figure 12-34

- *Node definition:* shows the definition of the (logical rule in English) node to the selected node.

Select to *view the tree View* → *Tree* (Figure 12-35). The middle column shows the percentages and numerical values of training data while that on the right shows data validation (Figure 12-36).

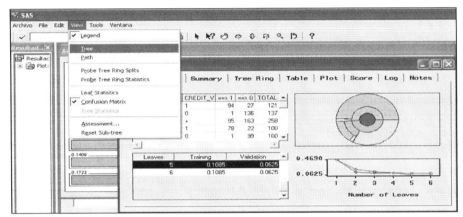

Figure 12-35

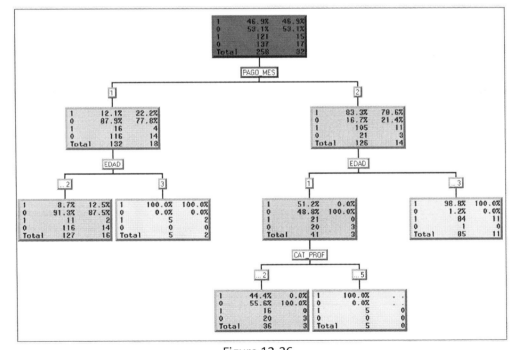

Figure 12-36

A decision tree diagram contains the following features:

- *Node root:* is the node that contains all the comments just prior to the first division. In this case shown as 258 customers, 121 returned credit (46.9%), while 137 were unpaid (53.1%).

- *Branches:* once selected the variable that best discriminate, details are parties in two or more branches in accordance with the values of the variable. In the former case the variable that most discriminate is if the customer perceives his remuneration on a monthly basis (2) or weekly (1).

- *Node:* contain the split data from other branches and nodes.

- *Nodes sheet:* they are terminal nodes and contain the general classification of the tree once fulfilled all logical rules defined by the previous nodes.

12.3 INTERACTIVE TRAINING (INTERACTIVE TRAINING)

The decision tree node is able to offer an automatic result, as seen so far, but we can also carry out analysis in an interactive way. If we choose this option, (select the tree node's decision with the right button of the mouse and select *Interactive Training*), the node automatically generates the best tree based on the predefined criteria.

This option provides a number of advantages over the auto option:

- It allows to force entry into the model of a certain variable.
- It allows to force partition of a variable in a particular way.
- Allows you to prune a tree previously built.

This choice can be justified by a prior knowledge of the problem that assures us that certain variables are relevant because certain breakpoints in a variable have one mathematical or economic sense greater than other points, etc. The interactive training window opens in the subwindow *All* showing the outline of the figure 12-37.

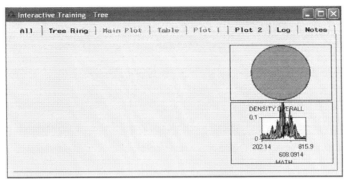

Figure 12-37

The window displays a graph of vacuum tree ring a density diagram of the response variable (or percentage in the case of binary or categorical variables). This last graph can be examined in the *Plot 2*window.

The interactive training has its own toolbar that you can use to build the tree (Figure 12-38).

Figure 12-38

12.3.1 Creation of   rules

The button *Create rule* 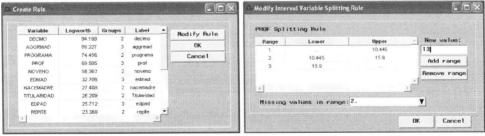 of toolbar strength to a variable into the tree and modify breakpoints. You can also access this option by clicking with the right button of the mouse the rings of tree graph and selecting *Create rule*. The figure gets 12-39. First select the variable whose input we want to force taking into account that the variables that best discriminate are those with a high *Logworth* . Once selected the variable we'll click on *Modify Rule*. In the new window you can add ranges or modify the value of the existing ranges (Figure 12-40).

Figure 12-39   Figure 12-40

Once launched a division by a new variable can do any of the following options.

12.3.2 Try the new ring of the tree

To do this in the main menu select *View → Probe Tree Ring Splits* or *View → Probe Tree Ring Statistics*. We can also click on the toolbar button *Show Info About Points* and move along the ring where the statistics of each node will be displayed.

12.3.3 See the tree after the division

To do this select *View → Tree.*Gets the shaft (Figure 12-41).

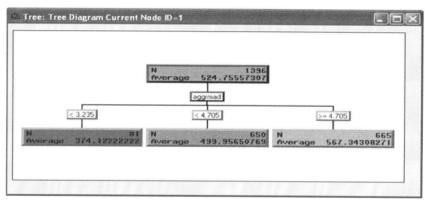

Figure 12-41

In this way we will be building the tree.

12.3.4 Change division current

Once the partition of the data we want to change this or add new branches to the partition. To this end we landed to the *Main Plot* tab and the chart will use the context menu that provides the right button of the mouse which allows us to choose the options of Figure 12-42.

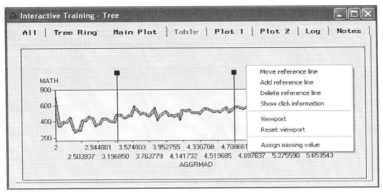

Figure 12-42

- ***Move reference line***: allows you to move the line that defines the partition to a new position. To do this select the line with the left mouse button and drag it to the new position.

- ***Add reference line***: adds a new branch or partition the data.

- ***Delete reference line***: deletes the reference line. So once you choose the option click in the point where the reference line crosses the goal line.

- ***Show information click***: displays a text box that reports the value of the variable from the density of the target value and the target value for each point of the density line.

- ***Viewport***: activates a zoom to see in detail specific areas of the graph. Do this once selected the option, select with the mouse the area we want to enlarge to see details.

- ***Reset viewport***: allows you to return to the original graphic.

- ***Assign missing value***: allows you to assign a lost value to one of the branches to our choice.

To choose another index variable select the node that you want to divide and select again to create rule by repeating the process.

12.3.5 Train the rest of the tree once generated or enforced rules and conditions wanted

To finish building the tree automatically will make click in the automatic training of the toolbar icon 🏛 .

Alternatively select the tree with the mouse right button choosing the *Train*option. The new tree will be generated by keeping unaltered the options that were defined by the analyst.

12.3.6 Prune the tree

One of the many advantages of the interactive training is that it allows the pruning of the tree, that is, the Elimination of rules irrelevant for the purposes of the analysis. To do this, once selected the node below which you want to prune select option prune the toolbar ✂ .

Alternatively select the tree with the mouse right button choosing the *Prune*option.

12.3.7 Save the tree created

After the tree is completed, this can be kept as *input* for a training or further construction or as final model. This selecciona-remos *File* → *Close* and choose one of the two options (Figure 12-43).

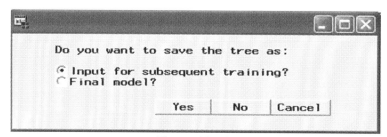

Figure 12-43

Chapter 13

NEURAL NETWORKS WITH SAS ENTERPRISE MINER

13.1 DESCRIPTION OF A NEURAL NETWORK

A *neural network* can be defined as a set of highly interconnected elements of information processing, which are able to learn the information that feeds them. The main feature of this new technology of neural networks is that it can apply to a large number of problems that can range from complex problems to theoretical sophisticated models such as image recognition, voice recognition, financial analysis, analysis and filtering of signals, etc. In this chapter we will see applications of neural networks for the improvement of the techniques of classification, discrimination, prediction, etc.

Neural networks are trying to emulate the nervous system, in a way which are able to reproduce some of the major tasks that develops the human brain, to reflect the fundamental characteristics of the same behavior. They really try to model neural networks is one of the physiological structures of the brain, Neuron and support groups structured and interlinked of several of them, known as networks of neurons. In this way, they build systems that present a certain degree of intelligence. However, we must insist on the fact that artificial neural systems, like any other tool built by man, have limitations and have only a superficial resemblance to their biological counterparts. Neural networks, in relation to the processing of information, inherited three basic characteristics of networks of biological neurons: massive parallelism, nonlinear response of neurons against the received inputs and processing information through multiple layers of neurons.

One of the main properties of these models is their ability to learn and generalize from real-life examples. I.e., the network learns to recognize the relationship (which does not cease to be equivalent to estimate a functional dependence) that exists between the set of inputs provided as examples and their corresponding outputs, so that, after learning, when the network presents you a new entry (even if it is incomplete or possess any error), based on the functional relationship established in the sameIt's able to generalize it offering a way out. As a result, can be defined an artificial neural network as an intelligent system able to not only learn, but also to generalise.

A neural network consists of processing units that are called neurons or nodes. These nodes are organized into groups that are called "layers". There are usually three types of layers: an input layer, one or more hidden layers and a layer of output. Connections are established between adjacent nodes in each layer. The input layer, which presents data to the network, consists of input nodes that receive the information directly from the outside. Output layer represents the response of the network to a given as this information transferred to outside input. Hidden or intermediate layers are responsible for processing information and interposed between the input and output layers are the only ones who have no connection with the outside.

13.2 NETWORKS NEURAL WITH SAS ENTERPRISE MINER

SAS Enterprise Miner allows to work with neural networks through multiple nodes located in the category *Model* (Figure 13-1).

Neural Network node allows you to use neural networks for optimization and forecasting through Multilayer Perceptrons, radial basis and generalized linear models functions.

The *Princomp/Dmneural* node allows you to use neural networks to calculate principal components and later use in the optimal setting of a regression model with a view to the prediction.

The *Two Stage Model* node allows you to use neural networks for general a model in c stages in order to predict a class variable and a continuous variable. You can use the perceptron multilayer, generalized linear models and radial basis functions.

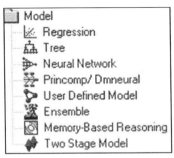

Figure 13-1

SAS Enterprise Miner also allows you to work with neural networks through the node *SOM/Kohonen*, overlooking classification tasks. This node is located in the category *Modify* (Figure 13-29).

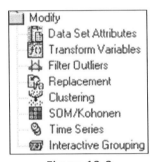

Figure 13-2

13.3 OPTIMIZATION AND ADJUSTMENT OF MODELS WITH NETS: NEURAL NODE   NETWORK

The *Neural Network* node allows you to use neural networks for the optimization and adjustment of models through Multilayer Perceptrons, radial basis functions and generalized linear models. As shown in Figure 13-1, is located in the *Model* of the SAS Enterprise Miner menu category.

As an example, we will use the data from the file*Credits*to set the logical rules that will allow you to help make the decision on when you decide to assign or not credit. Once imported file, assign to the variable *customer* role *ID* in the model while the *CREDIT_V* variable will be the variable target (*Target*) and the other variables will be *inputs*.

Once we already have our work in SAS (*creditos.sas7bdat*file) format data in a specific library (library *work* representing the subdirectory *c:\libros\miningt*), open the project P1 (*File → Open*) and using *File → New → Diagram* create diagram D14. Then we put the *Input Data Source* node that is assigned the data set *creditos.sas7bdat* of the library work in the diagram. Then join the data with the partition node (*Data Partition*) and will randomly assign 80% data training, 10% to validation and 10% test. Once this task will connect the node of data with neural networks node partition (*Neural Network*) as shown in Figure 13-3.

To assign to the variable*Customer*type*id*, the variable*CREDIT_V*type*Target*and the rest of the variables type*input*, double click on the *Input Data Source* node and choose the *Variables*tab. Then you click with the right button of the mouse on each variable to be of type *input*Select *Set Model Role* and then *Input*. Repeat the process with the variable of type *target* (Figure 13-4). To assign randomly 80% data training, 10% to validation and test 10% we double click on the *Data Partition* node and fill in the *Variables* tab as shown in Figure 13-5.

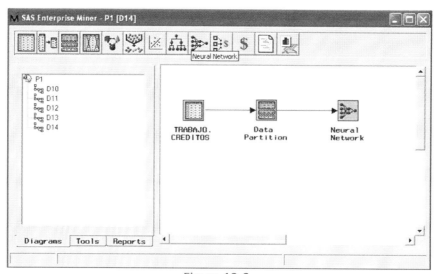

Figure 13-3

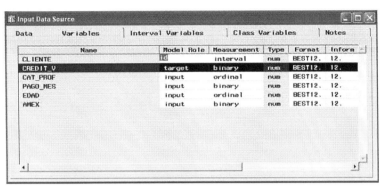

Figure 13-4

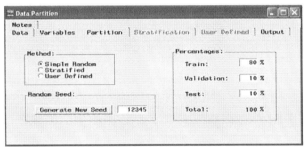

Figure 13-5

To set the specifications of the network open *Neural Network* node by double-clicking on it in the diagram. Gets the entry screen of the node on which tab *Data* specifies the location of the predecessor data that will be used to train, validate, test and give new answers (Figure 13-6). The Sub *Options* (Figure 13-7) specifies if it is carried out a training prior and in this case the maximum number of rows that is dedicated to the interactive training. 2,000 Observations are selected by default. To use the entire sample is necessary to disable the box *simple Use of data sets*. To configure the sample size and random seed generator sample select *set*.

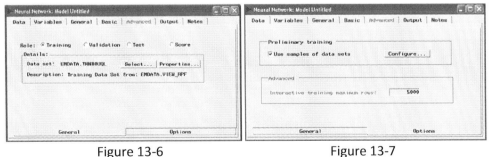

Figure 13-6   Figure 13-7

On the *Variables* tab are the variables involved in the tree and its properties and on the *General* tab we activate the advanced user interface and choose the criteria for selection of models of profit and loss. (Figure 13-8). The following model selection criteria are eligible:

- *Average Error:* choose the model with the smallest error in the validation sample.

- *Misclassification Rate:* choose the model with the lowest rate of error in the validation sample.

- *Profit / Loss:* if two or more decisions in the matrix of losses or gains are defined the objective will be to maximize the profit matrix (minimize the loss matrix) of the validation data.

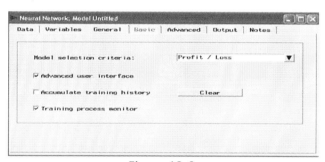

Figure 13-8

As in Figure 13-8 we have chosen the advanced user interface tab is accessible*Advanced,*that will leave by default the typical architecture of the multilayer perceptron with three neurons in the hidden layer. This tab leads to a window (Figure 13-9), which has five subwindows on the sub-tabs located on its bottom (*Initialization, Optimization, Network, Train* and *Prelim*).

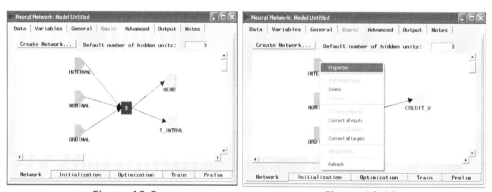

Figure 13-9   Figure 13-10

Network: In the subwindow (Figure 13-9) can carry out the following tasks:

- **Create the network:** allows you to set the same options as in the basic window (Figure 13-20). We chose architecture *Multilayer Perceptron*.

- **Diagram the network:** allows to make connections that you want in the chart. By default the variables of each type are grouped in nominal, ordinal and continuous nodes. Each variable output nominal and ordinal has, where appropriate, its own node. Continuous variables are grouped on a single node with the name *T_intrvl* which can subsequently be unbundled. All the variables, both *inputs* and *outputs* can be added and separated nodes. The neural network architecture diagram is extremely similar to the flowchart from *Data Mining* we build in the work area. We can connect the nodes, delete connections or select different nodes and connections at the same time. The right button of the mouse activates the context menu of Figure 13-10 with the following options:

  - **Properties**: opens a dialog box with the properties of the node or connection. These properties allow you to separate or grouped variables as well as deciding if the standardization of the variables processed there, options of initialization on each node and choose the activation function and function to combine the signals received by the tab *Hidden* (Figure 13-11).
  - **Add hidden layer:** allows you to add new hidden layers.

  - **Delete:** deletes the selected item.

  - **Redraw:** returns to draw the diagram.

  - **Connect selected:** connects the selected nodes.

  - **Connect all inputs:** connects all *inputs* to the hidden layer or variable output selected.

  - **Connect all hidden:** connects all *inputs* to the hidden layer is selected an *input* or connecting all the nodes *output* to the hidden layer in the case of an *output*.

  - **Connect all targets:** connecting the node *input* selected to all target nodes either connects the selected hidden layer or all nodes (all *outputs*) output layer.

○ *Merge nodes*: merges the selected nodes of the same type in one only.

○ *Refresh*: updated the diagram shown on the display.

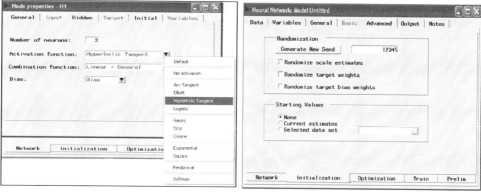

Figure 13-11   Figure 13-12

*Initialization:*It defines the options to initialize the training of the neural network (Figure 13-12).

The two fields on this screen are described below.

• *Randomization*: can generate a random number to distribute the amount of weights randomly (*Generate New Seed*) or by entering a number that set the weights a previous training. We also specify if we want to be randomized estimates of scale, the weights of the *outputs* and weights of bias (*bias*).

• *Starting values*: *None* is the default option in which there is no defined pesos. *Current estimates* starts with the most recent weights training and *selected data set* select a directory where we will select the data file with the weights of a library of data from SAS (Figure 9-11).

*Optimization:*Specifies the target optimization, function type, memory (*weight decay parameter*) parameter and parameter convergence (Figure 13-13). Options on this screen are explained below:

• *Optimization Step:* phase and form of training.

○ *Train:* the model is trained when you select.

o **Preliminary**: carries out the process of optimization of the weights of the algorithm initialization.

o **Train and Preliminary**: holds first optimization of weights and then uses those weights to carry out training.

o **Early stopping**: defines a set of parameters of training to accelerate the convergence of complex models.

o **Evaluate function**: calculates the value of the function target using the current weights.

• **Objective Function**: training is carried out objective of minimizing one of the following functions.

o **Default**: node chooses a target function depending on how the variable output is measured.

o **Deviance**: the difference between the likelihood for the current network and the likelihood for a saturated model which has a weight for each case in the training data.

o **Maximum likelihood**: minimization of the negative value of the logarithm of the likelihood of the model.

o **M Estimation**: is used to obtain robust estimations when values in the output can contain *outliers*.

• **Weight Decay Parameter**: allows you to enter a parameter's memory when changing weights. This parameter prevents sudden on the surface of the error jump while you can assume the fall in local minima.

• **Convergence Parameters**: to access these options you should select the button *set* (Figure 13-14). The upper sub-tabs are:

o **NLP:** sets the parameters for a process of nonlinear optimization (Figure 13-14).

o **Adjustments:** allows you to adjust parameters for each of the functions absolute convergence objective (fig. 13-15).

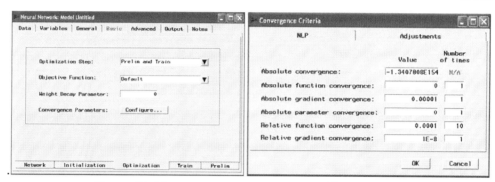

Figure 13-13   Figure 13-14

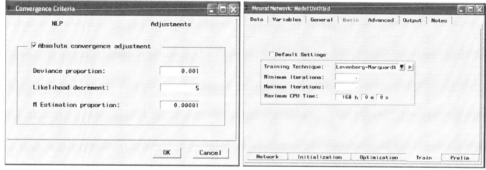

Figure 13-15   Figure 13-16

Train:It allows you to specify various options for the training (Figure 13-16). If you select the *Defaults Settings*box, the node will use the values by default. If this box is unchecked you can choose between the following possibilities.

- ***Training technique***: allows you to select one of the following algorithms of optimization.
  - ***Conjugate Gradient***
  - ***Double Dogleg***
  - ***Trust Region***
  - ***Levenberg-Marquardt***
  - ***Newton-Raphson w / Line Search***
  - ***Newton-Raphson w/Ridging***
  - ***Quasi-Newton***
  - ***Standard-Backprop***
  - ***RPROP***
  - ***Quickprop***
  - ***Incremental Backprop***

The algorithms most commonly used in the literature are the Levenberg-Marquardt used to problems with not more than one hundred parameters, quasi-Newton for medium *Data Mining* problems of around 500 parameters and *Conjugate Gradient* for problems requiring more than 500 parameters. The number of parameters is often related to the number of data on the problem. Next to these traditional models there are several amendments to the classic algorithm of monitored traffic tend to accelerate training. Other classic algorithms such as the Newton-Raphson may finally be used.

- **Minimum Iterations:** allows you to define a minimum number of interactions. The default is *missing*, which means that the node select this number based on the size of the training and the parameters of the network data.

- **Maximum Iterations:** allows you to define a maximum number of interactions. The default is *missing*, which means that the node select this number based on the size of the training and the parameters of the network data.

- **Maximum CPU Time:** by default is set to 168 hours (7 days).

Prelim: In this window (Figure 13-17) can be deployed to the previous training options and changes that the *Train*tab. In addition it is possible to specify the number of scans preliminaries that we want in order to obtain a proper initialization of weights training.

The *Output* tab leads to a window that contains two subwindows on the sub-tabs on the bottom of the figure. In the subwindow *Data* is selected, similarly to other nodes, the files in which the data will be stored. In the subwindow *Variables* (Figure 13-18) we can ask to save any of the following results to be used in a subsequent node or to perform sensitivity analysis of the results.

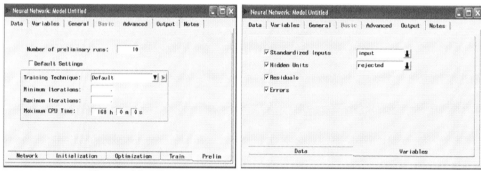

Figure 13-17   Figure 13-18

In Figure 14 - 8 had not chosen the advanced user interface, would be accessible the *Basic* tab in which are the basic elements to set up training (Figure 13-19).

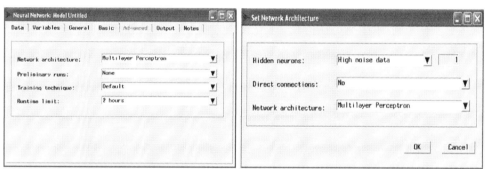

Figure 13-19   Figure 13-29

The options in this screen are explained to acontinucion:

- ***Network architecture***: allows, once deployed (Figure 13-20) Options window, choose the neural network architecture.

  o ***Hidden neurons***: is used to specify the number of neurons in the hidden layer. This selection it can perform automatically depending on the level of noise in the data or select Set *number* and enter the desired number directly.

  o ***Direct connections***: in this case each neuron of the input layer is directly connected to the output layer. This option disables the possibility of finding non-linear relationships.

o ***Network architecture:*** display the following options:

- Generalized linear models.
- Multilayer Perceptrons.
- Ordinary basic radio functions with equal widths.
- Ordinary basic radio functions with unequal widths.
- Normal Basic radio functions with equal heights.
- Normal Basic radio functions with equal volumes.
- Normal Basic radio functions with equal widths.
- Normal Basic radio functions with equal heights and widths.
- Normal Basic radio functions with uneven heights and widths.

- ***Preeliminary runs:*** this option is useful for finding good initial values for weights in neural network avoiding learning trapped in local minima. To select this option, it is necessary to specify a number of initializations displaying the settings dialog.

- ***Training Technique:*** select one of the four available algorithms: Conjugate-Gradient, quasi-Newton, Levenberg-Marquadt, Standard-Backprop or leave the option by default.

- ***Runtime limit:*** allows you to set a time limit of training can vary between 10 minutes and 7 days or even not setting limit and stop it when required by the user.

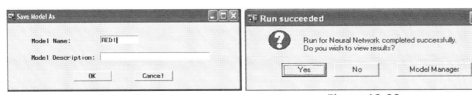

Figure 13-21   Figure 13-22

Already defined the specifications of the network neural and saved with a name (Figure 13-21), only subtracts its execution. To *run networks of automatic node* when the node is open select *Tools → Run* or will click the icon to run the analysis ✗ .

If the node is closed its execution also possible. To do this in the main menu select *Actions → Run* or activate the context menu by clicking with the right button of the mouse on the node and selecting *Run*. In any of the options when the node is running is displayed, unless this option has been disabled, the training monitor. This monitor displays graphically the process of adjustment from the descent along the surface of the problem error (Figure 13-23). After the execution, we can choose to see the results (Figure 13-22).

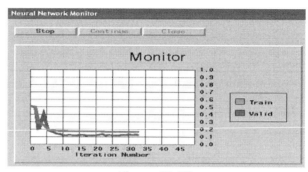

Figure 13-23

If we choose to see the results we obtain the *results Viewer*, which presents several tab as described below:

Model: Displays the description of the model and the variable target in its sub-tab *General* (Figure 13-24). The *Network* sub-tab contains the description of all the parameters of the architecture of the neural network (Figure 13-25).

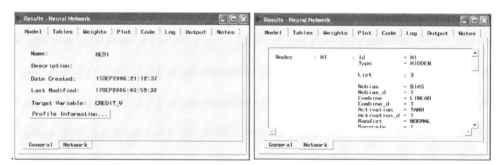

Figure 13-24   Figure 13-25

Tables: In the tables window show the statistical adjustment of the process of training, validation, and test (Figure 13-26). If we click on the black arrow on the right of the field *Fit statistics* get a pop-up menu (Figure 13-27) with the following options:

- **Current estimates**: shows the objective function value and the value of the pesos (parameters) to the trained neural network.

- **Prelim statistics**: shows the statistics of the previous training.

- **New estimates**: shows the change in weights and the settings of the model across all iterations of the training process.

- **History estimates**: shows all followed training history, from the stage preliminary to training, to adjust the weights.
- **Current statistics**: shows the statistics of the goodness of fit of the model.

- **New statistics**: shows the process of adjustment of the statistics of goodness of fit of the model.

- **History statistics**: shows the process of adjustment of the statistics of goodness of fit of the model including statistics preliminary.

- **New plot**: statistical summary for parameters and statistical goodness of fit along all the training.

- **History plot**: Statistics summary for parameters and statistical goodness of fit over all training and training preliminary.

- **Input training data**: shows the data used for training.

- **Input data validation**: shows the data used for the validation.
- **Input testing data**: shows the data used for the test process.

- **Output training data**: original, adjusted training data and errors.

- **Output validation data**: original, adjusted validation data and errors.

- **Output testing data**: original, adjusted test data and errors.

| Model | Tables | Weights | Plot | Code | Log | Output | Notes |

Fit statistics ▼

	Fit Statistic	Training	Validation	Test
1	[TARGET=CREDIT_V]			
2	Average Profit	0.4689922481	0.46875	0.5757575758
3	Misclassification Rate	0.0968992248	0.03125	0.1818181818
4	Average Error	0.2083430182	0.1298054024	0.9413980668
5	Average Squared Error	0.0673142055	0.0403207036	0.1214369573
6	Sum of Squared Errors	34.734130048	2.5805250296	8.0148391791
7	Root Average Squared Error	0.2594498131	0.2008001583	0.3484780585
8	Root Final Prediction Error	0.2927449116		
9	Root Mean Squared Error	0.2765987968	0.2008001583	0.3484780585
10	Error Function	107.50499737	8.3075457563	62.132272409
11	Mean Squared Error	0.0765068944	0.0403207036	0.1214369573
12	Maximum Absolute Error	0.9447455626	0.8008493768	0.9999999972
13	Final Prediction Error	0.0856995832		
14	Divisor for ASE	516	64	66
15	Model Degrees of Freedom	31		
16	Degrees of Freedom for Error	227		
17	Total Degrees of Freedom	258		
18	Sum of Frequencies	258	32	33
19	Sum Case Weights * Frequencies	516	64	66
20	Akaike's Information Criterion	169.50499737		
21	Schwarz's Baysian Criterion	279.6467445		

Figure 13-26

| Model | Tables | Weights | Plot | Code | Log | Output | Notes |

Fit statistics ▼

	Fit Statistic		lidation	Test
1	[TARGET=CREDIT_V]	Fit statistics		
2	Average Profit	Current estimates	0.46875	0.5757575758
3	Misclassification Rate	Prelim. estimates	0.03125	0.1818181818
4	Average Error	New estimates	98054024	0.9413980668
5	Average Squared Error	History estimates	03207036	0.1214369573
6	Sum of Squared Errors		05250296	8.0148391791
7	Root Average Squared Error	Current statistics	08001583	0.3484780585
8	Root Final Prediction Error	New statistics		
9	Root Mean Squared Error	History statistics	08001583	0.3484780585
10	Error Function		75457563	62.132272409
11	Mean Squared Error	New plot	03207036	0.1214369573
12	Maximum Absolute Error	History plot	08493768	0.9999999972
13	Final Prediction Error			
14	Divisor for ASE	Input training data	64	66
15	Model Degrees of Freedom	Input validation data		
16	Degrees of Freedom for Error	Input testing data		
17	Total Degrees of Freedom			
18	Sum of Frequencies	Output training data	32	33
19	Sum Case Weights * Frequencies	Output validation data	64	66
20	Akaike's Information Criterion	Output testing data		
21	Schwarz's Baysian Criterion	279.6467445		

Figure 13-27

Weights: This window contains two tabs: *Table* and *Graph*. The *Table* (Figure 13-28) tab contains the weights once completed the training. These weights or connections are arranged according to the connections between each neuron in the input (*input*) layer and the neurons in the grey output and these to the output (*output*) layer. The tab*Graph*contains a graphical representation of the relative contribution of each weight to the final result (Figure 13-29). Colours Express if the weight is positive or negative.

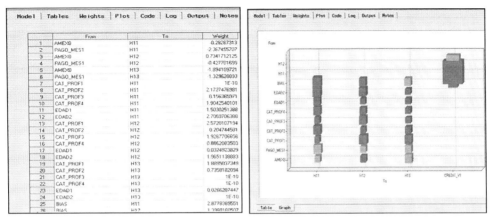

Figure 13-28   Figure 13-29

Plot: By default this window shows the process of adjustment of the error function means when the objective function is minimized (Figure 13-30). In each iteration, the result is updated until there are no perks to continue the process.

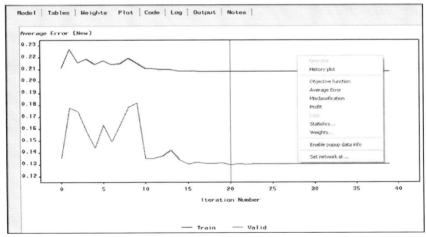

Figure 13-30

The context menu activated by clicking on the graphic with the right mouse button activates other options to graphically represent.

- ***New plot:*** draws a new chart with the selected variables.

- ***History plot:*** draws a graph with the history in the setting of the selected variables.

- *Objective function*: draws a graph with the objective function adjustment process.

- *Average function*: draws a graph with the process of adjustment of the average error function.

- *Misclassification*: draws a graph with the adjustment of the rate of error of classification in each sample.

- *Profit*: shows the value of the benefit in each iteration.

- *Loss*: shows the value of the losses in each iteration.

- *Statistics*: allows you to select the statistics which setting you want to draw.

- *Weights*: allows you to select the weights whose setting you want to draw.

- *Enable popup data info*: when this option is enabled when you click a point in the chart shows the number of iteration and the target value at that point. *Disenable popup data info* disables this option.

- *Set network at*: displays a series of options such as browse the network on the desired iteration and examine the network at the minimum of the function of error in the validation sample.

*Code:*The code window automatically generates SAS code that was sent to run the node (Figure 13-31). The *Training* option generates SAS code to train the model. The *Scoring* option shows the passage of generation of outcomes in the SAS DATA STEP.

Log: Shows the SAS log of process optimization (Figure 9-25).

*Output:*This window contains the output generated by SAS from the sent code. This result includes:

- The history of the process preliminary adjustment.
- The algorithm (the neural network weights) initialization parameters.
- Criteria to carry out optimization Levenberg-Marquart.
- Statistics of the process of adjustment of the algorithm.
- Final weights.
- Objective function value in the latest iteration.

The output of the example is as follows:

08: 57 Pm Friday, September 15, 2006 26 SAS System

Procedure NEURAL

Execution of seed value of
training function random number of criteria of
 preliminary home goal iteration completion

    1 12345 0.211176770867 20
    2 1190861051 0.22719159682 20
    3 998823970 0.215761009645 20
    4 1425928522 0.218819508158 20
    5 679865644 0.214304877758 20
    6 422345732 0.217671879857 20
    0.214530807261 20 7 1042897464
    8 69139770 0.215164001944 20
    9 335245709 0.219794327804 20
    10 2039838345 0.215464563868 20
                      08: 57 Pm Friday, September 15, 2006 27 SAS System

Procedure NEURAL

Home of optimization
Estimators of the parameter
                         Function restrictions restriction restriction
     Objective of the dimension from the dimension from the dimension number
observations parameter estimator active top bottom gradient

    1 AMEXO_H11 - 0.240598 - 0.000789.   .   _
    2 - 2.094752 0.000175 PAGO_MES1_H11.   .   _
    3 AMEXO_H12 0.389627 - 0.000124.   .   _
    4 PAGO_MES1_H12 - 0.140027 - 0.000073962.   .   _
    5 AMEXO_H13 - 2.073916 - 0.000078984.   .   _
    6 - 0.279044 0.000574 PAGO_MES1_H13.   .   _
    7 CAT_PROF1_H11 1E - 10-0.000182 - 1E-10.   Lower BC _
    8. 2.239986 0.000017131 1E-10 CAT_PROF2_H11.   _
    9. CAT_PROF3_H11 0.028934 - 0.000022672 1E-10.   _
    10. CAT_PROF4_H11 1.672774 - 0.000124 1E-10.   _
    11. 1.814981 0,000525 1E-10 EDAD1_H11.   _
    12 EDAD2_H11 2.712413 0.000445 1E-10.   _
    13. CAT_PROF1_H12 2.578040 - 0.000033604 1E-10.   _
    14. 0.504210 0.000144 1E-10 CAT_PROF2_H12.   _
    15. CAT_PROF3_H12 1.518576 - 0.000106 1E-10.   _
    16. CAT_PROF4_H12 0.619115 - 0.000021206 1E-10.   _
    17 EDAD1_H12 0.067998 - 0.000240 1E-10.   _
    18. EDAD2_H12 1.792368 - 0.000053064 1E-10.   _
    19. CAT_PROF1_H13 0.652617 - 0.000041624 1E-10.   _
    20. CAT_PROF2_H13 0.384451 - 0.000231 1E-10.   _
    21 CAT_PROF3_H13   1E-10   0.001011   1E-10   . Lower BC _
    22 CAT_PROF4_H13   1E-10   0.001035   1E-10   . Lower BC _
    23 EDAD1_H13 - 10 0.000444 1E-10 1E.   Lower BC _
    24 EDAD2_H13 1E - 10 0.001073 1E-10.   Lower BC _
    25. BIAS_H11 2.865239 - 0.000651.   .   _
    26. BIAS_H12 1.410057 - 0.000027774.   .   _
    27 - 1.786858 0.000082654 BIAS_H13.   .   _
    28 H11_CREDIT_V1   6.042685   -0.000452   .   .   _
    29 H12_CREDIT_V1   -4.556905 -0.000010786   .   .   _
    30 H13_CREDIT_V1   -3.104712   0.000481   .   .   _
    31 BIAS_CREDIT_V1   2.769563   -0.000372   .   .   _

Value of Objective Function = 0.2111767709

Procedure NEURAL

Levenberg-Marquardt optimization

Iterations 0 should
Maximum iterations 100
Maximum invocations of the function 2147483647
Time 604800 maximum CPU
Criterion gradient ABSGCONV 0.00001
Criterion gradient GCONV 1E-8
Criterion gradient 0 GCONV2
The function 0 ABSFCONV criteria
Criterion of function FCONV 0.0001
The function 0 FCONV2 criteria
Parameter 0 FSIZE
Criterion of change of parameter ABSXCONV 0
Parameter 0 XCONV change criteria
Parameter 0 XSIZE
Function ABSCONV 0.0013901477 criteria
Initial region of confidence 1 radio factor
Tolerance of singularity (SINGULAR) 1E-8
Accuracy of restriction (LCEPS) 1E-8
Linear (LCSING) unit 1E-8 restrictions
Releasing active restrictions (LCDEACT).

Levenberg-Marquardt optimization

Set to update More scale (1978)

Estimates of parameter 31
Lower limits 18
Upper limits 0

Home of optimization

Active restrictions (+) 4 function objective 0.2111767709
Max Abs Gradient Element 0.0010733276 Radio 1

Iteration	reset	func.	Called restrictions Active	function objective fun. obj.	change Max abs	Element / pred. gradient / about current	Change Lambda
1	0	3	5	0.21076	0.000413	0.00401	0.0348 0.945
2	0	4	5	0.21020	0.000565	0.0130	0.0138 0.835
3	0	5	5	0.20998	0.000222	0.0479	0.00436 0.222
4	0	6	4'	0.20882	0.00116	0.00573	0.00231 0.770
5	0	8	4	0.20870	0.000117	0.00357	0.00952 0.755
6	0	9	4	0.20858	0.000124	0.00297	0.00410 0.884
7	0	10	4	0.20843	0.000147	0.0111	0.00130 0.793
8	0	12	3'	0.20839	0.000042	0.00427	0.00500 0.769
9	0	13	4	0.20837	0.000023	0.0107	0.00210 0.518
10	0	14	3'	0.20834	0.000024	0.0118	0.00154 0.400
11 *	0	15	3'	0.20833	0.000017	0.0168	0.00114 0.264
12 *	0	17	4	0.20832	8. 954E-6	0.00930	0.0188 0.169
13	0	18	3'	0.20829	0.000023	0.00368	0.00527 0.596
14 *	0	20	3	0.20829	4. 37E-6	0.000621	0.201 0.695
15 *	0	22	4	0.20829	1. 715E-7	0.000256	0.261 0.341
16 *	0	23	3'	0.20829	1. 036E-7	0.000087	0.0595 0.796
17	0	24	4	0.20829	6. 505E-8	0.000893	0.0311 0.496
18	0	25	3'	0.20829	1. 606E-7	0.000350	0.0267 0.824

```
19 * 0 26 4 0.20829 1. 25E-7 0.00113 0.0136 0.551
20 * 0 27 3' 0.20829 7. 801E-7 0.000557 0.00496 0.921
21 0 29 4 0.20829 5. 039E-8 0.00125 0.0241 0.279
22 * 0 30 3' 0.20829 2. 315E-7 0.000496 0.0205 0.777
23 * 0 32 4 0.20829 5. 517E-8 0.00102 0.0297 0.387
24 * 0 33 3' 0.20829 1. 706E-7 0.000405 0.0318 0.796
25 0 35 4 0.20829 5. 315E-8 0.000870 0.0342 0.455
26 0 36 3' 0.20829 1. 345E-7 0.000341 0.0308 0.809
27 * 0 37 4 0.20829 1. 136E-7 0.000928 0.0155 0.619
28 0 38 3' 0.20829 2. 477E-7 0.000379 0.0169 0.870
29 * 0 39 4 0.20829 1. 054E-7 0.00179 0.00769 0.297
```

                          Optimization results

Iterations 29 41 function invocations
Invocations of the Jacobian 31 4 Active restrictions
Function Objetive 0.2082866033 Max Abs Gradient Element 0.0017940834
Lambda   0.0076877421 Actual Over Pred Change   0.297003074
Radio   0.0066361286

 Convergence criterion (FCONV=0.0001) satisfied.

NOTA: At least one element of the (projected) gradient is greater than 1e-3.

                        08: 57 Pm Friday, September 15, 2006 31 SAS System

                          Procedure NEURAL

                        Optimization results
                      Estimators of the parameter
                                            Function restriction
              Objective of the dimension number
      observations parameter estimator active gradient

                  1 AMEXO_H11 - 0.257131 - 0.000500
                  2 PAGO_MES1_H11 - 2.392911 - 0.001310
                  3 0.733225 0.000240 AMEXO_H12
                  4 - 0.426302 0.000536 PAGO_MES1_H12
                  5 AMEXO_H13 - 1.804353 - 0.000135
                  6 PAGO_MES1_H13   -1.413130   0.000161
                  7 CAT_PROF1_H11   1E-10   0.001010   Lower BC
                  8 CAT_PROF2_H11   2.153513   -0.000738
                  9 CAT_PROF3_H11   0.151181   -0.000746
                 10 CAT_PROF4_H11   1.902728   -0.000748
                 11 EDAD1_H11   1.492679   -0.001339
                 12 EDAD2_H11   2.705477   -0.001346
                 13 CAT_PROF1_H12   2.584303   -0.000314
                 14 CAT_PROF2_H12   0.200228   0.000307
                 15 CAT_PROF3_H12   1.947512   0.000306
                 16 CAT_PROF4_H12   0.898843   0.000308
                 17 EDAD1_H12   0.032145   0.000412
                 18 EDAD2_H12   1.970760   0.000415
                 19 CAT_PROF1_H13   2.009222   -0.000101
                 20 CAT_PROF2_H13   0.720500   0.000085835
                 21 CAT_PROF3_H13   1E-10   0.000203   Lower BC
                 22 CAT_PROF4_H13   1E-10   0.000204   Lower BC
                 23 0.025731 0.000112 EDAD1_H13
                 24 EDAD2_H13 1E - 10 0.000332 Lower BC
                 25 2.877422 0.001794 BIAS_H11
                 26. BIAS_H12 1.404961 - 0.000559
                 27. BIAS_H13 - 1.359450 - 0.000175
                 28 H11_CREDIT_V1   14.712253   -0.000043900
                 29 H12_CREDIT_V1   -7.627579   -0.000000723
                 30 H13_CREDIT_V1   -9.134602   0.000039444

```
      31 BIAS_CREDIT_V1        4.009858        0.000133

          Value of Objective Function = 0.2082866033
                First Order Lagrange Multipliers

                                           Multiplier
                  Active restriction Lagrange
          Lower BC CAT_PROF1_H11 0.001010
          Lower BC     CAT_PROF3_H13        0.000203
          Lower BC     CAT_PROF4_H13        0.000204
          Lower BC     EDAD2_H13            0.000332
                        Sistema SAS      20:57 Friday, September 15, 2006  32
```

As in other nodes for the creation of models, neural networks node also allows the use of the *Model Manager* utility.

To choose the architecture *Multilayer perceptron* (Figure 13-20), the adjusted model is very comprehensive and calculated estimators considering all combinations of all values of the variables involved in the model. If you instead choose architecture of *Generalized Linear Model* using *Advanced* → *Network* → *Create Network* (Figure 13-31), obtained a regular general linear model estimates (considering only the intersections of categories of independent qualitative variables) as shown in output arising then.

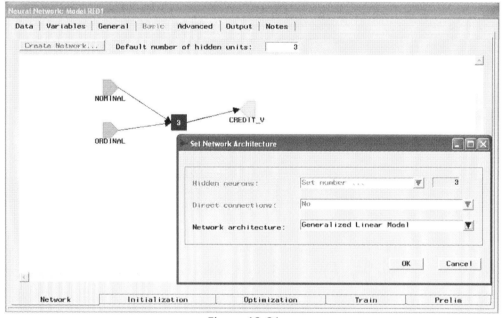

Figure 13-31

When you run the network, the output obtained in the *Output* tab is as follows:

```
                              08: 57 Pm Friday, September 15, 2006 33 SAS System

                      Procedure NEURAL

Execution of seed value of
training function random number of criteria of
 preliminary home goal iteration completion

          1               12345    0.284019332715        18      FCONV
                                   Sistema SAS        20:57 Friday, September 15, 2006  34

                      Procedure NEURAL

                    Home of optimization
                  Estimators of the parameter
                                        Function restrictions restriction
     Objective of the dimension from the dimension number
observations parameter estimator top bottom gradient

       1 0.148876 0.000010647 AMEXO_CREDIT_V1.               .
       2 PAGO_MES1_CREDIT_V1 - 1.870673 - 0.000039094.             .
       3 CAT_PROF1_CREDIT_V1          0       0.009132        1E-10
       4 CAT_PROF2_CREDIT_V1     0.411481     -0.000036074    1E-10          .
       5 CAT_PROF3_CREDIT_V1          0       0.005557        1E-10          .
       6 CAT_PROF4_CREDIT_V1     0.640014     0.000018549     1E-10          .
       7. 1.914427 0.000040673 1E-10 EDAD1_CREDIT_V1.
       8. 1.303736 0.000025305 1E-10 EDAD2_CREDIT_V1.
       9 BIAS_CREDIT_V1          1.289612     -0.000035562           .               .

                              Sistema SAS        20:57 Friday, September 15, 2006  36

                    Procedure NEURAL
                 Levenberg-Marquardt optimization
            Iterations 0 should
            Maximum iterations 100
            Maximum invocations of the function 2147483647
            Time 604800 maximum CPU
            Criterion gradient ABSGCONV 0.00001
            Criterion gradient GCONV 1E-8
            Criterion gradient 0 GCONV2
            The function 0 ABSFCONV criteria
            Criterion of function FCONV 0.0001
            The function 0 FCONV2 criteria
            Parameter 0 FSIZE
            Criterion of change of parameter ABSXCONV 0
            Parameter 0 XCONV change criteria
            Parameter 0 XSIZE
            Function ABSCONV 0.0013901477 criteria
            Initial region of confidence 1 radio factor
            Tolerance of singularity (SINGULAR) 1E-8
            Accuracy of restriction (LCEPS) 1E-8
            Linear (LCSING) unit 1E-8 restrictions
            Releasing active restrictions (LCDEACT).

                    Levenberg-Marquardt optimization

                Set to update More scale (1978)

                9 Parameter estimators
                Lower limits 6
```

```
                    Upper limits 0

                      Home of optimization

        Active restrictions 2 function objective 0.2840193327
        Max Abs Gradient Element 0.0091321906 Radio 1


                                                              Change
                                            Element / pred.
                Called restrictions function change gradient / about
  Iteration reset func.      Active objective fun. obj.   Max abs current Lambda


        1 0 2 2 0.28402 3. 965E-8 0.000030 0 0.256
        2 0 3 2 0.28402 2. 221E-8 0.000023 0 0.259
        3 0 4 2 0.28402 1. 209E-8 0.000017 0 0.256
        4 0 5 2 0.28402 6. 733E-9 0.000013 0 0.258
        5 0 6 2 0.28402 3. 69E-9 9. 425E-6 0 0.256


                          08: 57 Pm Friday, September 15, 2006 37 SAS System

                      Procedure NEURAL

                      Optimization results


Iteration 5 8 function invocations
Invocations of the Jacobian 7 2 active restrictions
Function Objetive 0.2840192483 Max Abs Gradient Element 9. 4251954E-6
Lambda                           0  Actual Over Pred Change        0.2563529384
Radio                    0.000598374

 Convergence criterion (ABSGCONV=0.00001) satisfied.
                          Sistema SAS        20:57 Friday, September 15, 2006  38



                      Procedure NEURAL
                      Optimization results

                     Estimators of the parameter
                                        Function restriction
           Objective of the dimension number
  observations parameter estimator active gradient


        1. AMEXO_CREDIT_V1 0.148621 - 0.000002497
        2 - 1.870098 0.000009362 PAGO_MES1_CREDIT_V1
        3 CAT_PROF1_CREDIT_V1           0       0.009159     Lower BC
        4 CAT_PROF2_CREDIT_V1     0.414633      0.000008536
        5 CAT_PROF3_CREDIT_V1           0       0.005558     Lower BC
        6 CAT_PROF4_CREDIT_V1     0.636314     -0.000003673
        7 EDAD1_CREDIT_V1         1.913749     -0.000009425
        8 EDAD2_CREDIT_V1         1.304362     -0.000005166
        9 BIAS_CREDIT_V1          1.289578      0.000007493

            Value of Objective Function = 0.2840192483

            First Order Lagrange Multipliers


                                       Multiplicador
                 Restricción activa       Lagrange

        Lower BC      CAT_PROF1_CREDIT_V1      0.009159
        Lower BC      CAT_PROF3_CREDIT_V1      0.005558
```

```
Projected gradient

Dimension gradient
    free projected

       1 0.000045110
       2 0.000049937
       3 0.000031834
       4 0.000009876
       5 0.000060193
       6-0.000023238
       7-0.000030922
```

If all the variables considered are of type range, the procedure *Neural Nerwork* adjusts a usual multiple linear regression model. As an example, we will consider the same structure of neural network of Figure 13-3, but now the *Input Data Source* input data set is the set of data *belgica.sas7bdat*. *Input*were chosen as *TargetMATH* and *READ* and other variables as variables in this node.

As it tries to fit a regression which deals with model to explain the scores in mathematics *MATH* according to the rest of the quantitative variables of the file, choose *MATH* dependent variable and independent variables the rest of the quantitative variables of type file interval, by filling in the *Variables* of the node *Neural Network* tab as shown in Figure 13-32. On the tab *Advanced* se choose architecture of *generalized linear Model* using *Advanced* → *Network* → *Create Network* (Figure 13-33).

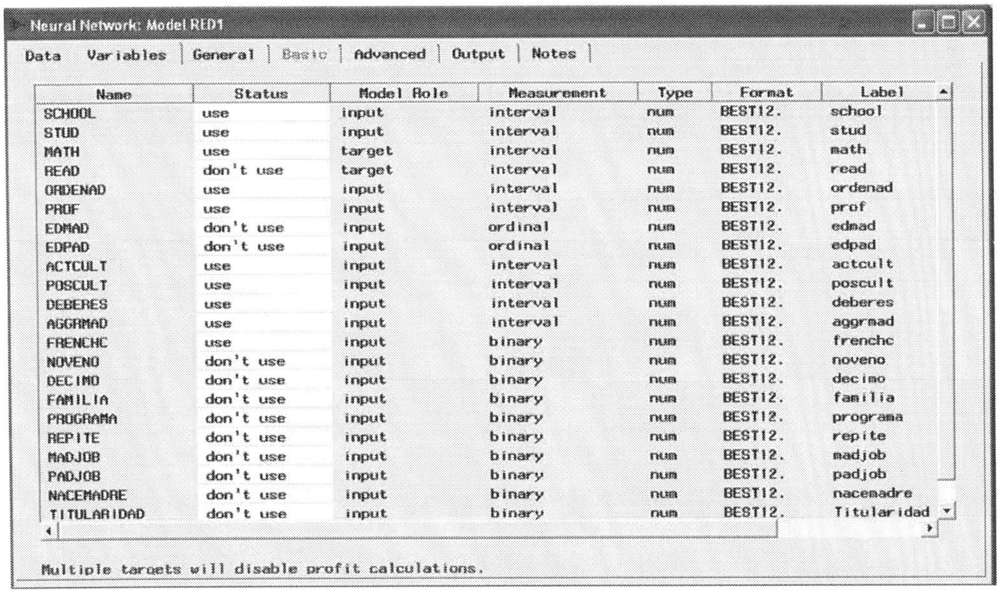

Name	Status	Model Role	Measurement	Type	Format	Label
SCHOOL	use	input	interval	num	BEST12.	school
STUD	use	input	interval	num	BEST12.	stud
MATH	use	target	interval	num	BEST12.	math
READ	don't use	target	interval	num	BEST12.	read
ORDENAD	use	input	interval	num	BEST12.	ordenad
PROF	use	input	interval	num	BEST12.	prof
EDMAD	don't use	input	ordinal	num	BEST12.	edmad
EDPAD	don't use	input	ordinal	num	BEST12.	edpad
ACTCULT	use	input	interval	num	BEST12.	actcult
POSCULT	use	input	interval	num	BEST12.	poscult
DEBERES	use	input	interval	num	BEST12.	deberes
AGGRMAD	use	input	interval	num	BEST12.	aggrmad
FRENCHC	use	input	binary	num	BEST12.	frenchc
NOVENO	don't use	input	binary	num	BEST12.	noveno
DECIMO	don't use	input	binary	num	BEST12.	decimo
FAMILIA	don't use	input	binary	num	BEST12.	familia
PROGRAMA	don't use	input	binary	num	BEST12.	programa
REPITE	don't use	input	binary	num	BEST12.	repite
MADJOB	don't use	input	binary	num	BEST12.	madjob
PADJOB	don't use	input	binary	num	BEST12.	padjob
NACEMADRE	don't use	input	binary	num	BEST12.	nacemadre
TITULARIDAD	don't use	input	binary	num	BEST12.	Titularidad

Figure 13-32

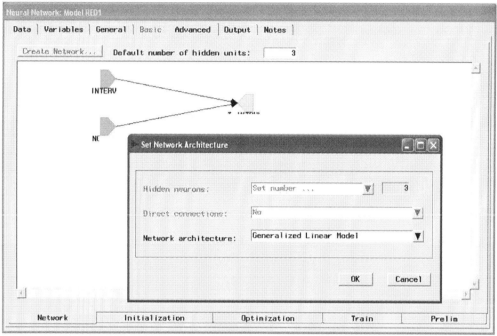

Figure 13-33

When you run the network tab*Output* you get estimates from a usual linear model. These estimates are presented below:

```
                        08: 57 Pm Friday, September 15, 2006  19 SAS System
                          Procedure NEURAL
Execution of seed value of
training function random number of criteria of
 preliminary home goal iteration completion

         1              12345    6459.963650953          1        ABSGCONV
                                 Sistema SAS      20:57 Friday, September 15, 2006  20


                          Procedure NEURAL
                          Home of optimization
                          Estimators of the parameter
                                                       Function
               Number of target
           observations parameter estimator gradient

               1 actcult_math 6.578258 2. 223024E-12
               2 aggrmad_math 47.531983 - 1. 311E-11
               3 deberes_math 4.062924 7. 104148E-11
               4 ordenad_math - 0.187665 - 7. 30685E-11
               5 poscult_math 4.909899 - 4. 25728E-11
               6 prof_math          -3.715439     2.926204E-11
               7 school_math        -0.011685       7.44691E-9
               8 stud_math - 0.191509 1. 733156E-11
               9 frenchc0_math - 41.129208 - 1. 1417E-12
              10 BIAS_math 288.876878 - 1. 73245E-12

           Value of Objective Function = 6459.963651
```

Procedure NEURAL

Levenberg-Marquardt optimization

Iterations 0 should
Maximum iterations 100
Maximum invocations of the function 2147483647
Time 604800 maximum CPU
Criterion gradient ABSGCONV 0.00001
Criterion gradient GCONV 1E-8
Criterion gradient 0 GCONV2
The function 0 ABSFCONV criteria
Criterion of function FCONV 0.0001
The function 0 FCONV2 criteria
Parameter 0 FSIZE
Criterion of change of parameter ABSXCONV 0
Parameter 0 XCONV change criteria
Parameter 0 XSIZE
Function ABSCONV 9.7702640882 criteria
Initial region of confidence 1 radio factor
Tolerance of singularity (SINGULAR) 1E-8

Levenberg-Marquardt optimization

Set to update More scale (1978)

Estimates of parameter 10

Home of optimization

0 Active restrictions function objective 6459.963651
Max Abs Gradient Element 7. 44691E-9 Radio 1
Optimization results

Iterations 0 3 function invocations
Invocations of the Jacobian 1 0 active restrictions
Function 6459.963651 Max Abs objective Gradient Element 7. 44691E-9
Lambda   0 Actual Over Pred Change   0
Radio   1

 Convergence criterion (ABSGCONV=0.00001) satisfied.
                                        Sistema SAS   20:57 Friday, September 15, 2006 22

Procedure NEURAL

Optimization results
Estimators of the parameter
                                                        Function
           Number of target
        observations parameter estimator gradient

                1 actcult_math 6.578258 2. 223024E-12
                2 aggrmad_math 47.531983 - 1. 311E-11
                3 deberes_math 4.062924 7. 104148E-11
                4 ordenad_math - 0.187665 - 7. 30685E-11
                5 poscult_math 4.909899 - 4. 25728E-11
                6 prof_math   -3.715439   2.926204E-11
                7 school_math   -0.011685   7.44691E-9
                8 stud_math - 0.191509 1. 733156E-11
                9 frenchc0_math - 41.129208 - 1. 1417E-12
               10 BIAS_math 288.876878 - 1. 73245E-12

            Value of Objective Function = 6459.963651

The adjusted model turns out to be:

MATH = 288,8 +6,5*AGRICULT*+47,6*AGGRMAD*+4,06*DEBERES*-0,18*ORDENAD*+4,9*POSCULT*-3,71*PROF* - 0,011*SCHOOL*-0,19*STUD*-41,12*FRENCH0*+*ERROR*

13.4 ANALYSIS ON PRINCIPAL COMPONENTS THROUGH NEURAL NETWORKS: NODE PRINCOMP / DMNEURAL

The *Princomp/Dmneural* node allows you to use neural networks to calculate principal components and later use in the optimal setting of a regression model with a view to the prediction. It is located in the Model category from the menu of SAS Enterprise Miner (Figure 13-1).

Through this node is activated an algorithm that is able to perform two tasks. Firstly it allows an analysis of principal components in order to pass the results to successive nodes or be used as *inputs*. The second task of the node is that it can use the results of the analysis of major components as *inputs* to predict a binary or continuous variable using a non-linear additive model. This algorithm was devised to overcome the slowness that sometimes present artificial neural networks in the process of *Data Mining*.

Its advantages are greater the more correlated are the data and the greater the training database. Through training the first *Dmneural* process is a principal components analysis. Then choose those components that present a good prediction for the response in a linear regression using as a criterion the coefficient of determination. Finally, the components are passes along the neural network using 8 activation functions.

Then we will discuss the implementation and the results derived from applying the *Princomp/Dmneural* node to the *Belgium*data file. In this typical analysis, given the number of variables it is interesting to perform a reduction of information, which can be a step prior to analysis with neural networks. Once we already have our work in SAS (*belgica.sas7bdat*file) format data in a specific library (library *work* representing the subdirectory *c:\libros\miningt*), open the project P1 (*File → Open*) and using *File → New → Diagram* create diagram D15. Then we put the *Input Data Source* node that is assigned the data set *belgica.sas7bdat* of the library work in the diagram. Then join the data with the partition node (*Data Partition*). Once this task will connect the node's data with the main components node partition *Princomp/Dmeural* as shown in Figure 13-34.

Once imported the file we double click on the node *Input Data Source* and choose the tab *Variables*. We will then take the result in reading comprehension (READ) as dependent variable or *target*. *STUD* and *SCHOOL* variables are variables of tag (*id*). The *MATH*variable, corresponding to the result in mathematics, as well as binary variables are not used in this example. It is for this reason that to all of them we will assign them the role of *rejected* being *inputs* the remaining (Figure 13-35).

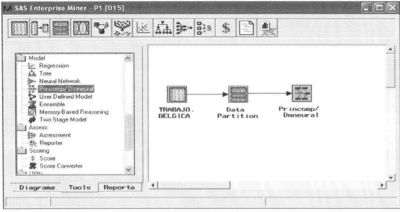

Figure 13-34

Name	Model Role	Measurement	Type	Format	Informat	Variable Label
SCHOOL	id	interval	num	BEST12.	12.	school
STUD	id	interval	num	BEST12.	12.	stud
MATH	rejected	interval	num	BEST12.	12.	math
READ	target	interval	num	BEST12.	12.	read
ORDENAD	input	interval	num	BEST12.	12.	ordenad
PROF	input	interval	num	BEST12.	12.	prof
EDMAD	input	ordinal	num	BEST12.	12.	edmad
EDPAD	input	ordinal	num	BEST12.	12.	edpad
ACTCULT	input	interval	num	BEST12.	12.	actcult
POSCULT	input	interval	num	BEST12.	12.	poscult
DEBERES	input	interval	num	BEST12.	12.	deberes
AGGRMAD	input	interval	num	BEST12.	12.	aggrmad
FRENCHC	rejected	binary	num	BEST12.	12.	frenchc
NOVENO	rejected	binary	num	BEST12.	12.	noveno
DECIMO	rejected	binary	num	BEST12.	12.	decimo
FAMILIA	rejected	binary	num	BEST12.	12.	familia
PROGRAMA	rejected	binary	num	BEST12.	12.	programa
REPITE	rejected	binary	num	BEST12.	12.	repite
MADJOB	rejected	binary	num	BEST12.	12.	madjob
PADJOB	rejected	binary	num	BEST12.	12.	padjob
NACEMADRE	rejected	binary	num	BEST12.	12.	nacemadre
TITULARIDAD	rejected	binary	num	BEST12.	12.	Titularidad

Figure 13-35

We then double click on the node *Data Partition* and the *Partition* tab will assign random 70% of the training data, 15% to validation and a 15% (Figure 13-36). We will then open the node*Princomp/Dmneural*and on the tab*General*we will activate the procedure*Dmneural*along with all the options (Figure 13-37). In the tab *Output* Activate the option *Process or Store* (Figure 13-38).

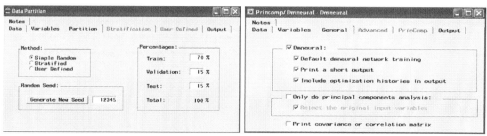

Figure 13-36   Figure 13-37

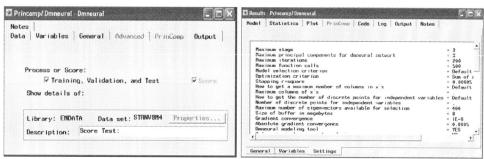

Figure 13-38   Figure 13-39

Once selected these options we will be able to run the node. After appoint and terminate the analysis we will open the output window. The *Model* tab displays the characteristics of the trained model. In particular the *Settings* window displays each selected options (Figure 13-39). The *Statistics* tab displays some statistics summary of the analysis (Figure 13-40). The *Plot* tab we can draw various scatterplots. It is particularly interesting to visualize the setting making the prediction of the dependent variable (Figure 13-41).

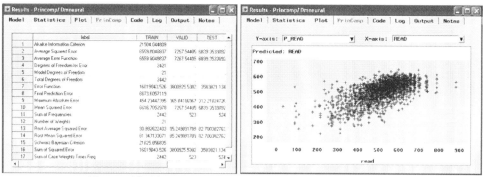

Figure 13-40   Figure 13-41

Finally, the *Output* window displays the results of all neural networks trained by varying the functions activation as well as setting that reaches each of them (Figure 13-42).

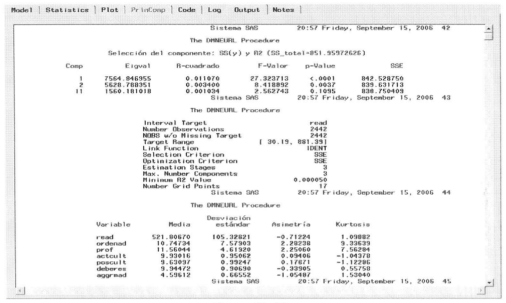

Figure 13-42

As we know this node also allow us to perform only a principal components analysis. To this end, first we go to the data node and define the variables EDMAD and EDPAD as of interval (Figure 13-43). Then in *Princomp/Dmneural* node in the *General* tab select the option *Only do principal component analysis* (Figure 13-44). Selecting this option will activate the *PrinComp*tab. In it we will indicate that we will use the matrix of correlations. This is justified since in this case the variables whose information we want to reduce are not measured in the same units (Figure 13-45).

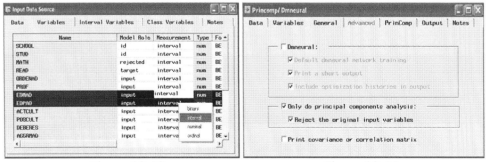

Figure 13-43   Figure 13-44

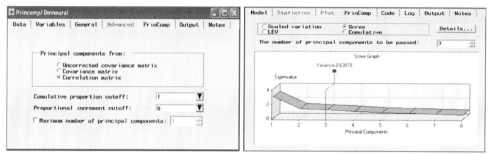

Figure 13-45   Figure 13-46

And finally, once closed the node, we shall proceed to the execution of the principal components analysis. Then we will open the results Viewer. In the *PrinComp* tab we select the *Scree Plot*. In it we can see how by selecting three components (in the field *The number of main components to be passed*) explain 64,464% of the total variance in the data (Figure 13-46). The option *Details...* contains the eigenvalues (*Eigenvalues*), and the percentage of the total variance explained (Figure 13-47). The eigenvectors (*Eigenvectors*) or weights can obtain the original variables from the calculated components (Figure 13-48). For each individual factor scores are stored in files generated in SAS for validation and test both the training data.

Eigenvalues and Eigenvectors

⊙ **Eigenvalues** ⚬ **Eigenvectors**

	_NAME	EigenValue	Difference	ProportionalEigenvalue	CumProportionalEigenvalue	LogEigenvalue
1	PRIN1	2.8744725771	1.6954251768	0.3593090721	0.3593090721	1.055869206
2	PRIN2	1.1790474003	0.1222516271	0.147380925	0.5066899972	0.1647068245
3	PRIN3	1.0567957732	0.2211564478	0.1320994717	0.6387894688	0.0552414746
4	PRIN4	0.8356393254	0.1998600151	0.1044549157	0.7432443845	-0.179558188
5	PRIN5	0.6357793103	0.0559691683	0.0794724138	0.8227167983	-0.452903772
6	PRIN6	0.579910142	0.1160232214	0.0724897678	0.895205566	-0.544862115
7	PRIN7	0.4638969206	0.0894183695	0.0579858651	0.9531914311	-0.768114462
8	PRIN8	0.3744685511		0.0468085689	1	-0.982247455

Close

Figure 13-47

Eigenvalues and Eigenvectors

⚬ Eigenvalues ⊙ **Eigenvectors**

	NAME	PRIN1	PRIN2	PRIN3	PRIN4	PRIN5	PRIN6	PRIN7	PRIN8
1	orderad	-0.291025572	0.3685451586	0.4830429973	0.1873576422	0.6819903503	0.17329417	-0.125340738	0.0138978913
2	prof	-0.389799291	0.3076627459	0.3373295717	0.0800902639	-0.457261118	-0.133199159	0.5852825698	0.2526044838
3	edmad	0.4018050418	0.5126666506	-0.008826978	0.088088222	-0.047846233	-0.066039189	0.2441037254	-0.708280048
4	edpad	0.365767816	0.5477581478	-0.014113698	0.1493698598	-0.231729037	-0.147921958	-0.481235455	0.4863101367
5	actcult	0.323148015	0.262401048	0.5157874528	0.210250422	0.155697412	-0.700116707	0.0350125845	0.0280325906
6	poscult	0.3252914597	-0.079039127	0.5209604971	-0.400508447	-0.24501891	0.6277665101	-0.042243921	0.0148936474
7	deberes	0.2387193781	-0.360608767	0.2320769242	0.8505220038	-0.128555308	0.1334210885	0.0345355028	-0.014375075
8	aggrmad	0.4482199547	0.0388824063	-0.247617451	0.020293799	0.4110341682	0.1546921313	0.588520764	0.4434245794

Close

Figure 13-48

Closed the previous Windows using *Close*, the *Output* tab shows the SAS output with the eigenvalues and their proportion of explained variance.

```
                    The DMNEURL Procedure

                                        Deviation
            Average standard variable

                ordenad      10.74734      7.57903
                prof         11.56044      4.61920
                edmad         4.58804      1.39696
                edpad         4.72482      1.36093
                actcult       9.93016      0.95062
                poscult       9.63097      0.99247
                deberes       9.94472      0.90690
                aggrmad       4.59612      0.66552


                    The DMNEURL Procedure

                Correlation Matrix of eigenvalues

           Self-worth cumulative proportion difference

        1 2.87447258 1.69542518 0.3593 0.3593
        2 1.17904740 0.12225163 0.1474 0.5067
        3 1.05679577 0.22115645 0.1321 0.6388
        4 0.83563933 0.19986002 0.1045 0.7432
        5 0.63577931 0.05586917 0.0795 0.8227
        6 0.57991014 0.11602322 0.0725 0.8952
        7 0.46388692 0.08941837 0.0580 0.9532
        8 0.37446855 0.0468 1.0000
```

13.5 PREDICTION AND DISCRIMINANT ANALYSIS THROUGH NEURAL NETWORKS: NODE TWO STAGE MODEL

The node*Two Stage Model,*located in the Group*Model*Miner (Figure 13-1), menu allows to generate a model in two stages to predict a class variable and a continuous variable. The continuous variable is normally associated with the objective of class level. For example in the file *Belgium* can predict whether characteristics a child attend public or private school through the *property* variable that has two levels: public = 1; Private = 0, tending this continuous variable would be the result in the children in public schools *MATH*math. Cited two variables would be the rest of *input*type and *target* type. This model helps to summarize in a single node tasks that normally would implement in several. The node automatically recognizes the objective of class and the continuous estimating a value for both of these objectives in each phase respectively. Defining a transfer function and a filter you can specify how to apply the forecasting for the class defining as well if we want to use all cases for the prediction of the second stage.

Once we already have our work in SAS (*belgica.sas7bdat*file) format data in a specific library (library *work* representing the subdirectory *c:\libros\miningt*), open the project P1 (*File → Open*) and using *File → New → Diagram* create diagram D16. Then we put the *Input Data Source* node that is assigned the data set *belgica.sas7bdat* of the library work in the diagram. Then join the node*Two Stage Model*as shown in Figure 13-49.

Once imported the file we double click on the node *Input Data Source* and choose the tab *Variables*. We will then take *ownership* and *MATH* variables as variables of type *target*. The rest of the variables are of type *input* (Figure 13-50).

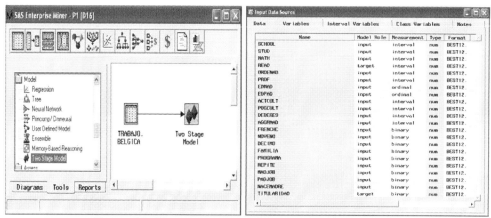

Figure 13-49   Figure 13-50

Now we run the *Two Stage Model* node by double-clicking on it. On the *Data* tab are active by default training data. On the *Variables* tab, you can specify the variables that we will use and not use in analysis, in addition to the usual options defined in the *Input Data Source* or *Data Set Attributes*node to be displayed. *Otput* tab you can select the data whose response you want to predict. We can also predict new databases if we then introduce in the flowchart node *Score*. To make predictions about the training data, validation, test and *score* simply activate the corresponding dialog (Figure 13-51) box.

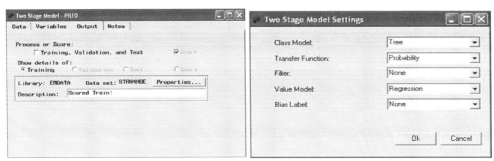

| Figure 13-51 | Figure 13-52 |

To access the scanning options (Figure 2-52) have to press in the tool menu icon either in the main menu select *Tools* → *Settings...*This window allows you to choose between the following options:

- **Class model:** specifies the model that we use in the first stage to fit the model with the categorical variable aim:

  - **Tree**: decision tree. It is the default.

  - **Regression**: . linear regression

  - **MLP**: with one or more hidden layers multilayer perceptron. The number of units in the hidden layer is function of the number of degrees of freedom. The combination of the entries in the layers hides, and output is linear and the function of activation in the hidden layer is the hyperbolic tangent.

  - **RBF**: neural network with radial base with a hidden layer function. The number of units in the hidden layer is function of the number of degrees of freedom. Use the combination radial-eq width and heights in the hidden layer and output function and activation in the hidden layer function is of type softmax. Not standardizes the variable aim.

  - **Glim**: model of neural network generalized linear and interactive. Because it has no hidden layer is characterized, not standardize neither the inputs and the outputs.

- **Transfer function**: determines how to incorporate the variable target outright in the second stage. By default, the selection is the probability of membership estimated to be the first model to be incorporated as input to the second model. You can also change this option and choose classification which introduces the final classification of the case.

- **Filter**: specifies the way in which the observations in the training data are introduced to train the model.

  - **None**: no observation is excluded and all observations used in the first stage are used in the second.

  - **Nonevent**: those observations that do not have the required value of type, which is specified in the order of the classes of the categorical variable, the variable lens of class are excluded from training in the second stage.

  - **Misclassified**: incorrectly classified in the first stage observations are excluded in the second.

  - **Missing**: with values lost in the variable aim continuous observations will be excluded in the second stage.

- **Value model**: allows you to choose the model that we will use to adjust the continuous variable in the second stage.

  - **Tree**: decision tree.

  - **Regression**: linear regression. It is the default option.

  - **MLP**: with one or more hidden layers multilayer perceptron. The number of units in the hidden layer is function of the number of degrees of freedom. The combination of the entries in the layers hides, and output is linear and the function of activation in the hidden layer is the hyperbolic tangent.

  - **RBF**: neural network with radial base with a hidden layer function.El number of units in the hidden layer is a function of the number of degrees of freedom. Use the combination radial-eq width and heights in the hidden layer and output function and activation in the hidden layer function is of type softmax. Also do not standardize the target variable.

  - **Glim**: model of neural network generalized linear and interactive. Because it has no hidden layer is characterized, not standardize neither the inputs and the outputs.

- **Bias adjustment**: determines the way in which the probability a posteriori of the prediction of the class variable and continuous variable prediction are combined to calculate the final predictions.

- **None**: No. Default option.

- **Multiple**: uses the probability a posteriori to adjust the value of the continuous variable using the following equation $\hat{Y} = \tilde{Y} * P(Z)$ where $\hat{Y}$ is the final prediction of continuous variable which depends of $\tilde{Y}$ which is multiplied the second stage model prediction by $P(Z)$ is the probability a posteriori model estimated in the first stage.

- **Filter**: the predicted values of the observations with the not analyzed category are assigned the value zero.

It is essential to point out that any of these combinations will reduce lift or Lift factor if we compare the results with the model without merging the responses.

Once selected all options we will be able to run the node. After appoint and terminate the analysis we will open the output window. The *Output* of the *results Viewer* tab shows the following output:

```
          Target= TITULARIDAD : Tree Variable Importance (max=20)

                                       NUMBER OF
                                       RULES IN      RELATIVE
     Obs     NAME          LABEL         TREE       IMPORTANCE

      1      prof          prof           3          1.00000
      2      school        school         8          0.89524
      3      aggrmad       aggrmad        3          0.87070
      4      ordenad       ordenad        6          0.77962
      5      math          math           0          0.66211
      6      frenchc       frenchc        1          0.37681
      7 ninth ninth 0 0.28790
      repeats 8 repeats 0 0.00000
      9 edpad 0 0.00000 edpad
     10 padjob 0 0.00000 padjob
     11 edmad 0 0.00000 edmad
     12 family family 0 0.00000
     13 program program 0 0.00000
     14 madjob 0 0.00000 madjob
     15 stud stud 0 0.0000
     16 tenth 10th 0 0.00000
     17 nacemadre 0 0.00000 nacemadre
     18      poscult       poscult        0          0.00000
     19      actcult       actcult        0          0.00000
     20      deberes       deberes        0          0.00000
                                      20:57 Friday, September 15, 2006  98
                      Classification Table

                            TRAIN     TRAIN
                 From  Into  Count    Percent
                  0     0     2373    68.0138
                  0     1      196     5.6177

                  1     0      148     4.2419
                  1     1      772    22.1267
                      Fit Statistics
```

```
Statistic                          Training

Average Squared Error                0.07
Total Degrees of Freedom          3489.00
Divisor for ASE                   6978.00
Maximum Absolute Error               0.99
Misclassification Rate               0.10
Sum of Frequencies                3489.00
Root Average Squared Error           0.26
Sum of Squared Errors              486.05
Sum of Case Weights Times Freq    6978.00
```

Target= READ : Regression Effects (max=40)

```
Obs    Effect                       Sign    T-Score
 1     math                          +      27.4951
 2 tenth 0 - 11.5330
 3 program 0 - 11.0717
 4 Intercept + 6.7322
 5 prof - 6.5095
 6 aggrmad + 5.8653
 7     noveno 0                      -       5.3034
 8     school                        -       4.5903
 9     poscult                       +       4.4367
10     actcult                       +       4.3660
11     nacemadre 0                   -       3.4430
12     frenchc 0                     -       3.0567
13 Predicted: Title = 1 - 2.6825
14 edmad 4 + 2.2597
15 edmad 2 - 1.9516
16 0 + 1.8205 family
17 edmad 3 + 1.7396
18 repeat 0 - 1.5484
19 madjob 0 - 1.5205
20 duties + 1.4003
21 edpad 3 + 1.3749
22 edmad 1 - 0.9746
23 padjob 0 - 0.7504
24 edpad 4 + 0.7435
25 edpad 2 + 0.5431
26 edpad 5 - 0.4678
27 edmad 5 + 0.4575
28 edpad 1 - 0.4545
29     stud                          -       0.2457
30     ordenad                       -       0.0224
                   Fit Statistics
   Statistic                        Training

   Average Squared Error              0.07
   Total Degrees of Freedom        3489.00
   Divisor for ASE                 6978.00
   Maximum Absolute Error             0.99
   Misclassification Rate             0.10
   Sum of Frequencies              3489.00
   Root Average Squared Error         0.26
   Sum of Squared Errors            486.05
   Sum of Case Weights Times Freq  6978.00
```

Final Prediction Analysis: Training data
Predicted event: 1
Bias adjustment: None

-- _from=0 _into=0 --

Procedure MEANS

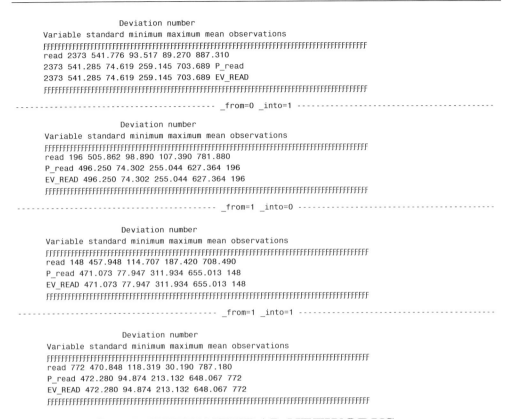

```
                         Deviation number
       Variable standard minimum maximum mean observations
       FFFFFFFFFFFFFFFFFFFFFFFFFFFFFFFFFFFFFFFFFFFFFFFFFFFFFFFFFFFFFFFFFFFFFFFFFFFFFFFFFF
       read 2373 541.776 93.517 89.270 887.310
       2373 541.285 74.619 259.145 703.689 P_read
       2373 541.285 74.619 259.145 703.689 EV_READ
       FFFFFFFFFFFFFFFFFFFFFFFFFFFFFFFFFFFFFFFFFFFFFFFFFFFFFFFFFFFFFFFFFFFFFFFFFFFFFFFFFF

----------------------------------------- _from=0 _into=1 -----------------------------------------
                         Deviation number
       Variable standard minimum maximum mean observations
       FFFFFFFFFFFFFFFFFFFFFFFFFFFFFFFFFFFFFFFFFFFFFFFFFFFFFFFFFFFFFFFFFFFFFFFFFFFFFFFFFF
       read 196 505.862 98.890 107.390 781.880
       P_read 496.250 74.302 255.044 627.364 196
       EV_READ 496.250 74.302 255.044 627.364 196
       FFFFFFFFFFFFFFFFFFFFFFFFFFFFFFFFFFFFFFFFFFFFFFFFFFFFFFFFFFFFFFFFFFFFFFFFFFFFFFFFFF

----------------------------------------- _from=1 _into=0 -----------------------------------------
                         Deviation number
       Variable standard minimum maximum mean observations
       FFFFFFFFFFFFFFFFFFFFFFFFFFFFFFFFFFFFFFFFFFFFFFFFFFFFFFFFFFFFFFFFFFFFFFFFFFFFFFFFFF
       read 148 457.948 114.707 187.420 708.490
       P_read 471.073 77.947 311.934 655.013 148
       EV_READ 471.073 77.947 311.934 655.013 148
       FFFFFFFFFFFFFFFFFFFFFFFFFFFFFFFFFFFFFFFFFFFFFFFFFFFFFFFFFFFFFFFFFFFFFFFFFFFFFFFFFF

----------------------------------------- _from=1 _into=1 -----------------------------------------
                         Deviation number
       Variable standard minimum maximum mean observations
       FFFFFFFFFFFFFFFFFFFFFFFFFFFFFFFFFFFFFFFFFFFFFFFFFFFFFFFFFFFFFFFFFFFFFFFFFFFFFFFFFF
       read 772 470.848 118.319 30.190 787.180
       P_read 472.280 94.874 213.132 648.067 772
       EV_READ 472.280 94.874 213.132 648.067 772
       FFFFFFFFFFFFFFFFFFFFFFFFFFFFFFFFFFFFFFFFFFFFFFFFFFFFFFFFFFFFFFFFFFFFFFFFFFFFFFFFFF
```

13.6 CLUSTER WITH NEURAL NETWORKS ANALYSIS : NODE SOM /KOHONEN

The node *SOM/Kohonen,* located in the Group *Modify* menu (Figure 13-2), Miner is an method to carry out analysis *cluster* artificial neural networks with unsupervised learning, that is, do not specify a results variable. This method allows also *Kohonen Vector Quantization* (VQ) . The term *SOM* comes from the English word *Self-organizing Map* while *Kohonen* is the surname of Teuvo Kohonen, analyst who proposed this kind of self-organized neural network. On this occasion provided the inputs of input, which can be of type binary, nominal, ordinal or continuous, but the network does not receive any information that will indicate what is the output. The network, which only consists of two layers and modifies the weights to be able to associate with the same unit of output more similar input vectors. It is often said that these networks are capable of auto - organize. The Kohonen VQ method is oriented to the clustering while the SOM method can be used as the dimension reduction method.

As an example, we will use data from the *World* file to group, from social and economic information, to various countries of the world in homogeneous groups. The objective is to know which countries are more or less similar according to the following variables: , *urban density, espvidaf, espvidam, alfabet, inc_pob, mortinf, tasa_nat, tasa_mort, tasasida* and *log_pib*. The rest of variables, except *country*, who has a paper label and they will be excluded from the analysis.

Once we already have our work in SAS (*mundo.sas7bdat*file) format data in a specific library (library *work* representing the subdirectory *c:\libros\miningt*), open the project P1 (*File →Open*) and using *File →New →Diagram* create diagram D17. Then the node *SOM/Kohonen* is obtained through the button *Tools* from the browser's project of Enterprise Miner as a sub-option of the *Modify* category or dragging the node itself on the area next to the *Input Data Source* node has been that previously assigned the data set *mundo.sas7bdat* of the library work. Then will be the union of the two (Figure 13-53).

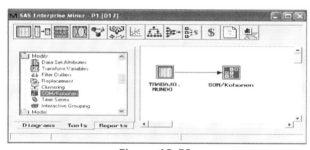

Figure 13-53

It will be necessary to declare variables , *urban density, espvidaf, espvidam, alfabet, inc_pob, mortinf, tasa_nat, tasa_mort, tasasida* and *log_pib* of type *input* and the *country* variable of type *id*, because that will be used as a label. This task is performed by double clicking on the *Input Data Source* node tagged as work.WORLD and choosing the *Variables*tab. Then you click with the right button of the mouse on each variable to be of type *input*Select *Set Model Role* and then *Input*. Repeat the process with the variables to exclude, that assigned type *rejected* and with the variable *country*which will be assigned type *id* (Figure 13-54).

Once connected nodes *Input Data Source* and *SOM/Kohonen* and defined the role of each variable will keep the information of the data node and open *SOM/Kohonen* node by double-clicking on it in the diagram. Gets the entry screen of the node in the *Variables* tab choose the variables that will be used and whether they will be or not standardized range or standard deviation (Figure 13-55).

Figure 13-54

Name	Status	Model Role	Measurement	Type	Format	Label
PA_S	use	id	nominal	char	$16.	país
POBLAC	don't use	rejected	interval	num	BEST12.	poblac
DENSIDAD	use	input	interval	num	BEST12.	densidad
URBANA	use	input	interval	num	BEST12.	urbana
RELIG	don't use	rejected	nominal	char	$8.	relig
ESPVIDAF	use	input	interval	num	BEST12.	espvidaf
ESPVIDAM	use	input	interval	num	BEST12.	espvidam

Figure 13-55

In the *Cluster* (Figure 13-56) window contains fields *Variable name* (name for the cluster identifier), *Variable label* (tag *cluster*) and *Role* (role that is assigned to the variable that is being used to form *clusters* that default is group or *group*). In the *General* window you can select the method, the size of the map and the number of *clusters* (Figure 13-57).

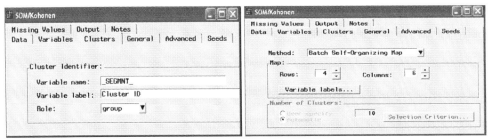

Figure 13-56   Figure 13-57

Then explains the fields in the window *General* (Figure 13-57).

Method: select one of the following options:

- *Batch self-organizing Map:* the most important options are the shape of the map and the size of the final neighbor. They are usually preferable large maps but it increases the time of training.

- *Kohonen self-organizing Map:* the most important options are the shape of the map and the coefficient of learning. It is important to start with a coefficient of high learning as 0.9.

- *Kohonen Vector Quantization:* the most important options are the number of *clusters* and the coefficient of learning. The choice of the number of *clusters* optimum is obtained by trial and error.

Map: select the number of rows and columns, which by default is 4 and 6, respectively. The optimal number is through a trial and error process. If the map is certainly very small groups not reflected the nonlinearities that contain data. If the map is very large analysis time will be elevated and the formation of empty *clusters* tend to hinder the interpretation of results. To resize this also proportionally change the size of the neighbor (*Neighborhood Options* on the *Advanced*tab). We can also rename the variables of row and column of the map in the *Variable labels*option.

*Number of Clusters:*It is activated by selecting the method of training Kohonen VQ. Default is determined automatically but can be specified by the user. We can also as node *Clustering* vary the method of *clustering, clustering cubic criterion cutoff* , and the minimum and maximum number of *clusters* in the *Selection Criterion*option.

In the *Advanced* window, you can select the advanced options in the subwindows: *Batch SOM Training, Neighborhood Options* and *Kohonen Training* (Figure 13-58).

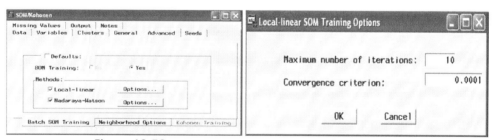

| Figure 13-58 | Figure 13-59 |

Then explains the Sub-Windows of the window *Advanced* (Figure 13-58).

Batch SOM Training:Default options are determined depending on the type of network selected in the *General*tab. For *batch SOM*: be active *SOM Training, Local-linear* and *Nadaraya-Watson*. The above options are disabled for *Kohonen SOM* . If *Local-linear* and *Nadaraya-Watson* are activated at the same time, first performed the *Nadaraya-Watson* training and after *Local-linear*. The criteria of convergence in both, well number of iterations well a criterion established, are defined in the option *Optitons* (Figure 13-59).

Neighborhood Options:When you select one of the methods SOM in the *General* window we can establish different options for neighbourhood deselecting *Defaults* (Figure 13-60).

- ***Kernel shape:*** default is *Epanechnikov* (1). Other forms are uniform (0), *biweight* (2), *triweight* (3), and others (value positive *k* defined by the analyst).

- ***Kernel metric:*** default is *Max* (0). Others are *Manhattan* or *cityblock* (1), (2) *Euclidean* and other positive values specified by the analyst.

- ***Size:*** neighbourhood value must be greater than or equal to zero. Selecting *Options* we can set the initial size, finish, number of steps until the final size and the number of iterations until the final size (Figure 13-61).

- ***Number of steps before reset:*** number of steps before the end.

It is *Row (j)* the row number of the *cluster j*- th, *Col (j)* the number of the column in the *cluster j*- th, *size* the size of neighbourhood, *k kernel* and form *p* the metric *kernel*. Then the function *kernel* is defined as:

$$K(j,n) = \left\{ 1 - \frac{\left[\left| Row(j) - Row(n) \right|^p + \left| Col(j) - Col(n) \right|^p \right]^{2/p}}{size^2} \right\}^{2k}$$

| Figure 13-60 | Figure 13-61 |

Thus for a uniform *kernel* $K(j,n) = 1$ when the distance between two seeds equals the size of neighbourhood (*size*) while for other *kernels* $K(j,n) = 0$ be satisfied again that the distance between two seeds equals the size of neighbourhood (*size*).

Kohonen Training:*SOM Kohonen* or *Kohonen VQ* is selected in the *General* window you can set various advanced options for Kohonen training in the subwindow *Kohonen Training* of *Advanced* (Figure 13-62) window.

- ***Learning rate****:* is used the training that varies the ratio of learning. This is initialized to Kohonen SOM 0.9 and 0.5 for VQ. It is reduced linearly in 0.02 during the first 1000 steps of training. The coefficient of learning, which should vary between 0 and 1, can be redefined by selecting *Options...*

- ***Maximum number of steps:*** default is 500 times the number of clusters. A step is the process carried out in each element.

- ***Maximum number of iterations:*** by default is 100. An iteration is the process carried out on all the training data.

- ***Convergence Criterion:*** default is 0.0001.

The training ends when it meets one of the convergence criteria.

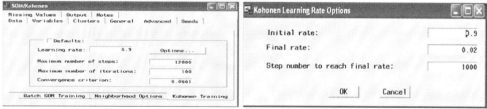

| Figure 13-62 | Figure 13-63 |

The *Seeds* window on the node SOM/Kohonen allows you to specify how to initialize the seeds of the *clusters* (Figure 13-64).By default they will depend on the type of network. *Principal Component*corresponds to *Batch SOM* . *Kohonen SOM* and *Kohonen VQ random*deserves. For other methods the initial seeds are cases of training without lost data separated by a minimum distance specified in the option *Minimum distance between seeds cluster* (*radius*).

Window *Missing Values* in the node *SOM/Kohonen* allows to set how to treat cases with missing data (Figure 13-65). Remarks presenting data lost in all the variables are excluded from the analysis. The fields in this window are explained below:
Imputation method: can choose between the following methods of imputation.

- **Nearest Cluster of Seed**: seed of the nearest *cluster* .

- **Ignore**: Ignore.

Processing of Missing Values during Training: there are 7 methods depending on any of them of the type of variable.

- **Ignore**: ignore the processing.

- **Category**: assign to a category.

- **Mean**: assign the average.

- **Median**: assign the median

- **Midrange**: assign the average value of the range.

- **Mode**: assign fashion.

- **Omit**: ignore the element.

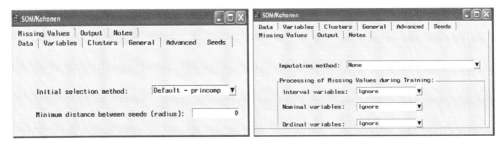

Figure 13-64   Figure 13-65

The *Output* window in the *SOM/Kohonen* node consists of two subwindows:

Clustered Data: sample libraries and files of results for data training, validation, and test (Figure 13-66). It is important to note that these results are stored in the same library to the project in which the diagram is contained. The data of the *cluster* results contain the original data, a segmentation variable and variable distance that is assigned the role rejected. Rows (*Row*), columns (*Column*) and variables rows: columns (coordinates on the map) are stored in the file *output* when a SOM method is used in training. If the lost data have been charged then will add a variable named *_IMPUTE_* to the results file.

Statistics Data Sets: this window lists the databases that contain the scan statistics *cluster* and seeds (Figure 13-67). The latter is especially useful to classify other data using SAS FASTCLUS command.

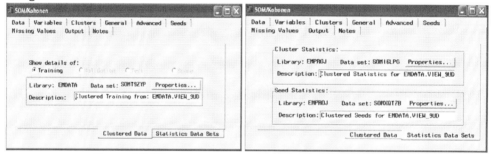

Figure 13-66   Figure 13-67

Once selected all the options we will be able to run the node. For our example we have been taking the options by default except in the tab *Cluster* where we have chosen the *Kohonen Vector Quantization* method and we have set 6 *clusters* (Figure 13-68). After running the analysis *results Viewer*opens.

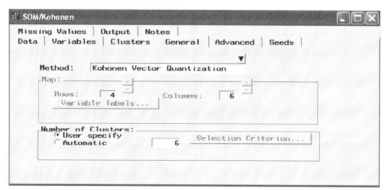

Figure 13-68

Run the node, we see that the results of the results Viewer are equivalent to the node for *clustering* already seen in the chapter on cluster analysis. For example, the *Map* (Figure 13-69) tab presents the same output.

If we click the right button of the mouse on any point of the *Map* window pie chart Gets the popup Figure 13-70, whose option *View Data* leads to the figure data table 13-71, presenting all the variables of the data file and the *cluster* to which they belong (CLUSTER_ID column).

The *Cluster Profile* from the previous pop-up menu option, takes us to a graph that presents the profile of formation of *clusters* in a tree way (Figure 13-72).

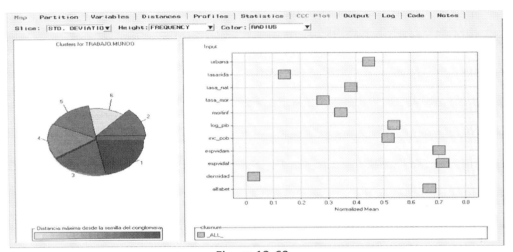

Figure 13-69

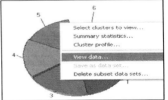

Figure 13-70

país	poblac	densidad	urbana	relig	espvidaf	espvidam	alfabet	inc_pob	mortinf	pib_cap	reg
Acerbayán	7400	86	54	Musulma	75	67	98	1.4	35	3000	
Afganistán	20500	25	18	Musulma	44	45	29	2.8	168	205	
Alemania	81200	227	85	Protest	79	73	99	0.36	6.5	17539	
Arabia Saudí	18000	7.7	77	Musulma	70	66	62	3.2	52	6651	
Argentina	33900	12	86	Católica	75	68	95	1.3	25.6	3400	
Armenia	3700	126	68	Ortodoxa	75	68	98	1.4	27	5000	
Australia	17800	2.3	85	Protest	80	74	100	1.38	7.3	16848	
Austria	8000	94	58	Católica	79	73	99	0.2	6.7	18396	
Bahréin	600	828	83	Musulma	74	71	77	2.4	25	7875	

Figure 13-71

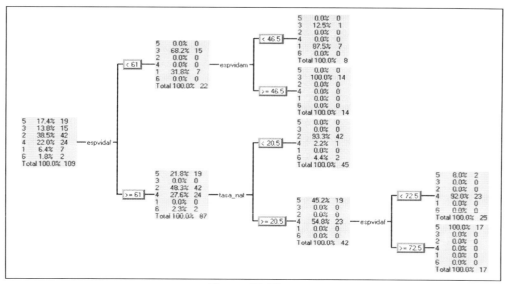

Figure 13-72

30371719R00201

Made in the USA
Lexington, KY
09 March 2014